9/14

Social Media in the
COURTROOM

Social Media in the

COURTROOM

A New Era for
Criminal Justice?

Thaddeus A. Hoffmeister

 PRAEGER

AN IMPRINT OF ABC-CLIO, LLC
Santa Barbara, California • Denver, Colorado • Oxford, England

Library of Congress Cataloging-in-Publication Data

Hoffmeister, Thaddeus (Thaddeus A.) author.
 Social media in the courtroom: a new era for criminal justice?/Thaddeus A. Hoffmeister.
   pages cm
  ISBN 978-1-4408-3005-1 (hardback) — ISBN 978-1-4408-3006-8 (ebook)
1. Online social networks—Law and legislation—United States. 2. Trial practice—
United States. 3. Evidence, Criminal—United States. I. Title.
KF390.5.C6H64 2014
347.73′5—dc23   2014014795

ISBN: 978-1-4408-3005-1
EISBN: 978-1-4408-3006-8

18 17 16 15 14   1 2 3 4 5

This book is also available on the World Wide Web as an eBook.
Visit www.abc-clio.com for details.

Praeger
An Imprint of ABC-CLIO, LLC

ABC-CLIO, LLC
130 Cremona Drive, P.O. Box 1911
Santa Barbara, California 93116-1911

This book is printed on acid-free paper ∞
Manufactured in the United States of America

Dedicated to A and Z.

Contents

Preface

As in other areas of society, social media has had an impact on the law. Some have gone so far as to say that "social media is having a transformative effect on the law and the legal profession."[1] While this statement may come across to some as hyperbolic, there is plenty of evidence to support the idea that social media plays a significant role within the legal system. Arguably, the most telling example is displayed in the courtroom where legal disputes are now being won or lost based on the attorney's mastery of social media.

Other examples of social media's impact can be found in the proliferation of cases that now have at least one social media reference. For instance, a search of the term "Facebook" in a 2007 LexisNexis legal database reveals 10 cases that use or cite the word. Those cases more than doubled to 22 for 2008. By 2012, 850 cases cited or referenced the word Facebook. In 2013, the number was 1,324.

Social media's reach is even felt in academia where a small but growing number of law schools have started to offer courses like *Social Media and Criminal Law* and *Law and Social Media*.[2] This is significant since law schools have long resisted curriculum changes, especially those geared toward teaching students practical, ready-to-use skills. Outside of academia, the legal bar, law firms, governmental agencies, and the like now routinely provide attorneys classes and training on social media.

Of the different areas of law most likely to be transformed by social media, criminal law is high on that list. This is because the field of criminal law reaches all segments of society and touches a wide spectrum of individuals from *Fortune* 500 CEOs involved in insider trading to panhandlers accused of improper solicitation. In addition, almost everyone involved in a criminal case, whether they are jurors, law enforcement, defendants, witnesses, attorneys, or judges, has already interacted or will interact with some form of social media. In fact, social media has even attracted the attention of criminal street gangs. This in turn has led commentators to coin new phrases and terms like "cyberbanging."[3]

This book explores social media's influence on criminal law by looking at how the key players in the criminal justice system, namely individual citizens, law enforcement, attorneys, and judges, interact with and use social media. This book is written primarily for those interested in social media or involved in the criminal law arena or litigation. However, the book will appeal to anyone who enjoys learning about technology and how it shapes and influences the legal system. This book may be read from front to back to obtain a comprehensive overview of the field or the chapters can be read individually, as each one serves as a quick and handy reference guide for the particular topic covered.

Of course, any book that examines technology runs the risk of becoming quickly dated. This is especially true here where the topic continues to evolve. To combat this problem, this book will not only examine the thorny legal and ethical questions that arise in the day-to-day use of social media in the criminal law context, but will also provide a 10,000-foot overview of social media's role in the criminal justice system as a whole. In addition, this book will attempt to forecast future changes that social media might bring to the field of criminal law.

Some may question the need for a book on social media and the law, much less one that only examines a subcomponent of the law—criminal law. They may wonder about the actual influence of social media. Others may consider social media a passing fad or just another form of communication. This in turn leads them to question whether an entire book can be dedicated to examining social media and criminal law.

As will be discussed in greater detail later, social media impacts every stage of the criminal justice process from the initial commission of the crime all the way through to the investigation and prosecution. To date, social media has been used to empower crime victims, assist virtual deputies, establish alibis, impeach witnesses, prove motives, investigate criminals, carry out crimes, monitor jurors, violate court rules, advertise attorney services, commit ethical violations, enhance sentences, apprehend suspects, and run undercover sting operations.

A deeper question does exist as to why social media should be treated differently from other forms of communication. Put another way, why not a book about the impact of the telephone on criminal law? What makes social media so unique? Is social media inherently different from all other forms of communication past or present, and if so, how is it different?

Chapter 3, which explores social media–related penalties, puts this issue squarely into focus. This chapter examines the efforts of several states to restrict the social media access of certain convicted criminal defendants. These same states, however, make no effort to restrict the criminal defendants' use of other forms of communication such as the mail, telephone, or television.

Thus, the question becomes, why the distinction among the various forms of communication? Is this an overreaction due to a lack of familiarity with new technology or is social media fundamentally different? In certain instances courts, attorneys, and legislators have definitely overreacted. However, in examining the complete picture, many have or are starting to realize that while social media shares similarities with past forms of communication, it is truly unique and worthy of individualized treatment.

SOCIAL MEDIA VS. OTHER FORMS OF COMMUNICATION

One of the distinguishing features of social media is privacy or lack thereof. Social media, more so than any other form of communication, works to erode the privacy of its users. This occurs in a variety of ways.

First, social media has redefined the word "friend." With social media, users create online friendships with people that they don't really know in the traditional sense; that is, most people who use social media have not interacted with (beyond accepting a friend request) or physically met all of their online friends.

The large number of friendships through social media has resulted in a breakdown of traditional barriers that kept strangers apart.

Second, social media has lowered the barrier for self-disclosure. Some go as far as saying that social media has created a new paradigm where the default position is to share one's life experiences from the most routine to the most intimate with the rest of the world. According to two legal commentators,

> [s]ocial media has created a new psychology in which the constant revelation of opinion and personal information is expected.[4]

With social media, it has now become the norm that individuals will share their innermost feelings with others online. A recent Pew Survey revealed that

[t]eens are increasingly sharing personal information on social media sites, a trend that is likely driven by the evolution of the platforms teens use as well as changing norms around sharing.[5]

Third, social media makes information conveyed by its users readily available for others to access and find. In contrast, with traditional forms of communication like the telephone and mail, the information conveyed was rarely made available to the general public nor was it stored in one convenient location like the Internet to be accessed and readily searched by others. Telephone calls resided with individual users or the telephone company, while mail resided with the United States Postal Service or with individual users. It was and is a crime to read someone else's mail or listen in on someone else's phone calls without permission.

Fourth, social media combines an individual's personal and professional life, which results in the sharing of information between the two. With other forms of communication, users are better able to keep these different worlds separate—the same is not true with social media. For example, many employers believe that an individual's social media account, as opposed to a résumé or interview, will offer them more insight into a potential job applicant's background and ability. Thus, employers with greater frequency are making hiring decisions based on what they find on social media. To date, a large number (69 percent according to a recent survey) of employers have rejected job applicants because of what they wrote or displayed on social media. In contrast, how many people lost a job opportunity because of a letter they wrote or how they answered their own personal phone?

Besides privacy, other distinguishing features of social media include the speed by which a user may contact large numbers of people. In a matter of seconds, users of social media can reach millions of people, most of whom they have never physically met. No other form of communication offers individuals, acting in their own capacity, the ability to communicate with such large numbers of people so quickly. This ability to reach out to so many people with only a few keystrokes will be discussed in greater detail in Chapter 2, which examines how virtual deputies use crowdsourcing to assist in the apprehension of criminal defendants.

The size and magnitude of social media also distinguishes it from other forms of communication. There is a wide array of social media platforms ranging from YouTube to Craigslist to LinkedIn to Myspace. The sheer size of social media and the growing number of social media providers is unparalleled in the history of human communications. As will be discussed in Chapter 3, this size creates a target-rich environment for criminal defendants who prey on unsuspecting victims. With social media, criminal defendants can greatly expand the reach of their criminal activities to include contacting victims thousands of miles away.

Social media's size and reach is also one of the reasons it has become so intertwined in the daily lives of Americans. In fact, using social media has become the most popular online activity.[6] More than half of Americans have at least one online profile.[7] In addition, 91 percent of adults who go online regularly use social media.

The pervasiveness of social media has not gone unnoticed by the courts. In *John Doe et al. v. Nebraska*, a class action lawsuit challenging the social media restrictions placed on registered sex offenders, the trial judge noted how much individuals including the plaintiffs now regularly rely on social media both in a personal and professional context. The court in *John Doe v. Prosecutor, Marion County, Indiana* went even further, stating that

> the use of computer-based social networking web sites, instant messaging, and chat rooms has become ubiquitous in today's society.[8]

Even the United States Supreme Court has commented on the role of social media in America. In *Citizens United v. Federal Elections Commission* the high court stated that

> [s]oon, however, it may be that Internet sources, such as blogs and social networking Web sites, will provide citizens with significant information about political candidates and issues.[9]

Most would find it extremely challenging to go an entire day without engaging in some form of social media, whether checking in with Foursquare, sending a tweet, or reading a blog post. This, in turn, raises serious concerns for judges who must instruct jurors about using and accessing social media while on jury duty. Chapter 4 examines the challenges in keeping jurors from improperly accessing and using social media during trials. This same dilemma does not arise with other methods of communication past or present.

Social media also has a social component (hence the name *social* media) that has no direct comparison to any past or present form of communication. This social component is facilitated by two key factors. First, social media providers allow and encourage users to build up their individual social media sites by expanding networks and sharing information with others. This primarily occurs when users update their sites with both professional and personal information. One legal commentator has noted that without a steady stream of user-provided content, sites such as Facebook and Twitter would be empty shells. Accordingly, these sites are constantly trying to get more [content], inviting users to update, upload, post and publish.[10]

This regular updating and expanding facilitates social interaction with others.

The second key factor to the social component is the human desire to be social. On the Maslow hierarchy of human needs, only sustenance and safety come before the need to interact socially.[11] Of the various forms of communication, social media affords users the best methods for social interaction. This is because social media, more so than any other form of communication, allows users to approximate face-to-face interaction. With social media and its ability to simulate in-person contact, users create and maintain friendships and relationships entirely online regardless of whether the parties are in the same city or thousands of miles away.

Having or maintaining relationships solely through social media may seem strange to "Digital Immigrants" (those who immigrated to the Internet). However, it is not unheard of among "Digital Natives" (those raised with the Internet). There was even a documentary film (*Catfish*) dedicated to exploring how these relationships work. The approximation of human interaction appears to be the driving force behind the success or failure of these social media relationships.

Of course, the ability to simulate in-person human interaction comes with its own set of perils. To date, numerous people have used social media successfully to impersonate others both real and fictional. This practice of online impersonation and identity theft will be discussed in greater detail in Chapter 3.

If one were to try to draw a corollary between social media and other forms of communication, the best comparison might be to a hybrid form of communication that combines the attributes of sending an email, making a telephone call, and watching television. Like television, social media allows users to reach a wide audience. However, unlike television, social media allows users to craft and control the message conveyed to others. Like the telephone, social media allows users to create a personal connection or bond with another person. However, unlike the telephone, social media allows the user to create this same bond with large numbers of people. In addition, like email, social media allows users to control, at least initially, who receives the information disseminated. However, unlike email, social media allows users to disseminate large amounts of information in different formats.

This attempt to compare social media to other forms of communication will be one of the reoccurring themes throughout the book. For example, Chapter 12 examines how courts address the question of authenticating a Myspace page. In formulating an answer, some courts attempt to analogize social media to other methods of communication like email. While the analogy works in some instances, it widely misses the mark in others.

Whether one looks at social media's size, reach, privacy implications, omnipresence, or communal aspect, it becomes fairly clear that social media is unlike any other form of communication past or present and thus deserves to be treated differently.

Introduction

Part I begins with an exploration of social media's influence on private citizens who for one reason or another find themselves involved in the criminal justice system. Individuals falling into this category include crime victims, criminal defendants, and jurors. To date, crime victims have used social media in generally one of two ways: to express their opinion about crime and the criminal justice system and to assist law enforcement.

On the other end of the spectrum from crime victims are those who commit crimes. Criminal defendants use social media in a variety of ways. Some rely on social media to plan, organize, and conduct illegal activity, while others merely use it to boast and talk about past and future crimes. A typical social media–related crime involves the defendant either (1) relaying information to another, for example, harassment; or (2) gathering information about a victim, for example, identity theft.

In addition to examining the methods by which social media facilitates criminal conduct, Part I also looks at the penalties and restrictions a court may impose on a criminal defendant's use of social media. For example, several states have attempted to prohibit certain convicted criminal defendants from using social media or require them to list their criminal convictions on the personal social media sites they use (Digital Scarlet Letters). This issue has arisen most prominently with respect to those convicted of sex-related crimes.

Part I concludes by exploring social media's impact on juries. Social media has had two distinct influences on jurors. First, it has led to greater encroachment on juror privacy as attorneys, in larger numbers, are turning to social media to assist them with investigating and monitoring jurors.

Second, it has led to increased instances of juror misconduct as jurors find it challenging, in the Digital Age, to adhere to the court's prohibitions against discussing the case with other jurors prior to deliberations and with outside parties prior to rendering a verdict.

Part II examines social media's influence on law enforcement. To date, law enforcement agencies across the country have turned to social media as a crime prevention tool. Agencies from the New York City Police Department to the Florida Fish and Wildlife Conservation Commission have established their very own social media units or dedicated personnel to investigate and monitor social media.[1] According to a recent survey of 600 law enforcement agencies, 92 percent reported using social media in some fashion. The most common use was criminal investigations (77 percent), followed by public notifications (64 percent), and then community outreach (62 percent).[2]

In the past, police officers walked city streets to safeguard residents. Today, law enforcement patrols a beat in the virtual world. These virtual streets consist of Facebook profiles and YouTube videos. This shift has occurred because many citizens now communicate and interact through social media.

Law enforcement is not alone in having to adapt to the growing role of social media in criminal law. Attorneys must navigate social media sites in order to better serve their clients, whether those clients are the state or criminal defendants. This is because social media has become instrumental in the prosecution and defense of criminal cases. Part III studies the influence of social media on prosecutors and criminal defense attorneys. To date, prosecutors have used social media to both obtain convictions and enhance a defendant's sentence. In contrast, defense attorneys have used social media to both humanize their clients and establish rock-solid alibis.

Part III also discusses the challenges that arise in obtaining and using information from social media. Chapter 7 looks at the three primary methods (independent research, discovery, and subpoena) relied on by attorneys for obtaining social media. Of those three methods, the subpoena raises the biggest hurdle for practitioners. This is due in large part to the Stored Communications Act (SCA). Written in the mid-1980s, the SCA greatly restricts what information social media providers can reveal to outside parties.

Besides raising a host of novel legal questions, social media also presents attorneys with a range of new ethical quandaries, which are explored in Chapter 9. Many of these ethical issues are not squarely addressed by the Rules of Professional Responsibility, which govern attorney behavior. For example, what advice, if any, can lawyers give their clients about using social media? Other ethical questions arise with respect to the information discovered on social media and whether it must be turned over to opposing counsel or the court. Chapter 9 tackles these questions and discusses whether or not the rules governing attorney ethics need to be updated to reflect the changes brought by social media.

Part IV looks at judges and social media. Of those involved in the criminal justice process, judges are arguably the least likely to use social media. However, this does not mean that they are immune from social media's impact. Judges need to learn about social media because they determine how courtrooms will operate. They decide whether or not to permit live blogging in their courtrooms. They are also responsible for instructing jurors about the use and misuse of social media during trial.

In addition and arguably most importantly, judges determine what information, if any, derived from social media will be admissible in a court of law. Chapter 12 is dedicated to examining how judges make this determination. The focus here is on authentication. The rules addressing the authentication of evidence were written many years ago before anyone had even thought about the concept of social media. This chapter discusses the methods by which social media evidence may be authenticated at trial.

SOCIAL MEDIA PLATFORMS

Prior to beginning the in-depth examination of social media's role in criminal law, this book will briefly examine some of the more popular social media providers, followed by a discussion on how to define and classify social media. This preliminary review will be helpful to those unfamiliar with the more common social media providers. It also helps establish the necessary foundational groundwork as many of these social media providers will be mentioned throughout the book.

Most of the social media platforms described next are free to users and available to anyone with Internet access. However, a few require payment for premium services that go beyond the basic level. Also, in order to place content or personal information on these social media sites, users generally have to agree to the Terms of Service (TOS) established by the social media platform.

Unlike traditional Web sites where the owner typically creates content to be made available for others to view, social media platforms allow individual users to create content inside a framework provided by the platform.[3] Within this framework, users, depending on the social media platform, create their own online identity, establish relationships, and share connections with other users.

Blog

A blog (a combination of the terms "web" and "log") is an online journal, diary, or bulletin board where the user ("blogger") makes personal or professional updates in the form of posts. These online posts are normally chronological and generally available to anyone with Internet access. A blog does not send messages, and there is no limit on the length of the posts made on a blog. Most blogs are interactive and allow visitors to leave comments. Also, blogs generally have text, images, and links.

Unlike social media platforms such as Myspace, LinkedIn, or Facebook, a blog is not hosted at one specific Web address. Instead blogs are created at various Web addresses and controlled by different companies like Blogspot, WordPress, and Tumblr. In 2011, there were approximately 156 million public blogs.

Craigslist

Founded in 1995, Craigslist is arguably one of the oldest if not the oldest social media provider still in existence. Craigslist is a virtual ad site that can be found in over 700 cities and 70 countries. Users of Craigslist advertise a variety of different things including jobs, housing, personals, items for sale, items wanted, services, community events, gigs, and résumés. Craigslist also has a section dedicated to discussion forums. The site receives approximately 50 billion page views per month.

Facebook

Founded in 2004, Facebook is one of the more popular social media platforms; it claims over a billion users. To use Facebook a user creates an online profile or page. With these profiles, users upload photos and video and provide commentary, which in some instances is instantly communicated to others. Facebook, which technically requires users to be 13 and older, offers a wide range of privacy settings that allow users to restrict who may view their Facebook profiles.

One reason for Facebook's popularity is that it provides the social interaction that humans crave. With Facebook, users can keep in touch with friends, family, and colleagues. This occurs through the routine viewing and updating of Facebook pages.

Most interactions begin when the Facebook user "friends" another person. Requests to friend are liberally granted and have led to a rather broad definition of what it means to be an online friend.

As a friend, an individual is given access to a Facebook user's online profile. This in turn allows an individual to post comments, links, pictures, or videos on a friend's profile page or share what she wants or feels with friends by writing in the status update area or posting to her own timeline.

If a friend is online and the individual wants to talk privately with that person, the individual clicks on the name and instant messages the friend. Once completed, the conversation is stored in the Messages section of Facebook to be accessed later. If the friend is not online, the individual can still send a message to the friend and that person will see it the next time she logs on.

Other features of Facebook that facilitate interaction among users include the "like" button and "tagging." With the like button, users are able to communicate their preferences (or likes) to other users. Individuals can like photographs, status updates, or posts on their own Facebook page or those of other users. With tagging, users of Facebook make identifications and connections. For example, when an individual uploads photographs she may "tag" or label those who appear in the photo. The tag establishes a link from the uploaded content (photographs, audio files, and video) to the profile page of the individual "tagged."

Foursquare

Foursquare is a geo-location social media provider that was founded in 2009. Users check in to certain locations and let others know their physical location. This allows users to find each other and get together for social events. Check-ins occur through GPS hardware in the user's mobile device or network location. Entities encourage check-ins by offering discounts or rewards to those who check in. As of April 2012, Foursquare had 20 million members and 2.5 billion check-ins.

LinkedIn

Founded in 2002, LinkedIn is an older social media platform. Like Myspace and Facebook, LinkedIn allows its users to create online profiles. However, LinkedIn, unlike Myspace and Facebook, is used almost exclusively for business or professional purposes. LinkedIn allows users to share work-related information with other users and keep an online list of professional contacts. LinkedIn, which is open to people 18 and over, claims over 175 million professional users.

Myspace

Founded in 2003, Myspace was a forerunner to Facebook. Although not as popular as it once was, Myspace had over 25 million users in 2012. Today, Myspace has a large presence in the music world.

Unlike its competitor Facebook, Myspace allows users to customize their profile. While Facebook limits users to plain text, a Myspace user has more ways to customize profiles, including using HTML and cascading style sheets. In fact,

> Myspace users have the sole discretion to decide what information they wish to include in their profile and have the ability to change it any time.[4]

Pinterest

Launched in 2010, Pinterest is a virtual bulletin board where users share photos. Pinterest allows users to share a picture with a related link and only a small amount of text. With Pinterest, users can create collections of things and follow collections created by other users. This is done through pinboards that rely heavily on photos. According to the Pinterest Web site, Pinterest allows users to plan weddings, redecorate homes, find styles, and save inspirations. In January 2012, comScore reported that Pinterest had 11.7 million unique users, making it the fastest site in history to break through the 10 million unique visitors mark.

Reddit

Founded in 2005, Reddit refers to itself as the front page of the Internet. This social media platform allows registered users (redditors) to submit content in the form of either a link or a text post. These posts are then voted "up" or "down" by other registered users. This allows the post to be ranked and determines the post's position on Reddit's page. According to Reddit, redditors vote on which stories and discussions are important; the hottest stories rise to the top, while cooler stories sink. Approximately 6 percent of online adults use Reddit.

Second Life

Launched in 2003, Second Life allows users to interact with each other through avatars, which are graphical representations of the user's alter ego or character.[5] This interaction occurs online in the Second Life social media platform. With avatars, users explore the world of Second Life, meet other residents, socialize, and create and trade virtual property and services with each other. Unlike a traditional computer game, Second Life has neither a designated objective, nor traditional game play mechanisms. As of April 2013, Second Life had around 600,000 active users.

Twitter

Created in 2006, Twitter was originally marketed as a means to let people share what they were doing in real life, in real time "in between emails and blogs." Twitter is a cross between blogging and instant messaging. Users of Twitter send out tweets, like blog posts, to followers. Unlike a blog post, a tweet must be 140 characters or fewer at a time. Unlike instant messages that disappear when the user closes the application, tweets are also posted on Twitter.com. Tweets are permanent and may be searched publicly.

Twitter allows its users to make their tweets public or private. Twitter also has a private message option similar to Facebook. Like instant messaging, information communicated via private messaging is only visible to the person a user sends it to. In many ways private messaging supplants email. As of February 2013, Twitter had 200 million users.

YouTube

Founded in 2005, YouTube allows individuals to share videos among friends, family, and the general public. The viewing may occur publicly or privately. At present, YouTube has the largest online video sharing site with over 800 million unique users who visit each month. Over 4 billion hours of video are watched each month, and 100 hours of video are uploaded to YouTube every minute. YouTube is also the second largest search engine in the world.

SOCIAL MEDIA DEFINED AND CLASSIFIED

The challenges with defining social media are threefold. First, as previously illustrated, social media encompasses a variety of platforms. Thus, any definition will have to be broadly worded to include all of these various formats. Second, social media is still evolving; therefore, any definition created today may need modification in the near future. Third, the terms "social media" and "social networking" have at times been used interchangeably, which makes it difficult to apply a fixed definition to either term.

For the purposes of this book, the term "social networking site" is a subset of social media and refers to a specific set of social media platforms such as Myspace, Facebook, and LinkedIn. This is in keeping with the generally accepted definition of social networking site. For example, in the 2007 case *Doe v. Myspace,* the court defined a social networking site as one that

> allows its members to create online "profiles," which are individual Web pages on which members post photographs, videos, and information about their lives and interests. The idea of online social networking is that members will use their online profiles to become part of any online community of people with common interests.[6]

Similarly, in 2008, Professors Danah M. Boyd and Nicole Ellison defined social networking sites as:

> web-based services that allow individuals to (1) construct a public or semi-public profile within a bounded system, (2) articulate a list of other users with whom they share a connection, and (3) view and traverse their list of connections and those made by others within the system.[7]

In contrast to social networking sites, the term "social media" is more broad-based and all inclusive. Many view social media as

> a catch phrase that describes technology that facilitates interactive information, user-created content and collaboration.[8]

Others see social media as

> the blending of technology and social interaction for the creation of value.[9]

Webster's Dictionary defines social media as

> forms of electronic communication (as Web sites for social networking and micro-blogging) through which users create online communities to share information, ideas, personal messages, and other content (as videos).[10]

The overarching themes with all these definitions of social media are (1) technology; (2) user creation; and (3) community.

The importance of precise definitions becomes more apparent in Chapter 3, which examines the government's ability to limit certain criminal defendants from accessing social media. To date, several states have passed laws banning sex offenders from social media. However, these laws have been routinely struck down by the courts. The sticking point for many of these courts centers on the broad definition given to social media. Courts have routinely found that these expansive definitions of social media intrude too far on the defendant's First Amendment rights.

Like attempting to define social media, categorizing social media is no easy task. This is due to the wide array of social media sites ranging from YouTube to Facebook to Twitter to Second Life. When categorizing social media some place it into functional building blocks such as (1) identity, (2) conversations, (3) sharing, (4) presence, (5) relationships, (6) reputation, and (7) groups. Others use a scheme involving a different set of categories: (1) collaborative projects (e.g., Reddit); (2) blogs and microblogs (e.g., Twitter); (3) content communities (e.g., YouTube); (4) social networking sites (e.g., Facebook); (5) virtual game worlds (e.g., World of Warcraft); and (6) virtual social worlds (e.g., Second Life).

Another form of classification places social media into platforms. At present, the platforms for delivering social media, which are steadily growing, fall into three overlapping categories.[11] The first category is directories. Here, social media functions as a résumé-listing service with ratings by clients and colleagues (e.g., LinkedIn and Avvo are social media platforms falling into the directory category). The second category is communication. Here, social media functions as a tool with which users can disseminate and write information on an ongoing basis (e.g., blogs, Facebook, and Twitter are social media platforms falling into the communication category). The third category is archiving and sharing. Here, social media is a tool for users to store, share, and redistribute video, slides, and documents (e.g., YouTube, Flicker, and Scribd are social media platforms falling into the archiving and sharing category).

Part I

Individuals

The first part of the book examines social media's impact on private citizens who find themselves in the criminal justice system for one reason or another. Generally speaking, individuals come in contact with the criminal justice system in one of three ways. The first and most common method is as a crime victim. Unfortunately, individuals in the United States have a 1 in 4.6 chance in their lifetime of becoming a crime victim. The other two ways in which private citizens come in contact with the criminal justice system, which will be discussed later in the book, are as a criminal defendant or juror.

1

Crime Victims

Those who have been victims of crime primarily use social media to voice their views about the perpetrator of the crime and the criminal act itself. For example, crime victims may send a tweet informing others that they have been robbed and then describe the robber and the property stolen. Not surprisingly, many of these communications involve the crime victims expressing displeasure or even outrage about their situation.

On occasion, this unhappiness carries over to the criminal justice system as a whole, as crime victims discuss their treatment by law enforcement, attorneys, court staff, and the judge. These communications via social media are therapeutic for the crime victims and, at times, educational for the public. Through social media, crime victims have been able to tell their stories. In *Reno v. ACLU* the Supreme Court noted that

> [t]hrough the use of chat rooms any person with a phone line can become a town crier with a voice that resonates farther than it could from a soapbox.[1]

This idea is magnified in the realm of social media where others can discuss and share the crime victim's story. This discussion can have both positive and negative consequences.

On the negative side, social media commentators sometimes rush to judgment. Unlike traditional media that rely on fact checkers and editors, and adhere to a professional code of ethics, users of social media are for the most part amateurs who, in many instances, arrive at conclusions without knowing the complete story or all of the facts. This concept will be discussed in greater detail later in the section on virtual deputies.

Another downside to crime victims using social media is the loss of privacy. Historically, a crime victim might share her story with law enforcement, relatives, and maybe a few close personal friends. Today, she can share it with the world. This not only works to erode her own privacy, but also that of all the parties involved.

On the positive side, social media discussions offer crime victims a second opportunity to right a real or perceived wrong. Furthermore, they get people to talk about the crime victim's problem and whether reform or change is needed. A recent juvenile criminal case in Kentucky illustrates both the advantages and disadvantages of crime victims using social media.

In August 2011, 16-year-old Savannah D. (the victim actually released her complete name to the public in order to bring greater public awareness to her situation) had drinks with two male juveniles and passed out at her own house party. While unconscious, she was photographed and sexually assaulted (digitally penetrated) by the two boys with whom she had been drinking.

Some months after the incident, Savannah started to hear rumors that the two boys had taken photos of her that night and shared them with others. Savannah confronted the boys by text about the rumors, but they denied that anything had happened. She ultimately went to the police, who subsequently interviewed the boys in February 2012. During the police interview, they admitted to the assault.

In June 2012, the two boys pled guilty to felony sexual abuse and misdemeanor voyeurism in juvenile court. During the hearing, the juvenile trial judge instructed everyone in attendance, including Savannah, not to discuss the incident with anyone for any reason. The state of Kentucky, like several other states, closes juvenile proceedings to the public and seals the records of juvenile defendants.

At the time of the initial plea in June 2012, Savannah disagreed with the sentences proposed for the two defendants. In her eyes, the punishment was too lenient; however, she felt powerless to stop the process from going forward. Thus, she decided to turn to Twitter and Facebook to voice her displeasure with the case. Among other things, Savannah tweeted the following:

I'm not protecting anyone that made my life a living Hell.[2]

She also tweeted the names of the two defendants. This was the first time that their names had been revealed to the general public. On her Facebook wall, she wrote:

[i]f reporting a rape only got me to the point that I'm not allowed to talk about it, then I regret it.[3]

As a result of Savannah's social media activity, an attorney for one of the defendants filed a motion to hold Savannah in contempt of court for violating the judge's gag order. The contempt charge carried a possible sentence of 180 days in jail and a $500 fine. Had this sentence been imposed, Savannah would have suffered a greater penalty than the young men who had sexually assaulted her. The contempt motion was quickly withdrawn, however, once Savannah's case caught the public's attention. Savannah received such a groundswell of support from the public that her online petition to get the contempt charges dropped set a record with 50,000 signatures within 24 hours.

Ultimately, the two teenage boys were sentenced in September 2012 to 50 hours of community service, sex offender treatment, and three years of supervised probation. In addition, the defendants had to disclose the names of anyone who viewed the photos of Savannah. The defendants are eligible to have the felony charge amended to a misdemeanor in 2015. This in turn would allow the defendants to request an expungement. During the initial plea discussion back in June, when Savannah initially turned to social media to voice her frustrations, the defendants were going to have their records automatically expunged when they turned 19½.

Savannah's case raises some very interesting points. First, it demonstrates how crime victims who feel underserved by the legal system can use social media to take their case to the court of public opinion. According to at least one legal commentator, the court of public opinion has been around for centuries,

[b]ut the internet, and social media in particular, has changed how it's being used.[4]

Prior to social media, crime victims had little opportunity to express to the world their views about the legal system or get their case before the court of public opinion. On occasion, crime victims garnered the attention of the media, but it was the media, not the crime victims, who told and shaped the story. With social media, Savannah told her story through her own lens. Her narration, among other things, resulted in a flood of online signatures. Her story also led the defense counsel to withdraw his motion for contempt. Savannah's story was ripe for telling in the court of public opinion where

having a good story is more important than having the law on your side.[5]

This case also placed a spotlight on the juvenile justice process. It made many in Kentucky and elsewhere reconsider the necessity of closing juvenile proceedings. Some feel that because of social media and the ease by which one can disseminate names to the public, the release of information from juvenile proceedings should be more tightly regulated. Others take the opposite viewpoint and believe juvenile proceedings should be more open, especially with respect to crime victims who want to talk about the crime and those who committed it. But again, this debate was only started because of a young woman's tweets and Facebook posts. It remains to be seen whether future juvenile proceedings will be able to safeguard the identity of juvenile defendants in the Digital Age.

Finally, this case highlights an issue that will be a reoccurring theme throughout the book and discussed in greater detail later—the tension between the First Amendment and social media. In the case of Savannah, it is questionable as to whether the judge could constitutionally restrict Savannah's First Amendment rights in the way that she did. However, Savannah's legal recourse was not to turn to social media but to appeal the judge's gag order. Interestingly, it appears that by taking the law into her own hands via social media Savannah ultimately achieved the outcome that she desired.

2

Virtual Deputies

In addition to giving crime victims a virtual soapbox, social media allows them to assist law enforcement in either preventing or solving crime. To date, crime victims have been successful in using social media to help in the recovery of their stolen property and the apprehension of criminal defendants.

Interestingly, crime victims are not alone in their desire to serve as "virtual deputies." Other citizens, who have not been the victims of crime, have also displayed a strong interest in using social media to help law enforcement. With private citizens patrolling social media, law enforcement greatly expands its investigatory reach. In talking about citizens using social media to assist law enforcement, a spokesperson from the Spokane County Sheriff's Office stated that

> [t]he more eyes we have, the more public help that we have, obviously, the more successful we're going to be.[1]

Virtual deputies sometimes act alone or recruit others such as immediate friends, family, and co-workers. For example, a virtual deputy might forward a Facebook photo of allegedly stolen property or a potential suspect to friends in an attempt to make some type of identification. Relying on the crowdsourcing (obtaining ideas from a large group of people) function of social media greatly expands the reach of virtual deputies and their ability to assist law enforcement.

It appears that virtual deputies become more vested and more willing to involve others if they view an actual crime being committed. According to a detective in the Waco (Texas) Police Department,

I think, just human nature, that angers people and makes them more willing to share that on their friends' list . . . [seeing the crime take place] increases the chance of getting people identified.[2]

In addition to expanding the ability of law enforcement to monitor more areas on the Web, virtual deputies have fewer constitutional restraints than the police. Private citizens, acting on their own accord, are not subject to the same Fourth Amendment restrictions as law enforcement. For example, if a private citizen unlawfully accesses a criminal defendant's social media account and finds incriminating information, the private citizen can turn that information over to the police, who can then use it to prosecute the criminal defendant. If, however, the police on their own unlawfully access a criminal defendant's social media account and find incriminating information, that information may be suppressed by the criminal defendant.

One fairly unique example of how virtual deputies operate comes from the Bahamas. In this instance, a virtual deputy came across Facebook photos of an American couple in the Bahamas grilling and eating iguanas. These particular iguanas happened to be protected by the Fisheries and Wild Animal Protection Act. The virtual deputy reported the couple to the Bahamian police and they were arrested. The arrest of the American couple most likely would not have occurred absent the assistance of the virtual deputy.

Virtual deputies, however, do have a downside. One concern for law enforcement is when virtual deputies acting on their own confront criminal defendants. Virtual deputies put themselves and others at risk when they attempt to make contact with criminal defendants rather than just inform the police and allow them to take the necessary steps for apprehension.

Another way in which virtual deputies put others at risk is when they misidentify criminal defendants or proceed on incorrect information. Consider the 2013 Boston Marathon bombing where images of the suspects were caught on video and in photos. In the rush to identify and find the perpetrators, social media sites like Reddit, 4chan, Facebook, and Twitter misidentified Sunil Tripathi (who had gone missing a month earlier) as a suspect in the bombing. This in turn led to a barrage of unwanted attention unleashed on Tripathi's family from both the media and the general public. It was not until the police actually released the identities of the true suspects that the Tripathi family was removed from the public spotlight.

Ultimately, Reddit acknowledged its missteps and issued an apology to the Tripathi family. Here is the statement posted by the Reddit general manager:

Though started with noble intentions, some of the activity on Reddit fueled online witch hunts and dangerous speculation which spiraled into very negative consequences for innocent parties. The Reddit staff and the millions of people on Reddit around the world deeply regret that this happened. We have apologized privately to the family of missing college student Sunil Tripathi, as have various users and moderators. We want to take this opportunity to apologize publicly for the pain they have had to endure. We hope that this painful event will be channeled into something positive and the increased awareness will lead to Sunil's quick and safe return home.[3]

Finally, there is the potential for jeopardizing police investigations and criminal convictions. This can occur in a variety of ways. For example, virtual deputies can unintentionally alert suspects to ongoing investigations by tweeting real-time information from police scanners. In addition, virtual deputies can lead police astray with false leads. Unfortunately, the misidentification of Sunil Tripathi was not the only incorrect information provided to law enforcement by virtual deputies shortly after the Boston Marathon bombing. This rush to assist the police after a major crime occurs often results in law enforcement spending countless hours tracking down bogus leads.

With respect to compromising a conviction, some virtual deputies make it more difficult for the government to prove its case in the courtroom. Take for example a situation where an individual is mugged by a local neighborhood juvenile thug. In this hypothetical situation, the entire case rests on the victim's identification of the perpetrator. The victim has an idea of what the juvenile looks like but wants to confirm the juvenile's identity. Rather than go to the police station and look at traditional mug shots or maybe a lineup, the victim takes it upon herself to identify the perpetrator by looking at the Facebook page of the local high school where she sees the juvenile's picture. At trial, it may be easier for defense counsel on cross-examination to discredit this type of self-help identification than one that adheres to proper police procedures and protocols.

RELUCTANT VIRTUAL DEPUTIES

Some private citizens have no interest or desire in reporting crimes that they come across while using social media. This in turn raises the question of whether or not one commits a crime by turning a blind eye to criminal activity on social media. Generally speaking, private citizens have no obligation to report crimes or criminal activity. The exception to this rule is when one has a special relationship with the crime victim, for example, husband–wife, parent–child, or teacher–student. This common law rule that individuals have no duty to report crimes or criminal activity has been modified in a few jurisdictions. The most noticeable modification occurs in Ohio, which makes it illegal for a person to "knowingly fail to report a felony" regardless of any special relationship with the victim.[4]

Ohio's failure to report statute was recently put to the test in the 2012 Steubenville football rape case in which two juvenile defendants were found delinquent (the juvenile equivalent of a guilty finding) of digitally penetrating an intoxicated 16-year-old girl at a high school party. The case came to the attention of investigators and the public at large after evidence of the assault including a video and photos appeared on social media. In fact, the social media evidence was critical to the actual conviction of the two juveniles because the victim remembered very little from the night in question.

One unique and unfortunate aspect of the case involved the role of bystanders who actually saw the girl firsthand or viewed videos and photos of her in a semiconscious state. One of the bystanders was a young college freshman who shortly after viewing the photos and videos of the young girl made his own video in which he said:

she is so raped right now.[5]

This young man's video was posted on YouTube on the same night as the assault.

Not surprisingly, this comment drew outrage from across the country. Groups and organizations like the National Organization of Women (NOW) have called upon the Ohio Attorney General to investigate and prosecute this individual as well as others who viewed the video and photos of the young girl and then failed to alert authorities or report that a crime had occurred.

Despite the push by groups like NOW to have this young man prosecuted under Ohio's failure to report statute, it has not happened to date. The state of Ohio is probably hesitant to charge him because of the precedent it might set. Furthermore, the young man never actually saw the young girl being assaulted. He was only speculating as to what might have happened to her. Thus, it might be difficult for the state to prove that this person had actual knowledge of a crime.

Other states don't go as far as Ohio but do carve out significant exceptions to the general rule prohibiting prosecutions for failing to report a crime. Massachusetts, Rhode Island, and Washington, for example, require those who witness certain violent offenses to notify authorities.[6] Another small group of states imposes an affirmative duty to act when an individual knows that another is in peril and that individual has the ability to call for help or render assistance.[7]

As more and more information is placed on social media, reporting statutes and the issues that arise from them will receive greater scrutiny. Currently,

Twitter users send [one] billion tweets every two and a half days.[8]

Instagram users upload 40 million images every day.[9] As for Facebook users, they share 684,478 pieces of content every minute.[10] With all this information on social media, it is highly likely that somewhere among all those photos, notes, and videos is evidence of criminal activity. What duty, if any, should be imposed on people who come across this information? Many are split on the issue.

Those against mandatory reporting statutes argue that society should not punish individuals for being bad samaritans or turn every citizen into an adjunct police officer. Furthermore, they worry that these laws will be selectively enforced. Will all crimes need to be reported or only a select few that grab the public's attention?

Finally, there is the issue of civil liability for improperly reporting a crime or misidentifying a criminal defendant. What happens if someone mistakenly reports another? As illustrated by the Tripathi family and the Boston Marathon bombing, this can happen and may occur more often in the future as an increasing number of individuals decide to become virtual deputies.

Those who support reporting statutes argue that they can be implemented fairly. Most don't recommend going as far as Ohio but instead suggest a compromise position somewhere in between. Thus, rather than have a blanket reporting requirement like Ohio, a state could take a more nuanced approach. For example, a state might limit failure to report statutes to situations involving violent crimes or children. Another approach would be to limit the statute to ongoing criminal activity discovered on social media as opposed to past criminal activity.

The previously mentioned example of the American couple in the Bahamas grilling and eating the protected iguanas provides a case study on how the middle-ground approach might work. In that situation, if the virtual deputy had failed to report what she saw on Facebook, she would not be subject to prosecution. The crime in question was not ongoing as the iguanas had already been killed. Furthermore, the crime did not involve violence or children. The outcome might be different if the virtual deputy had become aware of an ongoing crime or a future crime, for example, if the couple announced on Facebook that they planned to catch and then eat the iguanas. The outcome also would most likely be different if instead of posting photos of each other eating iguanas they posted photos of themselves hurting a child.

3

Criminal Defendants

On the other side of the spectrum from crime victims are those who commit crimes or are accused of committing crimes. This is the second most common method by which private individuals come in contact with the criminal justice system. This section of the book will examine how criminal defendants use social media to facilitate criminal activity. Additionally, this section will discuss efforts by the state to regulate the use of social media by those convicted of certain crimes.

For those bent on committing crimes, social media has opened up a whole new world. It has become the place where criminal defendants not only commit crimes, but also organize, plan, discuss, and even boast about their illegal activity. This is not to say, however, that social media has led to the creation of a vast array of new crimes. Quite the opposite; save for flash mobs and online impersonation, no new crimes have been created to date. What has changed is the method by which traditional crimes are now committed.

In the past, a crime like harassment might require a criminal defendant to interact physically or telephonically with the victim. Today, harassment can occur on social media without the criminal defendant ever speaking to or interacting with the victim. In fact, the criminal defendant doesn't even have to leave his house to harass.

Social media also allows the criminal defendant to harass the victim through third parties who may or may not know that they are harassing the victim. Third-party harassment works because, unlike past forms of communication, social media allows people to more easily (1) approximate human interaction, (2) conceal their true identity, and (3) take on the persona of another.

Consider the case of *United States v. Sayer* where the criminal defendant used social media to harass his ex-girlfriend.[1] In this case, Sayer posted ads on Craiglist's Casual Encounters (a section on Craigslist for meeting other people) that showed his ex-girlfriend in lingerie (prior to the breakup the defendant had taken consensual photos of the victim). The ad encouraged men to visit the victim at her home and included a list of sex acts the victim would perform when the men arrived. As a result of the ad, strange men would routinely appear at the victim's house looking for sexual encounters.

In order to avoid these encounters, the victim moved to Louisiana. However, strange men again started to show up at her new home. As had happened before, these men claimed that they had met the victim online. Shortly thereafter, the victim discovered a sexually explicit video of her on several adult pornography sites. As with the earlier pictures, the victim had consented to the video prior to her breakup with Sayer. The video posting included the victim's name as well as her Louisiana address.

Ultimately, Sayer was caught and successfully prosecuted for cyberstalking and identity theft. This case illustrates how one vindictive individual can use social media and third parties to torment an ex-girlfriend repeatedly without directly contacting her or ever physically leaving his own home. The case also demonstrates the reach of social media. In the Digital Age, removing oneself from the physical proximity of the criminal defendant may not be enough to prevent contact either directly or indirectly.

Generally speaking, social media crimes fall into one of two categories. Category I crimes involve defendants using social media to *relay* information to victims, co-conspirators, or the general public. Category II crimes, which will be discussed in greater detail later, involve the defendant using social media to *gather* information about victims, for example, identity theft.

CATEGORY I CRIMES (RELAYING INFORMATION)

With respect to Category I crimes, the term *relay* applies to any method by which an individual may deliver information to another. This includes such things as a *poke* or *friend request*. In one case from New York, a trial court determined that a defendant could be charged for violating a protection order when she sent a friend request to an individual who had a protection order against her.[2] According to the judge, the defendant's use of social media to reach the complainant was a form of contact just like speaking in person or by telephone, and the order of restraint had barred any type of contact.

When relaying information to victims, co-defendants or the general public, criminal defendants use a variety of techniques. For example, some may communicate directly with a victim on social media, while others communicate indirectly by merely posting information on social media in a public or quasi-public place where the victims or the public can view it. For example, in *Griffin v. Maryland*, which will be discussed in greater detail in Chapter 12, the girlfriend of the defendant allegedly posted the following on her Myspace page as a warning to anyone who planned to testify against her boyfriend in his upcoming trial.

JUST REMEMBER SNITCHES GET STITCHES!! U KNOW WHO YOU ARE!![3]

Also, when relaying information to victims, co-defendants, or the general public, some criminal defendants use their real names.[4] Others remain anonymous or create fictitious names.[5] A final group actually creates a false name or takes on the identity of the intended victim (e.g., online impersonation).[6]

Online Category I Crimes

Category I crimes are further divided into two subcategories. The first subcategory of crimes involves those that actually occur on social media, for example, harassment, threats, and stalking. The second subcategory involves crimes in which social media merely serves as a vehicle to communicate with victims and co-conspirators—the actual crime occurs offline, for example, flash mobs, sexual assaults, and homicides. *United States v. Drew*, discussed next, illustrates the challenges in prosecuting online Category I crimes like harassment.[7]

Harassment. In 2006, Lori Drew, a 49-year-old mother from Missouri, created a Myspace page with the picture of a fictitious 16-year-old boy named Josh Evans. Lori Drew created this account to befriend 13-year-old Megan Meier, a one-time friend and classmate of Lori Drew's daughter. Lori Drew believed that this bogus Myspace account would allow her to learn whether Megan Meier was spreading rumors about her daughter. Acting as Josh Evans, Lori Drew would flirt with Megan Meier on Myspace. The relationship eventually turned sour and Lori Drew, through Josh Evans, told Megan Meier that the world would be a better place without her. Shortly thereafter, Megan Meier committed suicide.

The federal government relied on the Computer Fraud and Abuse Act (CFAA) to charge Lori Drew with three felony counts of accessing protected computers without authorization to obtain information.[8]

At the time, the CFAA appeared to be the best federal statute to address Lori Drew's conduct. The U.S. Attorney from the Central District of California handled the prosecution because the Myspace servers were physically located in California. Missouri passed on the opportunity to prosecute because at the time the state's harassment statute did not address Lori Drew's conduct.

Under the government's theory of prosecution, Lori Drew violated the CFAA because she had entered into a contract or Terms of Service (TOS) agreement with Myspace in order to create Josh Evans's account. As discussed in the Introduction, most social media providers require users to enter into a TOS prior to setting up their accounts.

Pursuant to the Myspace TOS, Lori Drew was required to provide accurate and truthful information when registering for the account and

refrain from using any information obtained from Myspace services to harass, abuse, or harm other people.[9]

Lori Drew allegedly violated this TOS when she (1) created the bogus Josh Evans account and (2) used the account to harass Megan Meier. Thus, Lori Drew's communication with Megan Meier through Myspace's protected servers was without authorization or in excess of authorized access.

While the jury found Lori Drew guilty, it rejected the prosecution's theory that Lori Drew intended to harm Megan Meier, a required finding for a felony conviction under the CFAA. As a result, the jury only convicted Lori Drew of three misdemeanor counts. These convictions were later overturned by the trial judge on vagueness grounds. The trial judge determined that the CFAA as applied in the *Drew* case failed to give the defendant notice that breach of a website's TOS by itself could constitute a crime. In addition, the judge found that this verdict, if left intact, would result in unclear guidelines for law enforcement.

Although the government's prosecution of Lori Drew was ultimately unsuccessful, her case demonstrates how the government's broad reading of a statute allows it to criminalize inappropriate behavior that occurs on social media. Lori Drew's prosecution also shows the creative, albeit unsuccessful, approaches the government is willing to take to combat harassment via social media.

Lori Drew's acts were universally condemned across the country, however, many felt uncomfortable with her prosecution under the CFAA. Some believed that she should not be prosecuted at all. Others felt that she should be prosecuted but under a different legal theory. The concern over the case was not necessarily for Lori Drew but what her case meant for future defendants. Had the government succeeded in its prosecution of Lori Drew, then arguably anyone could be prosecuted for violating a TOS. Thus, lying on Myspace or LinkedIn about academic or professional credentials in order to impress some reader could lead to criminal charges if the social media provider's TOS prohibited such dishonesty or fraud.

As a result of the national attention garnered by Lori Drew's actions and the difficulty in prosecuting the case, several states and the federal government have or are attempting to modify their laws on harassment to cover situations like those found in *Drew*. For example, prior to the *Drew* case, a criminal defendant in Missouri had to harass a victim in writing or over the phone in order to be prosecuted. Now a criminal defendant in Missouri commits the crime of harassment if he or she:

(3) Knowingly frightens, intimidates, or causes emotional distress to another person by anonymously making a telephone call or any electronic communication; or

(4) Knowingly communicates with another person who is, or who purports to be, seventeen years of age or younger and in so doing and without good cause recklessly frightens, intimidates, or causes emotional distress to such person; or . . .

(6) Without good cause engages in any other act with the purpose to frighten, intimidate, or cause emotional distress to another person, cause such person to be frightened, intimidated, or emotionally distressed, and such person's response to the act is one of a person of average sensibilities considering the age of such person.[10]

This modified Missouri harassment statute does not require a pattern of misconduct. Thus, it applies to single isolated incidents. This statute also covers situations where the harasser poses as the victim and posts derogatory information about the victim or others. And, most importantly, at least for proponents of tougher laws on harassment via social media, this statute focuses on the victim's state of mind. Since most state statutes covering harassment via social media are fairly new, the courts are still grappling with their constitutionality; for example, section 5 of Missouri's new harassment statute was found to be unconstitutional.[11]

Online Impersonation.   Online impersonation is generally considered a hybrid crime containing elements of both identity theft and harassment.

Unlike traditional identity theft, online impersonation lacks an economic component. Instead, the defendant impersonates the victim for a noneconomic reason such as to harass. According to noted cyberlaw expert Susan Brenner,

> most jurisdictions define the crime [identity theft] solely in the terms of using another's identity for profit.[12]

It should also be noted that not all online impersonators have the intent to harass. As will be discussed shortly, some create fictitious online accounts for pure satire or to facilitate meeting others.

Online impersonations arise in a variety of different settings but generally take one of two forms. The first involves the impersonator pretending to be someone else in order to interact with the general public on social media. Some impersonations are fairly benign and could be considered parodies. At present, Twitter has become the most common social media platform for these types of impersonations.

One online impersonator has taken on the persona of the Queen of England and uses the following Twitter account (handle) "@Queen_UK." This person sends tweets such as

> [t]ake the day off, people. If anyone asks, tell them the Queen said it was OK

and

> [i]t's Gin O'Clock, kids. Down Tools.[13]

Other impersonations are less benign. A Philadelphia woman created a fake Facebook page in the name of her ex-boyfriend, a narcotics police officer. While impersonating him on Facebook she wrote,

> I'm a sick piece of scum with a gun

and

> I'm an undercover narcotics detective that gets high every day.[14]

This fictitious Facebook page was discovered and the woman was prosecuted and sentenced to a diversion program.[15]

Impersonation can also occur in non–social media settings. For example, in California a criminal defendant used information found on Facebook to take over the email accounts of unsuspecting females.[16] To accomplish his crime, the defendant told email providers, while pretending to be one of his victims, that he was locked out of his account. The email provider asked the defendant several security questions, which he answered based on the information he learned from the victim's Facebook page. Upon taking over the email accounts, he would search for nude or seminude photographs of the victims and send them to the victim's contact list. When asked by one victim why he sent out the pictures, the defendant replied,

Because it's funny.[17]

The second method of online impersonation involves the impersonator pretending to be someone else in order to interact with or establish a relationship with one specific person who may or may not be a "victim" depending on how that term is defined. This interaction can take the form of harassment (e.g., *United States v. Lori Drew*) or be more benign. In this latter category, the impersonator seeks to interact with the victim but does not believe it will be possible unless he creates a false online persona. This situation is apparently what occurred with Manti Te'o, the All-American linebacker from Notre Dame who was the runner-up for the Heisman Trophy in 2012.[18]

Te'o claimed that he was duped into believing that he had an online relationship with a Stanford undergraduate student named Lennay Kekua. Apparently, an acquaintance of Te'o's, Ronaiah Tuiasosopo, created the fictitious Lennay Kekua by using pictures of a former female high school classmate and setting up a bogus social media profile. Tuiasosopo, while masquerading as Lennay Kekua, maintained a social media dating relationship with Te'o for a number of months. It is not entirely clear why Tuiasosopo created Lennay Kekua, but it appears he did so in order to interact with Te'o online.[19]

Online impersonators are successful for three reasons. First, social media provides a cloak of anonymity. To date, neither social media providers nor the government has established a cost-effective method to verify social media users. Second, social media users, especially Digital Natives, have grown accustomed to meeting and interacting with complete strangers on social media. As discussed earlier, social media has led to a breakdown of the traditional social barriers that keep strangers apart.

Third and most importantly, social media permits users to connect and bond with each other in a manner not previously possible with other forms of communication. Through this bonding and connection users create and maintain intimate relationships with people thousands of miles apart.

Many users honestly believe, based on their social media interactions, that the individual at the other end of the laptop, tablet, or smartphone is who she says she is. However, as illustrated by Lori Drew, Ronaiah Tuiasosopo, and others, that assumption is not always correct.

While all states and the federal government have laws combating identity theft and harassment, only a few states have laws against online impersonation. California is one such state. The California law (Penal Code Section 528.5) reads as follows:

(a) Notwithstanding any other provision of law, any person who knowingly and without consent credibly impersonates another actual person through or on an Internet Web site or by other electronic means for purposes of harming, intimidating, threatening, or defrauding another person is guilty of a public offense punishable pursuant to subdivision (d).

(b) For purposes of this section, an impersonation is credible if another person would reasonably believe, or did reasonably believe, that the defendant was or is the person who was impersonated.

(c) For purposes of this section, "electronic means" shall include opening an email account or an account or profile on a social networking Internet Web site in another person's name.

(d) A violation of subdivision (a) is punishable by a fine not exceeding one thousand dollars ($1,000), or by imprisonment in a county jail not exceeding one year, or by both that fine and imprisonment.

(e) In addition to any other civil remedy available, a person who suffers damage or loss by reason of a violation of subdivision (a) may bring a civil action against the violator for compensatory damages and injunctive relief or other equitable relief pursuant to paragraphs (1), (2), (4), and (5) of subdivision (e) and subdivision (g) of Section 502.

(f) This section shall not preclude prosecution under any other law.[20]

To be prosecuted under the California law one must impersonate an *actual person*. Thus, the statute would most likely be inapplicable to situations like those of Manti Te'o or Lori Drew because both Lennay Kekua and Josh Evans were fictitious. This, however, may not be true for all jurisdictions. In Texas, criminal defendants may be prosecuted for online impersonation if they use

the name or persona of another.[21]

Assuming for the sake of argument that Lennay Kekua and Josh Evans had been real people, under the California statute Lori Drew might have been prosecuted but not necessarily Ronaiah Tuiasosopo. This is because in addition to the requirement that one impersonate an actual person, the criminal defendant must also have the purpose of

harming, intimidating, threatening, or defrauding another person.[22]

While Lori Drew arguably had the intent of harming Megan Meier, Ronaiah Tuiasosopo did not want to harm, intimidate, threaten, or defraud Te'o.

In many online impersonations the big issue is defining "harm." Some believe that the harm must be more than being a jerk. Others see it differently and consider emotional distress and financial damage as sufficient harm. Obviously, applying a lower standard to what constitutes harm will expose many more online impersonators to potential prosecution.

The reason for the varying approaches to defining harm is primarily due to two factors. First, there are few cases on this particular subject, so the law is still somewhat unsettled. Second, some jurisdictions categorize this crime as a felony (e.g., Texas), while others view it as a misdemeanor (e.g., California). If charged as a felony, it is far more likely that significant harm has occurred.

The growing trend of individuals impersonating others on social media raises interesting issues. First, some question whether this activity should even be criminal. Who has not at least once impersonated someone over the phone? Since society does not generally prosecute telephone impersonators, why should it prosecute social media impersonators? To answer this second question, one must go back to the Introduction to this book and explore some of the differences that distinguish social media from other forms of communication.

With social media it is much easier to impersonate another because social media allows users to approximate reality in ways unlike any other form of communication. In addition, this impersonation can occur over a longer period of time. More importantly, the impact of these impersonations can be quite significant. Arguably, Manti Te'o lost endorsements and his NFL draft stock went down after it was disclosed that he was involved in a bogus online relationship.

Assuming that society does want to criminalize online impersonations, should other states emulate California and enact similar laws? Many believe that the California model serves as the best approach because it affords both a civil and criminal remedy. Furthermore, it does not elevate online impersonation, which in many instances can be quite harmless, to a felony.

Some have also suggested expanding the law to reach situations like those of Manti Te'o and Lori Drew. While the Te'o and Drew impersonations involved fictitious people, they used pictures of real individuals. Thus, arguably they impersonated the persona of another. While such an expansion would definitely catch many more impersonators, it raises significant constitutional concerns, especially with respect to First Amendment rights.

Finally, should society require more from those who provide online impersonators the forum by which to operate? Most social media providers state in their TOS that users are prohibited from creating fictitious accounts. However, they make little effort to confirm the identities of their users. Is it time for society to expect more from social media providers?

At a minimum, some have suggested that if social media providers are not going to investigate or verify accounts, they should provide their users with notice of this fact. For example, social media providers could inform their users that they have not confirmed that the people they interact with are indeed who they purport to be. Also, social media providers could provide their users guidance on how to confirm the identity of the person that they are communicating with. Most social media providers take some additional steps to provide users information about the risks associated with social media, but this usually comes in the form of carefully scripted language buried in the TOS that few users read or know about.

This idea of placing more responsibility on the social media provider may gain greater traction as people discover the broad scope of immunity granted to social media providers by the Communications Decency Act (CDA) of 1996.[23] Section 230 of the CDA greatly limits the civil liability of computer service providers, including social media providers, from the acts of their users. The rationale behind Section 230, which was passed in the mid-1990s, is that legislators did not want to stifle the growth and use of the Internet by exposing social media providers and other Web site operators to potential liability. Thus, so long as the social media provider is not involved in the creation or development of the content, it will generally be immune from civil claims arising from third-party content or actions.

This point was illustrated in *Doe II v. Myspace, Inc.*[24] In *Doe II* several teenage girls were sexually assaulted by men they met on Myspace. As a result of these attacks, the young girls brought negligence action suits against Myspace. The trial court dismissed these claims citing Section 230 of the CDA. On appeal, the California appellate court upheld the dismissals stating:

> We conclude that section 230 immunity shields Myspace in this case. That appellants characterize their complaint as one for failure to adopt reasonable safety measures does not avoid the immunity granted by section 230. It is undeniable that appellants seek to hold Myspace responsible for the communications between the Julie Does and their assailants. At its core, appellants want Myspace to regulate what appears on this Web site. Appellants argue they do not "allege liability on account of Myspace's exercise of a publisher's traditional editorial functions, such as editing, altering, or deciding whether or not to publish certain material, which is the test for whether a claim treats a Web site as a publisher under Barrett." But that is precisely what they allege; that is, they want Myspace to ensure that sexual predators do not gain access to (i.e., communicate with) minors on its Web site. That type of activity— to restrict or make available certain material—is expressly covered by section 230.[25]

Threats.   Another common online Category I crime is issuing threats. Unlike harassment, threats generally involve

> conduct directed at the victim, rather than general communication about a victim.[26]

In order to prosecute someone for making a threat, the threat has to go beyond merely being objectionable or offensive. The threat must communicate a serious expression of intent to commit an act of unlawful violence to a particular individual or group of individuals.[27]

Over the past 10 years, the method of communicating a threat has evolved from word of mouth to voicemails to texts to social media. Individuals have used social media to send threats to a wide range of people from spouses[28] to teachers[29] to police officers[30] to witnesses[31] to sitting presidents.[32] These threats have occurred on a broad spectrum of social media platforms, including Myspace and blogs.

In one case, a criminal defendant was successfully prosecuted for threatening a judge in a music video posted on YouTube.[33] According to the Sixth Circuit Court of Appeals which upheld the defendant's conviction:

> No doubt, it is unusual or at least a sign of the times that the vehicle for this threat was a music video. Best we can tell, this is the first reported case of a successful § 875(c) prosecution arising from a song or video. One answer to the point is that the statute covers "any threat," making no distinction between threats delivered orally (in person, by phone) or in writing (letters, emails, faxes), by video or by song, in old-fashioned ways or in the most up-to-date. Nor would this be the first time that an old flask was filled with new wine—that an old statute was applied to a technology nowhere to be seen when the law was enacted.[34]

Most states and the federal government have laws to address threats made via social media. At the federal level, the Interstate Communications Act (ICA) makes it unlawful to

> transmit [. . .] in interstate or foreign commerce any communication containing any threat to kidnap any person or any threat to injure the person of another.[35]

This statute is limited to overt threats. Thus, it generally does not cover indirect threats made to the victim.

To be convicted of violating the ICA (§ 875(c)) the prosecution must establish that the defendant (1) knowingly made a communication in interstate commerce that (2) a reasonable observer would construe as a true threat to another.[36]

The prosecution of Anthony Elonis demonstrates how the ICA works in the context of a threat issued via social media. In *United States v. Elonis*, the federal government brought charges against the defendant Anthony Elonis for posting a series of ominous Facebook posts. In those posts, Elonis threatened his wife, a former employer, and the community as a whole. Here is a sample of what he posted:

> That's it, I've had about enough
>
> I'm checking out and making a name for myself
>
> Enough elementary schools in a ten mile radius

to initiate the most heinous school shooting ever imagined

And hell hath no fury like a crazy man in a Kindergarten class

The only question is . . . which one?

. . .

Fold up your PFA [Protection from Abuse Order] and put it in your pocket[.]

Is it thick enough to stop a bullet?[37] [this last threat was directed to Elonis's wife]

Prior to trial, Elonis filed a motion to dismiss the charges against him, arguing that his posts were

simply crude, spontaneous and emotional language expressing frustration, and that they were not sufficiently definite to constitute a true threat.[38]

The court denied the defendant's motion to dismiss, finding that

[w]hether the Facebook postings contain true threats is a question of fact for the jury and cannot be decided by the court.[39]

The case then proceeded to trial where the defendant testified that he never meant what he posted and that the words were taken from rap lyrics. Despite this testimony, the jury convicted Elonis on four of the five counts brought against him.

It should be noted that the Supreme Count has agreed to hear Mr. Elonis's appeal and other defendants have had more success in raising similar motions to dismiss. This is especially true if the alleged threat is (1) not made directly to the victim; (2) unlikely to be received by the victim; or (3) directed toward a public figure. In the *Elonis* case, those threatened by the defendant were likely to view the threats because they were friends with him on Facebook.

Stalking.   The third common online Category I crime is stalking. The term "Facebook stalker" has garnered a sort of benign humorous connotation in popular culture. However, individuals have been successfully prosecuted for using social media to repeatedly stalk or contact others.

The traditional difference between threatening and stalking is that the latter generally targets conduct and therefore requires a pattern, while the former only requires one threat to prosecute.[40] It should be noted that not all jurisdictions make this distinction. In fact, in some instances, threats, harassment, and stalking are all covered by one statute or overlapping statutes.

For example, the Telephone Harassment Act makes it unlawful for a person to use a communications device anonymously to

> annoy, abuse, threaten, or harass a person . . . who receives the communications.[41]

The Telephone Harassment Act, like the ICA and the CFAA, also applies to threats and stalking.

Examples of using social media to stalk another include a case from the Washington, D.C. area where a 14-year-old girl posed as a boy and started a relationship with another local girl.[42] After the victim's father discovered the relationship, he prohibited the 14-year-old girl from having any future contact with his daughter. However, the young girl continued to contact the victim via social media, going so far as to create bogus Facebook profiles pretending to be different boys. Eventually, the police were called and the young girl was charged with stalking.

The federal government and all states have some type of stalking statute. On the national level it is the Federal Interstate Stalking Punishment and Prevention Act (FISPPA).[43] As originally written it prohibited using the mail or commerce to put another in reasonable fear of death or serious injury. However, it was expanded in 2006 to criminalize causing "substantial emotional distress" to another person using an "interactive computer service."[44] Today, for a successful prosecution under FISPPA, the government must prove the following elements:

> Use of
>
> a. The mail
>
> b. Any interactive computer service, or
>
> c. Any facility of interstate or foreign commerce;
>
> To engage in a course of conduct, defined as a pattern of conduct composed of 2 or more acts, evidencing a continuity of purpose;
>
> That causes

d. Substantial emotional distress, or

e. Reasonable fear of death or serious bodily injury, to a person in another state or tribal jurisdiction or within the special maritime and territorial jurisdiction; and

Intent by the defendant to

f. Kill,

g. Injure,

h. Harass,

i. Place under surveillance with intent to kill, injure, harass, or intimidate, or

j. Cause substantial emotional distress to that person.[45]

United States v. Cassidy, discussed next, highlights some of the challenges that arise with FISPPA prosecutions when the alleged stalking or harassment involves a public figure and occurs on social media.[46] In *Cassidy*, the criminal defendant, who initially went by the alias Sanderson, met Alyce Zeoli in 2007. Zeoli, an enthroned Buddhist American tulku (a reincarnation of an enlightened being), teaches and leads the Kunzang Odsal Palyou Changchub Choling Center ("Center") located in Maryland. The meeting between Cassidy and Zeoli was facilitated by Zeoli's friends who believed that Cassidy was also a Buddhist American tulku.

After meeting and becoming fast friends with Cassidy, Zeoli invited him to drive with her to a retreat in Arizona. During the trip, Cassidy proposed to Zeoli but she declined his offer. He then suggested that the two pretend to be married. While on this trip, Zeoli also revealed intimate details about her personal life to Cassidy.

Shortly after the trip, it came to light that William Sanderson's real name was William Cassidy. Members of the Center also began to notice that Cassidy's conduct was inconsistent with the sect's teachings (e.g., he gossiped). Also, according to the criminal complaint filed against Cassidy, he told members of the Center that he had stage IV lung cancer, which led some members to take care of him. Yet, despite certain misgivings, Cassidy was appointed to the position of chief operating officer (COO) of the Center.

Shortly after his appointment as COO, Zeoli learned that Cassidy had never been a tulku. She confronted Cassidy about this fact and he left the

Center in February 2008. Subsequent to his departure, Cassidy started making disparaging posts and tweets about Zeoli and the Center. Some of the 8,000 tweets and blog posts were arguably threatening:

> ya like haiku? Here's one for ya: "Long, Limb, Sharp Saw, Hard Drop" ROFLMAO.

> Got a wonderful Pearl Harbor Day surprise for KPC... wait for it.

> Terrors in the night disturb Fat (A.Z.)'s sleep: she cannot sleep without taking something, and anxiety rules her body like a slavemaster.[47]

Other tweets and posts were critical and disparaging:

> [Zeoli] is a demonic force who tries to destroy Buddhism.

> (A.Z.) you are a liar & a fraud & you corrupt Buddhism by your very presence: go kill yourself.

> (A.Z.) IS A SATANIC CORRUPTER OF DHARMA: A SHE_ DEMON WHO MASQUERADES AS A "TEACHER"[48]

In 2011, Cassidy was charged with violating FISPPA. Specifically, Cassidy was charged with the intent to *harass* and *cause substantial emotional distress* to Zeoli in violation of FISPPA. Interestingly, the government did not charge the defendant with putting Zeoli in *reasonable fear of death or serious bodily injury*. This is most likely due to the fact that the posts and tweets, although disparaging, were not very threatening.

Prior to trial, counsel for Cassidy filed a motion to dismiss, arguing that the statute on its face and as applied violated Cassidy's First Amendment rights. The trial court found the statute unconstitutional as applied to Cassidy. Thus, it never decided whether the statute was unconstitutional on its face.

In dismissing the charges against Cassidy, the trial court first determined that Cassidy's tweets and blog posts, although in bad taste, challenged Zeoli's character and qualifications as a religious leader and thus were protected under the First Amendment of the United States Constitution. The court pointed out that not all speech is protected, for example, speech involving obscenity, fraud, defamation, true threats (as illustrated by *United States v. Elonis*), incitement, or speech integral to criminal conduct. However, Cassidy was charged with harassing Zeoli, not with placing her in reasonable fear of death or serious bodily injury.

The next step in the court's analysis was to determine whether FISPPA as applied to Cassidy's actions was a content-based restriction. The court ultimately determined that the statute as applied to Cassidy was a content-based restriction because it

limits speech on the basis of whether that speech is emotionally distressing to A.Z.[49]

As a result of this determination, the court examined the application of the FISPPA statute under the highest level of review—strict scrutiny. Thus, in order for the government to prevail against Cassidy's motion to dismiss, it had to show a compelling governmental interest, a very high standard to meet, as to why Cassidy should be prosecuted under FISPPA.

The government claimed that its compelling interest arose from the need to protect

victims from emotional distress sustained through an interactive computer service.[50]

The court pointed out, however, that this interest could just as easily be protected by having the victim ignore the defendant's blog or block his tweets.

The court then went on to examine whether the government could survive the defendant's motion to suppress under a lower level of review—intermediate scrutiny. Unfortunately for the prosecution, the court again found the government's argument for prosecuting Cassidy under FISPPA unconstitutional even with this lower level of scrutiny. Here, the court drew a distinction between using the telephone to harass someone and using Twitter or a blog. In explaining why Virginia's telephone harassment statute could be found constitutional while FISPPA as applied to Cassidy could not, the court stated:

harassing telephone calls "are targeted towards a particular victim and are received outside a public forum" . . . Twitter and Blogs are today's equivalent of a bulletin board that one is free to disregard, in contrast, for example, to e-mails or phone calls directed to a victim.[51]

The court's opinion did not end with finding the government's interest to be lacking at both levels of scrutiny. The court went on and assumed *in arguendo* that the government had a compelling interest. The court still found the indictment as applied to Cassidy unconstitutional because FISPPA, in this case, sweeps in the type of expression that the Supreme Court has consistently tried to protect.[52]

For example, the statute could cover statements Cassidy made about

KPC's beliefs and A.Z.'s qualifications as a leader.[53]

United States v. Cassidy might have resulted in a better outcome for the government if the defendant, rather than using social media, had employed traditional communication methods like the mail or the telephone. The court appeared troubled with prosecuting someone for making disparaging comments about a public figure in a public forum. The court noted

> that Twitter and Blogs are today's equivalent of a bulletin board that one is free to disregard, in contrast, for example, to e-mails or phone calls directed to a victim.[54]

The court went on to find that a blog is similar to a cyberspace bulletin board.

The government also might have defeated the defendant's motion to dismiss by changing its theory of prosecution from causing emotional distress to issuing true threats. As the court pointed out, true threats like obscenity, fraud, incitement, and speech integral to criminal conduct are not protected speech; however, that was not the basis for the government's indictment in this case. According to the court,

> the Government did not seek an Indictment on the basis that the Defendant intentionally used the Internet to put A.Z. in reasonable fear of death or serious bodily injury.[55]

William Cassidy's conduct, like that of Lori Drew and Anthony Elonis, occurred completely on social media. Put differently, all three were charged not for their offline actions but for their online actions: Lori Drew harassed Megan Meier on Myspace, Anthony Elonis issued threats on Facebook, and William Cassidy made disparaging comments through Twitter and the blogosphere. However, this is not always how Category I crimes are carried out. Sometimes the crime does not occur on social media. Instead, social media merely facilitates the criminal activity. The next section of the chapter will look at these types of Category I crimes where the actual crime itself, although involving social media, occurs offline rather than online.

Offline Category I Crimes

For offline Category I crimes, social media serves as a conduit for criminal defendants to interact with others. With respect to criminal defendants using social media to communicate with unsuspecting victims, this interaction occurs in one of two ways. Victims either respond to information posted on social media by criminal defendants or criminal defendants respond to information posted on social media by victims. The following examples illustrate these two methods.

Criminal Defendants Posting Information.   In the summer of 2011, a help wanted ad for a farmhand in north central Ohio was posted on Craigslist.[56] The ad promised the farmhand $300 a week, a trailer, and use of the farm. The job applicants who responded to the ad were instructed to bring all of their belongings with them to the initial interview because if hired they would be living on the farm.

When the job applicants arrived at a designated location on or near the farm, they were met by Brogan Rafferty (age 16 at the time) and Richard Beasley (age 52 at the time). After this initial meeting, these two defendants drove the job applicants to an isolated and remote area in the woods and executed them. The defendants then buried the victims in shallow graves and divvied up their possessions.

Of the four job applicants who met Rafferty and Beasley, only one would survive. The lone survivor, who escaped after being shot in the arm, reported the defendants to the police. This led to the ultimate capture of Rafferty and Beasley and their subsequent prosecution. Both Rafferty and Beasley were convicted at trial. Rafferty received a life sentence and Beasley was sentenced to death.

Victims Posting Information.   In the second week of April 2009, a New England medical student (Philip Markoff) reached out to several women who advertised personal services on Craigslist.[57] After making initial phone contact with these women, Markoff would make an appointment to meet them in person. Upon arriving at their respective hotel rooms, Markoff would rob the women. He killed one of the women after she put up a struggle.

Markoff was ultimately apprehended by high-tech police work. The police were able to link Markoff to the hotel room of the woman whom he killed by investigating cell towers, Craigslist accounts, and Internet protocol addresses. Markoff was never tried for his crimes because he took his own life while in police custody. Markoff's week-long crime spree garnered so much public interest that it was later dramatized in a made-for-TV movie, *The Craigslist Killer.*

Due to the actions of individuals like Markoff, Rafferty, Beasley, and others, there have been increased efforts to educate the public about taking precautions when first making face-to-face contact with people they only know from social media. Numerous entities across the country ranging from media outlets to law enforcement to civic organizations have offered the public suggestions and issued guidelines on how to safely use social media.

Communications among Criminal Defendants.   In addition to using social media to communicate with victims or the general public, criminal defendants also rely on it to communicate with each other and organize criminal activity. For example, a Philadelphia woman used social media to find a "hit man." She did this by posting the following on Facebook:

I will pay somebody a stack to kill my baby's father.[58]

Surprisingly, someone actually responded to the ad. Fortunately, the crime was never carried out as both the woman who posted the ad and the individual who responded to it were apprehended by law enforcement.

Another example of criminal defendants using social media to communicate with one another, one that has garnered a lot of attention recently, is the flash mob. Created in 2003 by Bill Wasik, senior editor of *Harper's* magazine, the flash mob was initially intended to be an act of spontaneous performance art. Communicating through social media, individuals would suddenly gather in one public location to participate in impromptu snowball or pillow fights or disco routines. According to Wasik:

[Flash mobs] were an important demonstration to the people who took part in them . . . especially in this kind of era of Facebook where we have these large communities of "friends" but our relationship with them are [sic] so virtual and they're so bound up in this very ephemeral or kind of just purely digital transactions. . . . There's something about flash mobs where those connections are suddenly made really explicit or really virtual and they remind us that we are still people who have bodies and still people who have the ability to create change in the real physical world.[59]

Recently, the flash mob has taken a sinister twist as large groups of teens have used social media to quickly gather at one location to vandalize, steal, and commit acts of violence. Flash mobs generate heightened concern among law enforcement and society as a whole because of the secretive (at times) and fluid nature in which they arise. Furthermore, flash mob participants can disperse just as quickly as they can assemble.

Some flash mobs involve co-conspirators who may not even realize they are participating in a flash mob. Consider the following Twitter flash mob. On August 12, 2011, well-known rapper The Game sent a tweet about a possible internship to his 580,000 followers.[60] The contact number listed in the tweet did not belong to The Game but rather to the Los Angeles County Sheriff's Department. As soon as The Game's tweet went out, the police were inundated with so many calls that regular callers could not get through. Once the police discovered the reason for the large number of calls, they contacted The Game, who then apologized for mistakenly tweeting the wrong number. Fortunately for The Game, no criminal charges were filed against him.

To date, several cities and states have passed or are considering legislation to address flash mobs. Interestingly, there is no cookie cutter approach to enacting such legislation. For example, in 2011, the Cleveland City Council passed an ordinance prohibiting the use of social media to incite people to riot, unlawfully congregate, or engage in disorderly conduct within the city.[61] This ordinance met with stiff opposition from the ACLU, who viewed it as vague and an infringement on an individual's First Amendment rights. This in turn led the mayor of Cleveland to veto the ordinance.

In response to the mayor's veto, the city council passed another ordinance without the social media language. This new proposal took a different approach and classified electronic media devices as a criminal tool when used to incite riots. Since the mayor neither vetoed nor signed this new ordinance, it ultimately became law.[62]

Another approach being considered by other jurisdictions is to hold each person in the flash mob accountable for the damage done by the group as a whole.[63] For example, if 30 teenagers show up at a convenience store and each one takes a candy bar, each teenager could be charged with the total number of candy bars stolen. This change in the law would make it easier to charge misdemeanor petty theft offenses, which often occur during criminal flash mobs, as felonies. This idea of holding co-defendants liable for the actions of others is also seen in the crime of conspiracy.

As with the new statutes addressing other Category I crimes, some question whether these laws will pass constitutional muster when challenged in court. Of the two approaches, the second method, holding one person liable for the entire conduct of the group, is more likely to be found constitutional because it is less likely to infringe on a defendant's First Amendment rights. Some believe that creating new legislation to target flash mobs is unnecessary. These opponents argue that rather than create new laws, jurisdictions would be better served by (1) improving law enforcement's ability to monitor social media activity and (2) enforcing current laws that target mob-like activity.

CATEGORY II CRIMES (GATHERING INFORMATION)

Most, but not all, social media–related crimes fall into Category I. Category II involves criminal defendants using social media to *gather* information about victims. Like Category I crimes, Category II crimes are further divided into two subcategories. In the first subcategory, the criminal defendant uses the information gathered from social media to commit modern crimes that many associate with the Internet (e.g., identity theft). In the second subcategory, the criminal defendant uses the information gathered from social media to commit traditional crimes that many do not necessarily associate with the Internet (e.g., burglary).

When using social media for Category II crimes, criminal defendants look for all types of personal identifiable information about victims ranging from photos to birthdates to names of friends. According to Frank Abagnale, a former con man turned FBI officer (portrayed in the 2002 film *Catch Me If You Can*),

[i]f you tell me your date of birth and where you're born [on Facebook], I'm 98% [of the way] to stealing your identity.[64]

To obtain certain personal information, criminal defendants must monitor social media over a period of time. This is especially true if the criminal defendant wants to learn the physical whereabouts or daily routine of the victim.

Modern Category II Crimes

As stated earlier, identity theft is generally considered an economic crime and thus different from online impersonation, although many people and some jurisdictions use the terms interchangeably.[65] Identity theft via social media takes numerous forms. Some of the more common schemes include using information discovered on social media to open financial accounts in the victim's name. Here, the criminal defendant is able to use a victim's social media site to learn enough personal information about the victim such as name, birth date, previous and current address, and certain other details to open bank accounts, credit cards, and so on in the victim's name.

Other identity theft schemes via social media include profile cloning. Here, a criminal defendant does the same digging on social media but instead of opening a credit card or bank account in the victim's name, he creates a fictitious social media account. Once this is done, the criminal defendant will send out some distress story via social media to the friends of the victim requesting that money be sent to some location. This crime is often referred to as a confidence scheme. Both of the aforementioned forms of identity theft may be prosecuted.

All states and the federal government have laws to combat identity theft. The federal statute 18 U.S.C. § 1028 criminalizes eight types of conduct involving fraudulent identification documents or the unlawful use of identification information. At present, subsection (a)(7) is most applicable to situations involving social media and reads as follows:

> Whoever in a circumstance described in subsection (c) of this section—(7) knowingly transfers, possesses, or uses, without lawful authority, *a means of identification* of another *person* with the intent to commit, or to aid or abet, or in connection with, any unlawful activity that constitutes a violation of Federal law, or that constitutes a felony under any applicable State or local law, shall be punished.[66] [emphasis added]

"Means of identification" includes

> any name or number that may be used . . . to identify a specific individual.[67]

"Person" refers to individuals both living and dead.[68] In prosecuting identity theft under this statute, the government must show that

> the defendant knew that the means of identification at issue belonged to another person.[69]

Traditional Category II Crimes

In addition to using social media to gather information on victims to carry out modern crimes like identity theft, criminal defendants also use the information collected to commit more traditional crimes like burglary. Historically, criminal defendants looking to burgle a residence had to stake out the place or look for telltale signs that the occupants were away, such as stacked up newspapers or mail. Today, burglars look to social media to determine whether or not an individual is out of town or away from his residence.

Some victims give criminal defendants obvious signs by actually stating on their social media account that they are going on vacation or pinpointing their exact location through geo-location social media platforms like Foursquare. Other victims give less obvious signs that nonetheless alert the criminal defendant of their absence, for example, posting pictures of exotic locales or allowing themselves to be tagged in photos. Once criminal defendants learn that the victim is away, they burglarize the victim's home. For those who feel the need to routinely post about life experiences, it has been suggested that they not do so in real time or wait until after they return from vacation.

CHALLENGES OF PREVENTING AND PROSECUTING SOCIAL MEDIA CRIMES

At present, many think that social media crimes are more difficult to prevent and prosecute than their offline counterparts.[70] This is due to a variety of reasons. First, some social media–related crimes involve the communication of information to others via public or quasi-public forums. Thus, any attempt to criminalize or prosecute such communications runs the risk of infringing upon a defendant's constitutional rights.

This was seen in *United States v. Cassidy* where the court dismissed the government's indictment, finding that it infringed on the criminal defendant's First Amendment rights. A key issue in *Cassidy* was the method used by the defendant to communicate his views. The court made note of the fact that rather than use the phone or email to make his disparaging comments, the defendant used public forums such as Twitter and blog posts. The court went on to compare these social media platforms to bulletin boards that the victim had the option of reading.

Second, the very nature of social media makes it challenging to attribute any specific comments to a particular individual. Many social media sites allow individuals to add information anonymously. In addition, as illustrated by online impersonation and identity theft, it is not difficult to pretend to be someone else when using social media. In fact, it regularly occurs. Most social media providers have no system in place to verify the identity of their users. This in turn makes it difficult for police to track down online imposters or anonymous users of social media.

Third, some jurisdictions have yet to update their laws to reflect the new methods by which people commit crimes via social media. For instance, very few states have laws regulating online impersonation. In fact, most states are in catch-up mode trying to pass new laws. Although Missouri has since modified its laws, it was unable to prosecute Lori Drew because the state's harassment statute, at the time, did not cover social media.

Fourth, social media affords criminal defendants a larger audience and a greater pool of victims. In the example of harassment, criminal defendants are no longer constrained by the volume of their voice. In *United States v. Elonis*, the criminal defendant was able not only to harass his estranged spouse but also his community as a whole by threatening via Facebook to shoot a kindergarten class. Other examples include the criminal defendants from Ohio who used Craigslist to find victims from both inside and outside of the state. Fortunately, one potential victim, who traveled all the way from South Carolina in response to the Craigslist ad, was able to escape and contact law enforcement.

Finally, the ease and speed by which social media crimes are committed encourages criminal defendants to continue to victimize others. In *United States v. Sayer,* the criminal defendant was able to use Craigslist's Casual Encounters site to repeatedly victimize his ex-girlfriend even after she moved far away from him. The criminal defendant in *United States v. Cassidy* made over 8,000 disparaging blog posts and tweets about Alyce Zeoli and the Center.

While at present it appears that criminal defendants have the upper hand with respect to employing social media, this advantage will most likely be short-lived. As Part II will demonstrate, law enforcement has been steadily adapting to the Digital Age and incorporating social media into almost every aspect of policing. Furthermore, legislators and prosecutors, as illustrated in Part III, are now taking proactive steps to prevent criminal defendants from exploiting social media for criminal purposes.

CRIMINAL PENALTIES TARGETING SOCIAL MEDIA USE

As the earlier part of this chapter demonstrates, criminal defendants have effectively used social media in a variety of ways to facilitate their illegal activities. This in turn has led some states to enact new laws limiting or targeting the use of social media by criminal defendants. These restrictions generally take one of four forms.

The first is sentencing enhancements. At least one state (Illinois) has increased the applicable penalties for violent crimes orchestrated by social media. The second is an outright ban on social media. Several states have passed laws prohibiting criminal defendants from accessing or using social media. Next comes monitoring of social media accounts. This is where the convicted criminal defendant must allow the court to monitor his usage of social media. The final method is the Digital Scarlet Letter. Here, the government requires convicted criminal defendants to list their crimes on any personal social media account they use.

The last three penalties, which will be the focus of this section, have been reserved primarily for those convicted of committing sex-related offenses. This is true even when social media plays no role in the crime at all. Courts have generally upheld these restrictions regardless of whether a link exists between the crime and social media so long as the criminal defendant is still under the jurisdiction of the court. One notable exception to the court's expansive power here is the case of *In re Andre B.*[71]

In re Andre B. involved a 15-year-old juvenile defendant who was convicted of improperly touching two young females. Social media played no role in the conduct of these crimes. Nevertheless, the court, as part of the juvenile's probation sentence, prohibited Andre B. from

> having or using a Myspace page, a Facebook page, or any other similar page; (3) participating in chat rooms, using instant messaging such as ICQ, Myspace, Facebook, Twitter, or other similar communication programs.[72]

Attorneys for Andre B. appealed his sentence, and a California appellate court struck down the probationary conditions, finding:

> There is no evidence or indication in the record that Andre used Internet chat rooms or social media to contact his victims or to learn how to carry out his actions underlying the true findings. We conclude that prohibiting Andre from using social media is overbroad and, as phrased, the prohibition has no bearing on his possible rehabilitation.[73]

Despite the ruling of *In re Andre B.*, most appellate courts adhere to the position that the trial judge has broad leeway in fashioning probationary requirements. Thus, restrictions on social media use are generally upheld. However, once criminal defendants are no longer on parole, probation, or court supervision the law is a little less clear with respect to imposing social media restrictions. Later sections will examine some of the issues that arise when courts attempt to restrict the social media activities of criminal defendants who are no longer under their direct jurisdiction.

However, prior to undertaking that discussion, this chapter will briefly examine sentencing enhancements.

Sentencing Enhancements

One tool legislators turn to when faced with a new crime, a surge in crime, or changes in how criminals commit crimes is to increase the criminal defendant's punishment upon conviction. This can be accomplished with sentencing enhancements where the defendant receives a higher sentence if certain facts, beyond the commission of the crime, are found by the court. For example, a judge might enhance a criminal defendant's sentence for any of the following reasons: commission of prior crimes, use of a weapon, harm to the victim, abuse of a position of trust, or involvement of a juvenile.

To date, sentencing enhancements have been met with mixed success. Some assert that sentencing enhancements lead to lower crime rates. Others question whether additional penalties actually prevent crime or just lead to higher rates of incarceration. This ongoing debate, however, has not stopped at least one state from applying sentencing enhancements to social media–related crimes.

In 2013, the state of Illinois created the first sentencing enhancement specifically targeting criminal defendants who use social media to organize violent crime.[74] With the passage of this new law, judges in Illinois now have the discretion to increase a criminal defendant's sentence if he uses electronic media to organize a group of people to commit a violent crime. A criminal defendant in Illinois who organizes a violent crime using an electronic communication now faces a three- to six-year sentence of incarceration rather than one to three years. According to the state representative who sponsored the new law,

> [t]hey [criminal gangs] are now using social networks to organize and mobilize violent activity. The intent of this legislation is to update our laws to reflect how people are using technology to organize crimes in our neighborhoods.[75]

Ban

To date, the most controversial penalty involving social media and criminal defendants is the ban. Several states across the country have enacted laws that prohibit certain sex offenders from accessing or using social media. One of the early cases to address the question of whether a state could ban a criminal defendant who was not under parole, probation, or court supervision from social media was *John Doe v. Prosecutor, Marion County, Indiana.*[76] In *Prosecutor, Marion County, Indiana* the plaintiffs (registered sex offenders) brought a class action lawsuit challenging the constitutionality of Indiana Code § 35-42-4-12(e). The statute prohibited certain registered sex offenders from knowingly or intentionally accessing a social networking site, instant messaging program, or chat room, if the offender knows that the site allows someone under the age of 18 to use or access it.[77] The statute defined a social networking site as follows:

> [A]n Internet web site that: (1) facilitates the social introduction between two or more persons; (2) requires a person to register or create an account, a username, or a password to become a member of the web site and to communicate with other members; (3) allows a member to create a web page or a personal profile; and (4) provides a member with the opportunity to communicate with another person. The term does not include an electronic mail program or message board program.[78]

Plaintiffs argued that this ban as applied to those no longer on parole, probation, or supervised release violated their First Amendment rights.[79] Specifically, the plaintiffs claimed that the statute affects three rights secured by the First Amendment: (1) the right to communicate; (2) the right to receive information; and (3) the right to associate.

On the initial question of whether the statute infringed on First Amendment rights, the district court agreed with the plaintiffs. However, the court then pointed out that certain First Amendment infringements are permissible if (1) they are narrowly tailored to serve a significant governmental interest and (2) alternative forms of communication exist. As to the first prong, the court determined that the ban was narrowly tailored because the statute did not prevent plaintiffs from all social media sites; for example, the court stated that plaintiffs could use LinkedIn, which, at the time, did not allow any users under the age of 18.

As for the second prong, the court, which ultimately determined that the statute was constitutional, found that the law allowed for alternative channels of communication. By way of example, the court pointed out that the plaintiffs could still

> congregate with others, attend civic meetings, call in to radio shows, write letters to newspapers and magazines, post on message boards,

comment on online stories that do not require a Facebook (or some other prohibited account), email friends, family, associates, politicians, and other adults, publish a blog, and use social networking sites that do not allow minors.[80]

On appeal, the Seventh Circuit Court of Appeals saw it differently. The appellate court determined that the ban was not narrowly tailored. The appellate court pointed out that

[t]he law does not differentiate based on the age of the victim, the manner in which the crime was committed, or the time since the predicate offense.[81]

Next, the appellate court determined that the ban was entirely too broad because it went beyond targeting improper communications to minors. The ban encompassed both protected speech and communication that had nothing to do with minors. The appellate court also noted that the state of Indiana had other ways by which to combat inappropriate communications between minors and sex offenders.

The Seventh Circuit Court of Appeals went on to make it abundantly clear that, although it found the current ban unconstitutional, the court was not foreclosing future efforts by the legislature to prevent sex offenders from using social media. The court stated that its decision

should not be read to limit the legislature's ability to craft constitutional solutions to this modern-day challenge.[82]

Thus, one takeaway from the appellate court's ruling is that the state is not prohibited from restricting or banning individuals from social media. However, such bans must be drafted with precision to avoid being overly broad. Subsequent to the decision by the Seventh Circuit Court of Appeals, the state of Indiana has reworked and significantly narrowed its ban. It remains to be seen whether this new law will be found constitutional.

Prior to the decision in *John Doe v. Prosecutor, Marion County, Indiana* the federal district court in Louisiana decided a very similar case in *John Doe v. Bobby Jindal et al.*[83] The Louisiana case involved a state statute that prohibited registered sex offenders found guilty of victimizing minors from using social networking sites, chat rooms, or peer-to-peer networking without permission from a probation or parole officer. In certain ways the Louisiana statute, which relied on a very expansive view of social networking, was more restrictive than the aforementioned Indiana statute. According to the Louisiana law, a social networking site included the following:

(a) Allows users to create web pages or profiles about themselves that are available to the general public or to any other users.

(b) Offers a mechanism for communication among users, such as forum, chat room, electronic mail, or instant messaging.[84]

The trial judge in *Bobby Jindal et al.* found the Louisiana law facially unconstitutional as it was both overbroad and vague. The court noted that the sweeping restrictions of the ban applied not only to traditional social media providers like Myspace and Facebook but also to online media outlets like newspapers because they allow communication among users in the form of comments and content forwarding. The court also noted that an individual violated the statute even if he mistakenly or unintentionally accessed the prohibited Web site. Finally, the court noted that the permission requirement in which an individual must receive approval from a probation or parole officer in order to view certain social media sites raises fundamental jurisdictional concerns, especially for those convicted criminal defendants no longer under court supervision.

In response to the *Bobby Jindal et al.* decision the state of Louisiana enacted a new ban with the passage of H.B. 620. This updated, more narrowly tailored law prohibits sex offenders convicted of offenses involving minors or video voyeurism from intentionally using social networking sites, which are defined as follows:

Social interaction with other networking website users, which contains profile web pages of the member of the website that include the names of or nicknames of such members, that allows photographs and any other personal or personally identifying information to be placed on the profile web pages by such members, and which provides links to other profile web pages on the networking website of friends or associates of such members that can be accessed by other members or visitors to the website.

A networking website provides members of, or visitors to, such website the ability to leave messages or comments on the profile web page that are visible to all or some visitors to the profile web page and may also include a form of electronic mail for members of the networking website.[85]

The definition of a social networking site created in H.B. 620 is quite narrow, especially in comparison to prior definitions used by both

Indiana and Louisiana. By limiting its definition, the state of Louisiana increases the likelihood that its new ban will be found constitutional. Here, it appears as though H.B. 620 primarily targets traditional social networking sites like Myspace and Facebook rather than all social media sites. Thus, it is unlikely that this new law will apply to sites like Craigslist.

H.B. 620, however, maintains the same draconian penalties from the last ban, which called for incarceration of up to 10 years without suspension of sentence or early release, and up to a $10,000 fine. It remains to be seen whether H.B. 620, like the new law in Indiana, will be deemed constitutional.

Those who support prohibiting convicted criminal defendants from using social media claim that such bans are necessary to protect vulnerable victims, especially children. Ban proponents point to the large presence of children on social media and the number of hours they spend using it. They also note that, unlike traditional forms of communication, social media allows children to make large amounts of information available to the general public. Professor James Grimmelmann, who has written extensively on law and technology, states that

> [a] fully filled-out Facebook profile contains about forty pieces of recognizably personal information, including name; birthday; political and religious views; online and offline contact information; gender, sexual preference, and relationship status; favorite books, movies, and so on; educational and employment history; and, of course, picture.[86]

To ban proponents social media has become a virtual billboard where sexual predators can lurk.[87] They believe that criminal defendants, especially sexual predators, will use the information posted on social media, no matter how trivial, to build a rapport and establish trust with potential victims.[88]

Some have also suggested that parents have less control over social media. In the offline world, parents for the most part regularly see what mail, if any, their child receives, the television shows they watch, and the friends they interact with. The same is not necessarily true for social media.

As discussed previously, social media has redefined the word "friend," so much so that normal social barriers that prevented interaction among strangers have eroded. With social media, a child may have hundreds or even thousands of so-called online friends that even she doesn't truly know, much less her parents.

The final and arguably the strongest argument for the ban concerns identity verification. As discussed in Chapter 2, criminal defendants have been very adept at impersonating others while using social media. In 2013, Facebook reported that 7–8 percent of its accounts or approximately 50 million were fictitious.[89] At present, there are few ways for users, especially children, to verify who they are communicating with when using social media. Thus, many believe that until social media verification procedures are in place the government should take all steps necessary to protect children.

Proponents of social media bans believe that they are constitutional despite being struck down in several states. As support for their argument, they compare the ban to other postconviction restrictions imposed on criminal defendants. These restrictions, like the ban on social media, prevent convicted criminal defendants from exercising rights that many consider fundamental. For example, if an individual is convicted of a felony, she can be prevented from sitting on a jury, voting, or possessing a firearm. This is true regardless of whether the individual was convicted of a white-collar crime like tax evasion or a typical street crime like robbery.

Advocates of the ban also point to the laws springing up around the country related to sex offenders. At present, many states and cities prohibit sex offenders from living or going near parks, playgrounds, schools, or daycare centers. This is in addition to the laws that require sex offenders to regularly register with local law enforcement. Proponents claim that the ban on using social media is merely an extension of these sex offender–related laws.

Opponents of the bans offer a variety of reasons for why they should be struck down. First and foremost, they raise the same constitutional arguments that the judges found persuasive in *John Doe v. Bobby Jindal et al.* and *John Doe v. Prosecutor, Marion County, Indiana*: The bans are (1) overbroad and vague, and (2) not narrowly tailored to serve a significant governmental interest. Opponents point out that these generic bans are not individualized. Instead, they institute blanket coverage regardless of the type of offense committed or whether the underlying crime involved either a child or social media.

Ban opponents also draw a distinction between restricting social media use and other postconviction penalties by pointing out that social media has become ubiquitous in society and that most people would find it difficult to go a day, much less a week without using some form of social media. This is true both personally and professionally as an increasing number of employers now use or require their employees to use social media. In contrast, an individual might not need to live in a certain neighborhood or go to a particular park, playground, daycare center, or school.

Regardless whether one is for or against a ban on social media use by convicted criminal defendants, the discussion raises some very interesting questions that are worthy of further debate. For example, should the ban go beyond those convicted of sex-related offenses? Some have argued that if society is truly concerned about victims, then criminal defendants should be banned from social media whenever they use it to carry out a serious crime. For example, if the criminal defendant uses social media to stalk or harm another, as in *United States v. Sayer*, he should be prohibited from using social media altogether in the future. The point here is that bans, if they are to be used, should not be restricted to sex-related crimes.

Other questions involve the role of social media providers. Should they play a more active role? At present, most social media providers prohibit sex offenders from using their site. Facebook's policy on sex offenders reads as follows:

> convicted sex offenders are prohibited from using Facebook. Once we are able to verify a user's status as a sex offender, we immediately disable their account and remove their account and all information associated with it.[90]

Some want social media providers to go further and take a more active role in discovering whether its users are sex offenders. Others believe that this is the government's responsibility. If it is left to the government, the next question becomes whether this is a federal or state issue. If only a few states pass bans, will the other states become havens for sex offenders? These are all questions that must be addressed in the near future, as social media continues to grow in popularity and people increasingly look for ways to restrict how criminal defendants use it.

Monitoring

In addition to outright bans, some courts subject criminal defendants to social media monitoring. This is more likely to occur when the criminal defendant is under some form of supervision by the court. In the juvenile law context, some judges require juvenile defendants to grant the court access to their social media pages. For instance, one judge in Galveston Juvenile Court in Texas requires juveniles under her supervision to "friend" her or grant her access to their social media accounts.[91] The judge then reviews the social media activities of the juveniles to determine whether they need to be returned to court.

If a convicted criminal defendant is no longer on parole, probation, or any other form of supervised release, it is very difficult for the court to monitor his social media activities without running afoul of the constitution. Although the United States Supreme Court has not addressed this issue directly, several federal district courts have found these types of requirements unconstitutional. In *Doe, Steve Morris v. Prosecutor, Marion County, Indiana* a federal district court in Indiana struck down a state law that required sex offenders to submit to searches of their personal computer and consent to monitoring. The court noted that sex offenders who are

no longer on parole, probation, or any other form of court supervision

were

entitled to full Fourth Amendment protection, without the lowered expectations of privacy.[92]

Similarly, in *Doe v. Nebraska*, the plaintiff successfully challenged a section of the Nebraska Sex Offender Registration Act that required registered sex offenders to consent to warrantless searches of their computers and to the installation of monitoring hardware or software. The court found this particular requirement of the Act (warrantless searches and monitoring) unconstitutional as applied to

persons who [were] not presently on probation, parole, or court-monitored supervision.[93]

Another form of monitoring, arguably less intrusive than computer searches, involves requiring sex offenders to turn over or register their online social media accounts and screen names with law enforcement. To some, this is an invasion of an individual's personal privacy and unlikely to improve public safety. Others see it differently and believe that such requirements serve as an extension of the sex offender registry. Furthermore, they claim that this information is beneficial to law enforcement because it allows them to better track sex offenders. At present, the courts are still grappling with whether this form of monitoring is constitutional when applied to those no longer under the jurisdiction of the court.

Digital Scarlet Letter

Due to the difficulty in banning criminal defendants from social media or subjecting them to monitoring, states are considering alternative ways in which to regulate a criminal defendant's use of social media. One state has decided to borrow from the past and require individuals to publicly display their past transgressions. As some may recall, this form of punishment was made famous in Nathaniel Hawthorne's romantic novel *The Scarlet Letter.*[94] In the book, the main character (Hester Prynne) was forced to wear a scarlet letter "A" on her chest for having had a child out of wedlock. This letter informed others in the 17th-century New England Puritan society that Hester had sinned by committing adultery.

In an effort to safeguard the online community from sex offenders, Louisiana has resurrected the scarlet letter. This new law, while based on the one used in Hawthorne's novel, has undergone some slight modern-day modifications. Rather than adorn the physical body of the criminal defendant with some type of sign or symbol, the Digital Scarlet Letter targets social media sites. This new law, the first in the country, requires sex offenders to indicate their criminal status on the social media site that they use. The law reads as follows:

> [an individual] shall include in his profile for the networking website an indication that he is a sex offender or child predator and shall include notice of the crime for which he was convicted, the jurisdiction of conviction, a description of his physical characteristics . . . and his residential address.[95]

If a convicted criminal defendant fails to include her prior convictions on her social media site, she could face 2–10 years of incarceration and a fine of up to $1,000.

The author of this new law believes it will pass constitutional muster because it merely expands the registration requirements already placed on sex offenders. Of course, there are some marked differences between requiring an individual to register as a sex offender and requiring him to include a list of his crimes on his social media site. First, the sex offender registry, as opposed to a Digital Scarlet Letter, is not readily identifiable with one individual. Furthermore, a registry requires the public to seek out information about sex offenders whereas the Digital Scarlet Letter does not require the public to go to an outside resource for information. Put another way, the Digital Scarlet Letter removes a step when attempting to determine an individual's sex offender status.

While this new law makes life more difficult for those convicted of sex-related crimes, it does offer some benefits to the criminal defendant. First, unlike a traditional sex offender registry, the Digital Scarlet Letter allows defendants to tell their side of the story through social media and offer an explanation for why their charges arose in the first place. The sex offender registry does not allow an individual to elaborate or explain how the charges arose; it merely states the crimes committed by the criminal defendant. Also, in comparison to the outright ban on social media, the Digital Scarlet Letter is a less punitive sanction as the convicted defendant can still use social media.

The new law, which is supported by social media providers like Facebook,[96] has a twofold purpose. First, like the original scarlet letter, the Digital Scarlet Letter was created to shame the convicted defendant. Second, the Digital Scarlet Letter works to safeguard other users of social media, especially children, by providing them with some type of notice about the person they are interacting with.

Some question whether the Digital Scarlet Letter will achieve its intended goals because like the ban on using social media, this law will be difficult to enforce. For example, the criminal defendant can access social media through another person's computer, phone, or tablet or create a false online identity. Others also question whether states will allocate the resources necessary to enforce such laws.

As for the constitutionality of the Digital Scarlet Letter, it remains to be seen whether the law will be upheld by the courts. Some might compare Digital Scarlet Letters to the special license plates issued to those convicted of certain traffic offenses like driving under the influence. To date, the use of those license plates has been upheld.[97] Obviously, however, differences exist between requiring a person to place a state-mandated message on a car as opposed to a social media site.

4

Jurors

The last method by which private individuals come in contact with the criminal justice system is by serving as a juror in a criminal trial. The introduction of social media into the jury box has had two profound effects on jurors: (1) erosion of juror privacy and (2) greater instances of juror misconduct.

In the Digital Age, attorneys increasingly investigate jurors before, during, and after trial. This is because social media has made it easier and cheaper to conduct such investigations. This topic of juror investigations via social media and the resulting loss of privacy felt by jurors will be discussed in greater detail in Chapter 8.

This chapter looks at the correlation between social media and juror misconduct. Chapter 4 begins by exploring the various ways jurors use social media to communicate with others. Next, the chapter examines why jurors feel the need to discuss what occurs in the courtroom on social media. Finally, the chapter concludes by analyzing possible ways in which to curtail juror communications on social media.[1]

Like attorneys, judges, witnesses, law enforcement, and defendants, jurors routinely use social media. However, unlike the other major players in the criminal justice system, jurors face far more restrictive rules regarding their use of social media. Unfortunately, jurors find it challenging to follow these rules. This inability to adhere to court rules regarding social media use has led to increased instances of juror misconduct.

JUROR COMMUNICATIONS

Citizens called to jury duty in a criminal trial get a firsthand look at the wheels of justice. As the arbiters of guilt or innocence, jurors are given the responsibility of listening to the evidence presented in court and then deciding the defendant's fate. In light of this important duty, one for which jurors receive no legal training, courts have created rules governing, among other things, what evidence jurors may use to make their decision and how they may communicate with one another and outside parties. The following section will briefly examine those rules and how they have been affected by social media.[2]

Generally speaking, individuals called to serve as jurors are prohibited from talking about the case with outside parties, including their own family members or those involved in the dispute such as the attorneys, until a verdict has been delivered in court. This rule is in place primarily to prevent outside parties from influencing the juror's decision making, since most communications involve an exchange of words or ideas. This concept is reflected in the case of *People v. Jamison* where the court explained why communications between a juror and a third party are restricted:

> The real evil the Court's instructions not to discuss the case was designed to avoid . . . [was] the introduction of an outside influence into the deliberative process, either through information about the case or another person's agreement or disagreement with the juror's own statements.[3]

Also, in most jurisdictions, but not all, courts prohibit jurors from talking with one another about the case until the deliberation stage, at which point both sides have submitted all of their evidence. This rule is in place for several reasons. First, it works to prevent premature judgment by the jurors. A strong belief exists, especially among the defense bar in both civil and criminal matters, that allowing jurors to discuss the case prior to deliberations puts defendants at a decided disadvantage, as they have yet to present their evidence.

Second, making jurors wait until deliberations to discuss the case gives jurors more flexibility during deliberations, as they are less likely to hold on to preconceived ideas. Third, prohibiting premature discussions by jurors increases the likelihood of quality and broad deliberations; and it reduces the chances that jurors will talk about the case outside the jury room and without the presence of all 12 jurors.

Unfortunately, these two aforementioned rules on juror communications have not been strictly adhered to. Human nature being what it is, jurors discuss the case with third parties, especially family members, prior to rendering a verdict. Furthermore, jurors talk about the case with other jurors prior to deliberations. For the most part, the court has turned a blind eye to jurors talking about the case with other jurors prior to deliberations and don't consider it a grave breach of a juror's duty.

The same cannot be said about jurors discussing the case with outside parties prior to deciding guilt or innocence. Here, the court is more likely to overturn a verdict if it discovers that a juror has communicated with a third party and that communication influenced the juror's decision making. This type of juror misconduct, however, was traditionally difficult to discover absent the juror or the third party coming forward and admitting wrongdoing. Social media, however, has dramatically altered this landscape.

With social media, today's jurors are more likely to violate the court's rules about improper communications. In fact, jurors have used social media to communicate with defendants, judges, attorneys, other jurors, relatives, friends, and the general public. Jurors, however, are also at a greater risk of being discovered violating the court's rules because of the digital trail they leave behind. To date, numerous instances exist of jurors caught making improper communications via social media.

In the corruption trial of former Baltimore mayor Sheila Dixon, several jurors used Facebook to interact with one another despite admonitions from the judge not to do so.[4] The media dubbed these jurors the Facebook 5. The jurors' transgressions became known shortly after the jury had rendered its guilty verdict. However, rather than appeal the verdict based on juror misconduct, the mayor and the prosecution entered into a plea deal.

In a two-day criminal trial in Michigan, a juror made the following Facebook post after the first day of trial:

Actually excited for jury duty tomorrow. It's gonna be fun to tell the defendant they're Guilty.:P.[5]

The juror's post was discovered prior to the jury's verdict, and the juror was subsequently removed from the case.

In England, a juror serving on a sexual assault case enlisted her Facebook friends to help her decide the defendant's guilt or innocence.[6] This particular juror set up a poll on her Facebook page asking her friends to vote on the criminal defendant's fate. This juror's post was discovered prior to the verdict, and she was subsequently removed from the case.

Besides using social media to contact other jurors, friends, and the general public, some jurors have gone so far as to reach out to court personnel.[7] In Texas, a juror, despite warnings from the judge not to contact anyone associated with the case, sent a friend request to the defense attorney whose client was on trial for murder. In addition to the friend request, the juror asked the attorney if he was single. Not surprisingly, this juror was subsequently removed from the jury.

As the aforementioned cases illustrate, juror communications via social media are problematic. Even the most innocuous communication can lead to an overturned verdict or mistrial, which takes both a financial and emotional toll on all of the parties involved. This is because when jurors use social media to communicate, they run the risk of interacting with an outside party or having their communications viewed by others.

With access to a juror's social media communication, another person can not only influence a juror, but also learn about the inner workings of the jury room and privileged information, such as informal vote counts or details of closed-door deliberations. This jeopardizes both jury deliberations and the integrity of the legal system itself. For example, who is going to place much faith in a verdict when one of the jurors attempts to friend or communicate with one of the parties or someone with a vested interest in the case? A trial may become less about who presents the best case and more about who does the best job monitoring the jurors' social media sites.

Another concern with jurors using social media is that such activity may hinder the traditional methods of juror decision making. For example, some jurors might not fully participate or might hold back their true feelings during deliberations if they knew that their views will be posted on someone's social media site. To address this problem and others raised by the improper use of social media by jurors, courts first need to better understand why jurors turn to social media when they are told not to. This topic will be discussed in greater detail next.

WHY JURORS DISCUSS THE CASE

When jurors are discovered violating the court's rules about improperly using social media, they offer a variety of reasons for their transgressions. Some jurors claim that they violated the rules on prohibited communications because they have grown too attached to social media. As discussed in the Introduction, social media is pervasive and has become quite integral to the lives of many people. According to a recent study, individuals spend

> more time on social networks than any other category of [Web]sites, accounting for 20% of their time spent on PCs and 30% of their mobile [use] time.[8]

For jurors falling into this category, going any extended period of time without communicating via a post, text, tweet, or blog is a challenge.

This desire for constant contact is so strong that it can almost be categorized as an addiction—one that they cannot give up even when called to serve on a jury. According to Judith Wright,

> [s]oft addictions are those seemingly harmless habits like checking your Facebook page or getting on your e-mail or Internet surfing . . . Just normal everyday activities that we so often overdo and we don't really realize the cost.[9]

Also, a few jurors falling into this category feel the need to constantly chronicle their daily activities for the general public. This desire by the so-called "Tell-All Generation" to put their lives on display to the world is not shed just because they are called to serve on juries. Rather, this change in daily routine may actually increase the appeal to reveal because jury duty

> in its own strange way may be an escape from the usual rhythms of city life.[10]

In the corruption trial of former Pennsylvania state representative Vincent Fumo, one sitting juror made several improper communications about the trial on both Facebook and Twitter. During a follow-up hearing in which the juror was questioned about his social media activity, the juror informed the court that

> [i]t's more for my benefit to just get it out of my head, similar to a blog posting or somebody journaling something. It's just to get it out there. And that's what a lot of Facebook ... it's just to get—a way to electronically get thoughts off your mind.[11]

Other jurors violate the court's rules about improper communications because they do not consider or realize that texting, tweeting, and blogging are prohibited forms of communication. Noted jury expert Paula Hannaford-Agor points out that

> [f]or some, tweeting and blogging are simply an extension of thinking, rather than a form of written communication.[12]

Not surprisingly, then, jurors continue to communicate with other jurors (prior to deliberations) and with outside parties (prior to the verdict) despite admonitions from judges.

In *State v. Dellinger*, a West Virginia juror never told the trial judge that she interacted with the defendant via Myspace despite being asked during voir dire whether she knew the defendant. During a later hearing to determine whether the juror's actions were grounds for overturning the defendant's conviction, the court asked the juror why she did not reveal that she knew the defendant and had interacted with him on Myspace. According to the juror:

> I just didn't feel like I really knew him. I didn't know him personally. I've never, never talked to him. And I just felt like, you know, when [the trial judge] asked if you knew him personally or if he ever came to your house or have you been to his house, we never did. . . . I knew in my heart that I didn't know him. . . . Maybe I should have at least said that, you know, that he was on Myspace, which really isn't that important, I didn't think.[13]

The final category of rule breakers involves jurors who are just plain curious or want more information before rendering a verdict. Just as an individual might turn to Foursquare or Yelp to learn about the best restaurants in a new town, jurors turn to social media to help them determine guilt or innocence. A juror might also turn to social media for assistance with an unfamiliar term or legal concept that was not adequately explained by the attorney or judge.

LIMITING OR CONTROLLING JUROR COMMUNICATIONS

To date, legal commentators from across the country have suggested a variety of ways to combat improper juror communications via social media: (1) requiring jurors to take an oath; (2) penalizing jurors; (3) investigating jurors; (4) allowing juror questions; and (5) improving jury instructions. The first three suggestions rely on punishment and oversight, while the last two focus on empowerment and education.

With juror oath taking, jurors sign an oath or affidavit acknowledging the instructions about improper communications. The purpose of the oath is to heighten awareness about the specific instructions pertaining to improper communications. One critique of this reform proposal is that it seems overly formalistic. Jurors should not have to enter into written agreements with the court to fulfill their civic responsibilities. Another critique is that oaths focusing on improper communications may lead jurors to falsely believe that these instructions are superior or more important than all other instructions given to jurors by the court.

The second suggestion involves penalizing jurors. Penalties can take various forms ranging from fines to public embarrassment to sequestration. The common theme with all penalties is that once imposed, they make citizens less inclined to want to serve as jurors. The average individual views jury duty as a burden that pulls so-called citizen volunteers away from their jobs, families, and friends to perform a sometimes stressful and other times mundane civic duty for which they receive minimal pay, if any at all. In fact, it is quite common for individuals to think of excuses, real or imagined, to get out of serving jury duty. Once jurors realize that, in addition to the possibility of sequestration, they run the risk of being penalized, the incentive to avoid jury duty will only increase. Therefore, penalties should be a last resort in preventing juror misconduct.

The third suggestion concerns investigating jurors and will be examined in greater detail in Chapter 8. The fourth recommendation involves juror questions. Allowing jurors to ask questions of witnesses reduces the detrimental impact of social media on jury service. This is because juror questions, like jury instructions, address the reasons that jurors use social media. When jurors have their questions answered, they are less inclined to turn to social media. Prohibiting questions leads jurors to seek alternative avenues for information like social media.

Admittedly, some questions that arise from a juror's inquiring mind cannot be answered directly due to restrictions imposed by rules of evidence and the constitutional protections guaranteed to parties and witnesses. This does not mean, however, that these questions should be ignored. For example, a juror might ask the court whether the defendant is presently incarcerated. It is unlikely that the judge would ever answer or pose such a highly prejudicial question. But the judge can use this situation to her advantage by turning it into a teaching point. The judge, even without going into the details of the question, can once again instruct the jury, including the juror who raised the question, that certain evidence must not be examined or considered by the jurors in order to protect the rights of the parties involved in the case. This timely reeducation of the jury is important because answers to questions like the defendant's incarceration may be obtained quickly and easily online.

The final suggestion centers on juror instructions. Of all the reform proposals suggested, improving jury instructions is the most common and popular measure. When crafting jury instructions to advise jurors about the prohibitions on improper communications, commentators have suggested using language easily understood by laypersons and avoiding overly technical terms. A sample set of model jury instructions, which were relied on in *United States v. Barry Bonds,* is included in Appendix D.[14]

In providing jury instructions about improper communications, some judges go beyond the current boilerplate language and include references to specific social media platforms. According to one legal commentator, people tend to forget that e-mail, twittering, updating your status on Facebook is also speech. . . . There's an impersonality about it because it's a one-way communication—but it is a communication.[15]

For jury instructions to be effective, they have to reflect the new methods by which members of society communicate and interact.

In addition to the instructions telling jurors that they cannot use social media, the instructions need to tell jurors *why* they cannot use social media to discuss the case. Jurors need to be told why practices that they regularly rely on, like communicating via social media, are incompatible with jury service. While a long discourse on due process is unnecessary, jurors need to know that improper communications by jurors can prevent them from being impartial and/or violate the rights of the defendant. Failure to provide an explanation of the court's instructions not only decreases the likelihood of juror compliance but also creates mistrust of the judicial system.

When providing the rationale behind the instructions, judges must advise jurors of the negative consequences of ignoring them. In addition, jurors should be told that failure to abide by the court's rules may lead to a mistrial, which is costly both in financial terms and in the emotional toll it takes on those involved in the process. Also, jurors need to be informed of the potential for contempt of court and the subsequent penalties assessed to jurors who violate the court's instructions.

Adding a self-policing section will also encourage compliance with jury instructions. While some jurisdictions have shied away from this approach for fear of creating distrust and apprehension among jurors, jury instructions should include language requiring jurors to report fellow jurors for failing to follow the rules of the court. This watchdog requirement is necessary because juror misconduct is difficult to detect and prevent. An added benefit of this rule is that if a juror violates the court's instructions, for example by communicating with a third party, the juror, for fear of being reported to the court, is less likely to reveal her findings to other jurors and thereby taint the entire jury.

Finally, as an aside, at least one judge has taken a rather unique approach to keeping jurors from using social media or the Internet during trial. The trial judge in the *Apple v. Samsung* high-stakes patent infringement case offered jurors a reward.[16] The judge promised jurors before the start of the trial that if they adhered to the court's instructions not to go online and research or discuss the case, at the end of the trial he would give the jurors a notebook of all the stories they had missed. According to the court librarian, who was tasked with gathering and keeping the stories until the end of the trial, this was a first for him. Also, it should be noted that although claims of juror misconduct arose in this case, they did not involve jurors improperly using social media or the Internet.

Part II

Law Enforcement

Like crime victims, criminal defendants, and jurors, law enforcement has also felt the impact of social media. Part II examines social media's influence on law enforcement by looking at two specific topics: (1) community relations and (2) crime prevention. With respect to community relations, police departments use social media to strengthen ties with the citizens they are responsible for protecting. Maintaining community relations through social media takes many forms ranging from educating citizens about criminal activity to promoting positive achievements of law enforcement personnel.[1] As for preventing crime, law enforcement relies on social media not only to track, monitor, and capture suspects, but also to run undercover sting operations and search for evidence. In addition, social media serves as a tool for law enforcement to defuse potentially dangerous situations.

5

Community Relations

Maintaining strong community relations is important to law enforcement for a variety of reasons. First, criminals are less likely to commit crimes around individuals they consider friendly to the police. Second, police cannot singlehandedly prevent and solve crimes; they need the assistance of the local community. As discussed in Chapter 2, private citizens who act as virtual deputies greatly expand law enforcement's investigative reach.

In high-profile crimes like the Boston Marathon bombing, public assistance is generally a nonissue as most are eager to help the police. However, the same cannot be said for low-level crimes or those crimes that do not generate large public interest. In many instances, citizens are disinterested or don't want to get involved because they either distrust the police or fear possible retribution in some form or another from criminal defendants. This lack of citizen engagement can be lessened somewhat if the police take the time to interact with local residents. This interaction is most likely to occur when the police maintain a presence in the community and cultivate relationships within it.

Historically, police–citizen interaction occurred when law enforcement patrolled neighborhoods by foot or car and met with the individuals they encountered. Today's citizens, however, are increasingly spending their time in virtual neighborhoods rather than physical ones. In some instances, people know more about their online friends than actual neighbors who live next door or in the same building. Thus, if law enforcement wants to connect with citizens in the Digital Age, they must go to where the people are—social media.

As discussed in the Preface, most police departments across the country understand this reality and have taken steps to strengthen their presence on social media. Examples of law enforcement using social media to interact with citizens can be found in numerous cities both large and small across the United States. In Seattle, the local police department has established 51 local neighborhood Twitter accounts that provide citizens with updates in almost real time about problem areas and suspected criminal activities. This might be thought of as a virtual police blotter via Twitter. According to the Seattle Police Department, residents

> want to specifically know what's going on in the areas around their home, around their work, where their children might be going to school. This is just a different way we could put out as much information as possible as quickly as possible.[1]

Besides Twitter, many departments use Facebook to communicate with the community. The Waco Police Department in Texas, like many other departments across the country, relies on its Facebook page to assist them not only with combating crime, but also with building rapport with the local community; for example, they inform residents about law enforcement activities that might go unreported or unrecognized such as police involvement with charitable causes. According to a detective from the Waco Police Department,

> [w]hat I hope the page accomplishes in the future, and in this past year, is maybe help people to not have as many stereotypes about the police department.[2]

Other examples of using social media to demonstrate a lighter side of law enforcement include so-called "Tweet Alongs." Here, police tweet everything that happens during a routine shift. Those who follow the Tweet Alongs quickly realize that police are real people and have a sense of humor. Consider the following exchange between a police officer and a local citizen on Twitter:

> Citizen: *If I declare a donut emergency does that mean you have to deliver donuts to me? I have bacon to trade.*

> Police Officer: *Watching our figures . . . Sorry. And we don't share donuts. Sorry.*[3]

One by-product of law enforcement's increased reliance on social media is greater accessibility for the general public. With social media, law enforcement can both deliver and receive information more easily to and from citizens. This transfer of information sometimes occurs in real time and citizens, if they prefer, can remain anonymous. According to the chief of the Yorkville Police Department located in Ohio,

> [i]f residents have a concern about something they can post it on [Facebook] or send us a message if there is an incident going on in town and they want to be anonymous, they can send it to us in a private message and we can go from there.[4]

In addition, social media facilitates conversations with local citizens. This was reflected in a recent undercover operation in Carlsbad, California, where the police department posted information on social media about a sting operation, in which they left a purse and valuables in a car at a location where a rash of burglaries had recently occurred. One person who viewed the posted information commented that he thought this was entrapment. The police, however, explained to the individual via social media why it was not entrapment. According to the Carlsbad Police Department spokesperson,

> [w]ithout a tool like this [social media], people will have this thought in their head. And this way, they can say it and we can explain [the law].[5]

Finally, social media allows the police to deliver their messages unfiltered by the media. Like crime victims, law enforcement can use social media to discuss an incident through their own lens rather than that of the media. With social media, law enforcement is more proactive and less reactive with getting out their message. In fact, social media allows law enforcement to get out in front of a story or incident, which results in fewer concerns about how they are portrayed by the media and others.

Obviously, not all police communications with the local community should occur through social media. Certain sensitive issues still require a human touch or a more personal response. Consider the following example from Georgia, which involved law enforcement using social media to contact family members about the death of a relative.

Ms. Lamb-Creasey was attempting to find her son (Rickey Lamb) who had gone missing.[6] Despite her best efforts and that of her daughter, they were unable to locate his whereabouts. However, both had received an email via Facebook from Misty Hancock informing each to call the Clayton County Police Department. Neither Ms. Lamb-Creasey nor her daughter recognized the name Misty Hancock, so they were hesitant to respond. Furthermore, the Facebook profile picture for Misty Hancock featured an Atlanta rapper named "TI."

After approximately 20 days of not hearing from Rickey or the police, Ms. Lamb-Creasey's daughter contacted Ms. Hancock and discovered that she was with the Clayton Police Department. She also learned that her brother had died weeks earlier in a traffic accident. Not surprisingly, both Ms. Lamb-Creasey and her daughter were bothered by the fact that the Clayton Police Department not only used social media to contact them about Rickey's death, but also used an account that was not readily identifiable with the police department. According to the Clayton Police Department, social media was the only way they knew how to contact the nearest known relative of Rickey Lamb. Ms. Lamb-Creasey disputed this claim, stating that she had had the same job for 13 years and was not a difficult person to find or contact.

6

Prevention, Apprehension, and Investigation

PREVENTION

In addition to using social media to further community relations, police have also relied on it, with mixed success, to reach criminal defendants and to defuse potentially dangerous situations. In Illinois, law enforcement employed Facebook to peacefully end a standoff with a juvenile murder suspect.[1] The teenager was holed up in his house and police negotiators were unable, at least initially, to communicate with him. However, the police learned that the suspect was, at the time of the standoff, on Facebook. The police went on Facebook and were able to interact with the suspect, which in turn led to a peaceful resolution to the standoff.

Other examples include employing Twitter as a crowd control measure. In New York, in 2009, Justin Bieber planned an album signing at a mall in Long Island. As part of the promotion plan, Bieber's manager, Scott Braun, sent the following tweet on behalf of Bieber:

> On my way to Roosevelt Field Mall in Long Island, NY to sign and meet fans! I'm pumped. See U There.[2]

Due to Bieber's popularity, more than 3,100 people (primarily young girls) showed up at the mall to see him and obtain an autograph.

Unfortunately, the police and mall security were not prepared to handle such a large number of people. After an officer sustained minor injuries, the police told James A. Roppo, a senior vice president for Def Jam

Records, the company releasing Bieber's album, to inform the crowd via Twitter that they should exit the mall. The police wanted the fans to leave because there was the potential for serious injury and they feared that some were getting dangerously close to a balcony.

Roppo refused to send the tweet. As a result he was arrested and the police charged him with felony assault, criminal nuisance, endangering the welfare of a child, reckless endangerment, and obstruction of governmental administration. The police then told Scott Braun, Bieber's manager, who was also at the event, to send out a tweet informing the crowd that the album signing had been cancelled. He initially refused and was also arrested and charged.

Ultimately, Roppo and Braun reached a plea agreement with the prosecutors. Pursuant to the agreement, the charges against the two were dropped in exchange for a public service announcement (PSA) by Bieber. In the PSA, Bieber discusses cyber responsibility, including cyber bullying. Bieber was a good choice for the PSA since he was initially discovered on YouTube.[3] Nassau County was also reimbursed for the expenses associated with sending police and fire personnel to the mall to handle the large influx of people.

In addition to illustrating how social media might be applied as a crowd control tool, this incident raises an interesting question about what affirmative duty may be placed on those who use social media. Chapter 2 examined individuals who come across crime or criminal evidence while using social media. As previously discussed, some states require individuals to report certain information regarding criminal activity to law enforcement or face potential prosecution themselves.

Here, the police imposed an even greater duty on Roppo and Braun. The police required them to use Twitter to contact private individuals and tell them to leave the mall and that the event was cancelled. Of course, unlike the virtual deputies in Chapter 2, Roppo and Braun had prior knowledge about the large numbers of people at the mall and the potential for harm to others. In fact, they were partially responsible for creating the riotous situation. However, the question remains, how far can the police go in requiring others to use social media? This question will likely need to be answered by the courts in the near future.

APPREHENSION

Besides serving as a tool to deescalate potentially life-threatening situations, social media has also been helpful to law enforcement in the area of apprehension. Social media assists with locating suspects in two ways.

First, it allows the police to track an individual's physical location. This tracking occurs by following the suspect's social media trail or footprint. In most instances it is the suspect himself who creates the trail, but this is not always the case. Sometimes the social media trail is created by friends of the suspect or people who have come in contact with him.

Some individuals make it fairly simple for the police to find them through social media while others, such as the previously discussed Boston Craigslist Killer, do not. Those situations falling into the easy category include a criminal defendant who decided to check his Facebook account in the midst of an actual burglary.[4] In fact, the burglar was brazen enough to use the victim's own computer. Upon arriving home, the victim noticed that the burglar had not only stolen some valuable items, but also had failed to completely log out of his Facebook account while using her computer. Not surprisingly, the burglar was quickly identified and apprehended. Interestingly, this is not the only case when a burglar accessed his social media account during an actual burglary, which says a lot about either the burglar's carelessness or the draw and power of social media.

In another example, the suspect's girlfriend created the social media trail for law enforcement. This situation involved a couple, Samantha Dillow and Dyllan Naecker.[5] Naecker had a warrant for his arrest in Maryland, so he decided to hide out at Dillow's place in Virginia. In an effort to keep tabs on the local police department to see if they suspected that Naecker was at her residence, Dillow became Facebook friends with the local sheriff's office. Apparently, she failed to realize that by doing this she made it possible for law enforcement to also keep tabs on her, which is what they did. After perusing her Facebook page and noticing a picture of Naecker, local law enforcement contacted Maryland officials to determine if he was wanted. Upon learning that Naecker was indeed wanted, law enforcement proceeded to Dillow's residence where they found Naecker hiding under a bed.

Other examples include a criminal defendant, Chris Creggo from Lockport, New York, who skipped out on the sentencing portion of his criminal plea.[6] In an effort to locate Creggo, the Lockport Police Department searched social media and quickly discovered that he had both a Facebook and a Myspace page. These accounts listed Creggo's new city and state of residence as Terre Haute, Indiana, and place of employment as a tattoo parlor called Body Art Ink. Creggo even went so far as to post the Lockport paper's wanted poster of him on his social media account. After reviewing these accounts, Lockport law enforcement contacted the U.S. marshals, who took Creggo into custody.

Not all social media trails are as easy to follow or discover as those previously mentioned. Many actually require the police to engage in a much more in-depth investigation. Consider the case of John McAfee, the antivirus company founder, who was wanted by the police for questioning in connection with the death of his neighbor.[7] McAfee was forced out of hiding when the police discovered a photo of him published on a blog. The photo in question was embedded with GPS metadata, which has been described as "data about data,"[8] that pinpointed McAfee's exact location in Guatemala.

The second method of suspect apprehension relies on virtual deputies (discussed in detail in Chapter 2) rather than law enforcement to track and locate suspects on social media. Many police departments attempt to facilitate the efforts of virtual deputies by posting photos of wanted suspects on law enforcement social media sites. Thus, rather than going to the local post office to find out who is the most wanted, virtual deputies can now check the social media site of their local police agency. In addition to photos, many police department social media sites include actual video surveillance of crimes taking place.

INVESTIGATION

In addition to assisting police with community relations, crime prevention, and suspect apprehension, social media facilitates the day-to-day investigative work of law enforcement. Across the country, police have come to rely on social media to combat criminals and illegal activity. To date, police have used social media to conduct undercover operations, monitor criminal defendants, and search for potential evidence.

In 2009, shortly after the Los Angeles Lakers won the NBA finals, a riot broke out in Los Angeles.[9] At the time of the riot, the police were unable to identify certain participants. However, after searching YouTube and Flickr, which contained pictures and videos of the riot, the police were able to identify previously unknown rioters.

In another example, police officers at the University of Illinois came across two students walking together at night.[10] One of the students, Marc, was urinating in public. When the officers approached the two students, Marc ran while the other student, Adam, did not. The police questioned Adam about Marc; Adam said he had just met Marc that night and did not know his last name.

The police eventually discovered Marc's identity and charged him with public urination. The police then went on Adam's Facebook page to see if he had been honest about not knowing Marc. The police discovered that Adam was a Facebook friend with Marc. Upon making this discovery, the police charged Adam with obstruction of justice for lying to the police.

Sometimes police use social media less as tool to capture criminals or thwart criminal activity and more as way to reconnect citizens with lost or stolen property. In Surrey, England, police came across a large number of stolen items, which they wanted to return to the rightful owners. However, they were not sure who owned the items, so they turned to social media. Specifically, they placed photos of the property on Pinterest and encouraged those who had been recently burglarized to view them. According to a local Surrey County constable,

> Pinterest offers an effective, efficient and convenient opportunity to view items at times suitable to the user, and is in a format that is widely accessible to the community as a whole.[11]

The social media investigations conducted by law enforcement are not limited to mining information or returning stolen property. Police also use social media to run undercover sting operations. In Wisconsin, for example, the police created a fictitious Facebook profile of an attractive young woman.[12] Using this fake Facebook profile, the police sent a friend request to a young male college student.

Although the college student did not recognize the Facebook profile, he nevertheless accepted the friend request—an all-too-often occurrence. Once the undercover officer became friends with the college student, he looked at the student's Facebook photos. The officer noticed one photo in which the underage college student held an alcoholic drink. The police officer used this photo to investigate and charge the student with underage drinking.

The use of fictitious social media accounts by law enforcement has become so common that police departments started issuing guidelines on the topic. The guidelines created by the New York City Police Department state that

> officers involved in probes involving social media may register aliases with the department and use a department-issued laptop whose Internet access card can't be traced back to the NYPD.[13]

The United States Department of Justice (DOJ) has also promoted the benefits of undercover operations on social media.[14] For example, during training sessions with local police departments, the DOJ will explain how social media allows law enforcement to communicate with suspects/targets, gain access to nonpublic information, and map social relationships/networks.

Some are uncomfortable with law enforcement using bogus social media accounts or going undercover on social media. They are especially bothered by the fact that in most instances creating a fake account violates the social media providers' TOS. For example, Facebook policy states that users

> will not provide any false personal information on Facebook or create an account for anyone other than yourself without permission.[15]

Myspace policy states that

> [b]y using Myspace Servers, you represent and warrant that (a) all registration information you submit is truthful and accurate.[16]

In addition, there is the example of Lori Drew discussed in Chapter 3. She was prosecuted, in part, for creating the fictitious Josh Evans, which was in violation of Myspace's TOS.

Law enforcement's social media tactics may be off-putting to some but they are not necessarily new or groundbreaking. While using social media is arguably cutting edge, at least for the time being, dishonesty and trickery have long been hallmarks of successful police sting operations. When running traditional undercover operations the police regularly hide their true identity from criminal defendants and outside third parties; to do otherwise might jeopardize the investigation. Such activity is generally permissible so long as the police do not entrap the suspect.

Consider a scenario where an undercover police officer impersonates a prostitute in an effort to get unsuspecting "johns" to offer her money for sex, which in most jurisdictions would constitute the crime of solicitation. Consider further that the undercover officer is working in the bar of an upscale hotel and has actually rented a room in the hotel. This type of sting would be nearly impossible to pull off if the undercover officer had to be truthful with the unsuspecting johns. The same holds true for outside third parties. Most hotels, if not all, prohibit guests from using their premises for illegal activities or undercover operations. If police are honest with the hotel or strictly follow the hotel's rules and regulations, they run the risk of compromising their investigation.

In conducting undercover operations on social media, law enforcement officers regularly pretend to be other people. As discussed earlier, this violates the online impersonation laws of several states. In addition, it runs contrary to the rules of most social media providers. However, without such duplicity law enforcement would find going undercover on social media difficult if not impossible to do.

As the prior discussion illustrates, at some level, police have to be given a certain amount of leeway in order to catch criminals. The question of how much leeway raises novel constitutional issues that courts are just now beginning to address. For example, how far can the police go with respect to using social media? Can they surreptitiously monitor a user's Facebook account or force the user to turn over a password to that account? Can the police friend unsuspecting defendants? The following two sections will examine how the courts work through these questions. In addition, these sections will explore how the Fourth and Fifth Amendments affect law enforcement's use of social media as a crime prevention tool.

FOURTH AMENDMENT

The Fourth Amendment states:

[t]he right of the people to be secure in their persons, houses, papers, and effects, against unreasonable searches and seizures, shall not be violated, and no Warrants shall issue, but upon probable cause, supported by Oath or affirmation, and particularly describing the place to be searched, and the persons or things to be seized.[17]

The Fourth Amendment, one of the 10 amendments of the Bill of Rights in the United States Constitution, serves as a bulwark against governmental intrusion into the privacy rights of citizens. Specifically, the Fourth Amendment prohibits unreasonable searches or seizures by the police. A search or seizure by law enforcement is reasonable if authorized by a search warrant or if an exception to the warrant requirement applies. A search warrant, issued by the court, must be supported by probable cause to believe that an offense has been or is being committed and that evidence will be found in the specific place to be searched or item to be seized.

To better understand the limits the Fourth Amendment places on law enforcement's use of social media to investigate citizens, it is first necessary to take a step back and look at three prior Supreme Court decisions: *Olmstead v. United States, Katz v. United States,* and *Smith v. Maryland.* All three cases involved the telephone and the Fourth Amendment. In each case, the criminal defendant argued with mixed success that the police violated his Fourth Amendment rights by either monitoring or intercepting his phone calls (including the numbers dialed) without a warrant. These three cases are important, for the purposes of this section, because they help set the stage for how courts will most likely apply the Fourth Amendment to similar situations involving social media.

The first case to be examined is *Olmstead v. United States*. In this 1925 case, Roy Olmstead, a lieutenant in the Seattle Police Department, was convicted of violating the federal prohibition laws. The police caught Olmstead in part because of wiretaps placed on phone lines leading to his house and place of business.

Olmstead appealed his conviction all the way to the Supreme Court. He claimed that federal agents, although they never physically entered his property, violated his Fourth Amendment rights when they intercepted his phone calls via wiretaps. Olmstead argued that a warrantless search occurred because federal agents listened to phone calls that took place in private places, that is, his house and place of business.

The Supreme Court found Olmstead's argument unpersuasive. This is because during that time period the majority of the Supreme Court justices took a very literal and traditional approach to the Fourth Amendment, limiting its application to searches of a "person, or his tangible, material effects." In affirming the defendant's conviction, the Supreme Court found that

[o]ne who installs in his house a telephone instrument with connecting wires intends to Project his voice to those quite outside, and . . . the wires beyond his house, and messages while passing over them, are not within the protection of the Fourth Amendment. Here those who intercepted the projected voices were not in the house of either party to the conversation.

We think, therefore, that the wire tapping here ... did not amount to a search . . . within the meaning of the Fourth Amendment.[18]

The *Olmstead* opinion was based on the idea of spatial privacy. Therefore, to violate the Fourth Amendment, the police had to conduct some physical intrusion or trespass without a warrant. Historically, this rule worked because most searches involved the police physically searching a person, the home, or some tangible object. However, the rule lost much of its effectiveness once law enforcement discovered new methods of searching. By the 1920s, the police, by tapping a phone line, were able to learn about conversations within an individual's home without ever physically entering the premises.

Justice Louis Brandeis, in a very prescient dissent, took the opposite view from the *Olmstead* majority and found that Olmstead's Fourth Amendment rights had been violated. According to Justice Brandeis,

[i]n the application of a Constitution, our contemplation cannot be only of what has been, but of what may be. The progress of science in furnishing the government with means of espionage is not likely to stop with wire tapping. Ways may . . . be developed by which the government, without removing papers from secret drawers, can reproduce them in court, and by which it will be enabled to expose . . . the most intimate occurrences of the home. . . . That places the liberty of every man in the hands of every petty officer.[19]

It took another 40 years before the Supreme Court would fully embrace Justice Brandeis's views on the Fourth Amendment. The opportunity came in *Katz v. United States* where once again the Court was faced with the question of whether law enforcement's use of a wiretap without a warrant violated the criminal defendant's Fourth Amendment rights.[20]

In *Katz,* the defendant, Charles Katz, worked as a bookie (a person who makes bets for other people) in Los Angeles. He regularly placed his bets by using one of three enclosed pay phone booths located on Sunset Boulevard. The police became aware of Katz's activities and decided to disable one of the phone booths he regularly used and place listening devices on the other two. With their equipment in place, the police intercepted and listened to the calls made by Katz for an entire week.

Katz was subsequently charged with illegal gambling. Prior to his trial, Katz moved to suppress the intercepted calls based on the Fourth Amendment's prohibitions against unlawful searches and seizures. He claimed that by listening to his phone calls the government conducted a warrantless search. The government argued that a search never occurred because they placed the listening devices on the outside of the phone booth and did not physically enter the booth. Based on the prior Supreme Court precedent in *Olmstead*, the trial court and the United States Court of Appeals for the Ninth Circuit rejected Katz's motion to suppress. Katz then appealed to the Supreme Court, which reversed his conviction.

In crafting the *Katz* opinion that overruled *Olmstead*, the Supreme Court determined that individuals have a constitutionally protected reasonable expectation of privacy regardless of where they are located.[21] With *Katz*, the Supreme Court greatly expanded the Fourth Amendment and applied its protections to both places and people.

Arguably, the most significant aspect of *Katz* is the concurring opinion of Justice Harlan, which established a two-part test to determine when a citizen's reasonable expectation of privacy has been established.[22] If both parts of the two-part test are met, the government must, absent some exception, obtain a warrant to search the protected area or information.

In the first prong, the individual must exhibit an actual subjective expectation of privacy. Here Katz had a subjective expectation of privacy. He thought his calls were private; he went into the phone booth and closed the door.

In the second prong, the expectation must be one society is prepared to recognize. Most in society would find Katz's belief that his phone calls were private to be reasonable. In the *Katz* opinion, the court went out of its way to illustrate how most Americans viewed the phone in the late 1960s. According to the Court,

> [o]ne who occupies [the telephone booth], shuts the door behind him, and pays the toll that permits him to place a call is surely entitled to assume that the words he utters into the mouthpiece will not be broadcast to the world. To read the Constitution more narrowly is to ignore the vital role that the public telephone has come to play in private communication.[23]

This two-part test, like most rules in the law, however, is not absolute. This reasonable expectation of privacy may be lost when an individual exposes the information in question to the public. The *Katz* Court noted this fact when it wrote,

> [w]hat a person knowingly exposes to the public, even in his own home or office, is not a subject of the Fourth Amendment protection.[24]

Another exception involves the third-party doctrine, which holds that a person does not have a reasonable expectation of privacy when information is voluntarily disclosed to a third party. This exception raises the third and final Supreme Court case in this section, *Smith v. Maryland.*[25]

In this 1979 case, the criminal defendant, Michael Lee Smith, was convicted of robbing Patricia McDonough. Shortly after the robbery, Smith began to harass McDonough on the phone and leave obscene and threatening messages. In an effort to stop the calls and collect evidence about the robbery, the police had the phone company set up a pen register to record the numbers dialed from the telephone at Smith's house.

The pen register, which was set up at the phone company, did not capture the content of the phone calls made from the Smith house, just the numbers dialed. Shortly after the pen register was installed, it recorded that someone at Smith's house had called the McDonough house. The police used this information to obtain a warrant and search Smith's house where they found further evidence linking him to the robbery.

At his trial for robbery, Smith filed a motion to suppress. He argued that the police executed a warrantless search in violation of his Fourth Amendment rights when they had the telephone company set up a pen register to record the numbers dialed from his house. The trial and appellate courts disagreed with Smith's argument, and his case ultimately made it to the Supreme Court.

In affirming the conviction, the Supreme Court determined that Smith did not have a reasonable expectation of privacy in the numbers dialed on his telephone. According to the court,

> [it] consistently has held that a person had no legitimate expectation of privacy in information he voluntarily turns over to third parties.[26]

The Court went on to determine that

> [w]hen [petitioner Smith] used his phone, petitioner voluntarily conveyed numerical information to the telephone company and "exposed" that information to its equipment in the ordinary course of business. In so doing, petitioner assumed the risk that the company would reveal to police the numbers he dialed.[27]

The decision in *Smith* was not unanimous. Several justices found the Court's opinion to be lacking and in conflict with *Katz*. For example, the criminal defendants in both *Katz* and *Smith* revealed information over the phone to third parties, that is, the telephone company. *Katz* involved an actual telephone conversation while *Smith* concerned the telephone numbers dialed. However, the Supreme Court only provided Fourth Amendment protections in the former, not the latter.

In his dissent, Justice Marshall also cast doubt on the premise that someone assumes a risk by using a modern-day tool that most could not live without in 1979. Justice Marshall wrote,

> [u]nless a person is prepared to forego use of what for many has become a personal or professional necessity, he cannot help but accept the risk of surveillance. . . . It is ideal to speak of "assuming"

risks in contexts where as a practical matter, individuals have no realistic alternative.[28]

Olmstead, Katz, and *Smith* not only serve as the starting point for any Fourth Amendment social media analysis, but also illustrate the difficulty in applying new ideas and inventions to a Constitution that was crafted well over 225 years ago. As illustrated by *Olmstead* and *Katz,* the Court struggles at times to properly apply the Fourth Amendment to advancements in technology. While phones and wiretaps may not seem that novel today, they were still fairly new concepts in the 1920s. The majority of the justices in *Olmstead* were unable to fully grasp their significance, which led them to adhere to a rather rigid formality when applying the Fourth Amendment. They relied on their 19th-century experiences and sensibilities to try to solve a 20th-century problem. As a result, it took the Supreme Court another 40 years to come up with the correct approach.

To date, the two-part test created by Justice Harlan in *Katz* has proven to be quite durable. More importantly, its use has gone beyond merely determining whether the police may intercept an individual's phone calls. The reasonable expectation of privacy test has become the standard by which to judge the constitutionality of law enforcement's actions with respect to the Fourth Amendment.

Smith's significance lies in the fact that the Supreme Court has yet to apply the third-party doctrine to social media or Internet communications. Thus, *Smith,* although over 35 years old, is the

reigning precedent to explain communications transmitted over the Internet.[29]

Smith's value, however, is somewhat diluted by the fact that no one, including judges, law professors, and practitioners, is quite sure how it applies in the context of social media.

Some believe that pursuant to *Smith* and the third-party doctrine social media users are not protected by the Fourth Amendment because they willingly reveal their communications to the Internet service providers (ISPs)—the functional equivalent of a telephone company. The ISP is the link between a computer and the Internet.[30] One legal commentator has noted that

[t]he only way that *Smith*'s reasoning based on third-party disclosure could make sense in the Internet age would be an undesirable (and likely factually incorrect) holding that people have no expectation of any privacy right in their Internet communications.[31]

While this is one possible reading of *Smith,* it is not the one generally accepted.

Most, but far from all, believe that the Supreme Court in the *Smith* decision created a division between content and noncontent information.[32] Content information (what a user sends another user), when communicated over equipment owned by a third party, is protected by the Fourth Amendment and not subject to the third-party doctrine. Noncontent information (what the entity or user transmits to facilitate the transmission), when communicated over equipment owned by a third party, is not protected by the Fourth Amendment and is subject to the third-party doctrine.

This content vs. noncontent distinction works with respect to the telephone because its use can be neatly segregated. A line can be drawn between content and noncontent information. The same, however, cannot be said for social media. Although the telephone and social media share many similarities, this area is not one.

One difference between social media and the telephone is the method by which law enforcement acquires information from the latter.[33] If law enforcement wanted to learn the numbers dialed from a certain phone, they traditionally relied on a pen register. This device captured only noncontent information. The risk of obtaining actual content was almost non-existent because the pen register did not collect actual conversations. In fact, law enforcement wasn't even aware whether an actual conversation existed.

It would be very difficult to apply a pen register–like device to social media. This is because social media and the telephone operate very differently, which raises the second and arguably the biggest difference between the two—functionality.

The telephone user has two basic options: dial a number and hold a conversation. In contrast, the social media user has a wide assortment of options that don't fit neatly into content and noncontent categories. For example, the social media user may post an emoticon or picture on her social media site or she may send an email, instant message, or video to another user. Do these functions involve content or noncontent information? The same question can be posed for geographic check-ins, tweets, wall comments, groups joined, pokes, status updates, and friend requests. Strong arguments can be made for and against calling this information either content or noncontent or both. Unlike the telephone, social media information does not fit neatly into content and noncontent categories.

In sum, *Smith* offers practitioners and the courts some general guidance on how to apply the third-party doctrine to online communications. However, because of the differences between how telephones and social media operate, *Smith*'s reach is fairly limited. At some point, the Supreme Court is going to have to step in and either overrule *Smith*, as it did with *Olmstead*, or provide better guidance on how to apply it in the Digital Age.

The next section looks at *United States v. Joshua Meregildo et al.*, one of the first reported cases to deal with social media and the Fourth Amendment.[34] Fortunately for the trial judge in *Meregildo*, this case was fairly straightforward and he was not faced with complicated issues such as distinguishing between content and noncontent information. However, *Meregildo* did raise the interesting question of what happens when an online friend proves to be not so friendly. The court in *Meregildo* held that, as in the offline world, a criminal defendant loses his Fourth Amendment protections when he willingly reveals information to a friend who in reality is working or cooperating with the government.

In *Meregildo*, law enforcement was investigating Melvin Colon, Joshua Meregildo, and others for Racketeer Influenced and Corrupt Organizations Act (RICO) violations related to drug activities and weapons. One of the defendants, Melvin Colon, had a Facebook page in which he maintained certain privacy settings. The general public could not view Colon's Facebook page, but his Facebook friends could see part of Colon's Facebook page including the messages and photographs that Colon and others posted. Working through a cooperating witness, who happened to be a Facebook friend of Colon, the government was able to see that

> Colon posted messages regarding prior acts of violence, threatened new violence to rival gang members, and sought to maintain the loyalties of other alleged members of Colon's gang.[35]

The government then used this information provided by the cooperating witness to request a search warrant to access more information from Colon's Facebook account. This led Colon to challenge the constitutionality of the government's methods of collecting evidence to support the probable cause determination for the warrant. Specifically, Colon viewed the government's use of a cooperating witness to discover information about his Facebook page as a violation of his Fourth Amendment rights.

In rejecting Colon's argument, the court determined that

> Colon's legitimate expectation of privacy ended when he disseminated posts to his "friends" because those "friends" were free to use the information however they wanted—including sharing it with the government.[36]

Additionally, the court found that

> [b]ecause Colon surrendered his expectation of privacy, the government did not violate the Fourth Amendment when it accessed Colon's Facebook profile through a cooperating witness.[37]

The *Meregildo* opinion should not be interpreted to mean that the court is never willing to apply Fourth Amendment protections to information placed on social media. Some courts have drawn a distinction between private messaging and posts to a wall, finding that a defendant has a reasonable expectation of privacy in the former. In a civil case, *R.S. v. Minnewaska Area School District,* the court held that the juvenile defendant had

> a reasonable expectation of privacy to [her] private Facebook information and messages.[38]

Of course, just as in *Meregildo*, if the person who receives the private message on social media decides to turn it over to law enforcement or make it public, the criminal defendant loses his Fourth Amendment protections.

FIFTH AMENDMENT

Between the Fourth and Fifth Amendments, the Fourth Amendment arises most often with respect to social media and criminal law. This is due primarily to the tactics employed by law enforcement. Rather than approach users directly, law enforcement's preferred methods of obtaining social media–related information involve either surveillance or requests made to social media providers. By relying on these two approaches, law enforcement raises potential issues with the Fourth but not necessarily the Fifth Amendment.

Furthermore, when law enforcement attempts to obtain information directly from a social media user, they usually do so with a warrant rather than a subpoena, thus further decreasing the chances of raising the Fifth Amendment. However, since law enforcement tactics may change in the future and Fifth Amendment issues do occasionally arise in the context of social media, it is still a topic worthy of discussion, however briefly.

The Fifth Amendment states in part,

> [n]o person . . . shall be compelled in any criminal case to be a witness against himself.[39]

As interpreted by the courts, this phrase prevents the government from forcing individuals to testify against themselves. For the state to violate an individual's Fifth Amendment rights, it has to compel the person to provide incriminating testimony. Compulsion does not include information the individual willingly conveys. Thus, a criminal defendant who voluntarily posts incriminating information on his social media site could not raise a Fifth Amendment claim when the government introduces that information later at trial. This is true even if the defendant does not testify.

Testimony is defined as the communication of facts or opinions. Testimony does not include physical evidence like an individual's hair, DNA, fingernail scrapings, handwriting sample, voice exemplar, and so on. However, as will be discussed shortly, the act of producing physical evidence may, in certain limited circumstances, serve as a communication.

Fifth Amendment issues generally arise in the context of the government issuing a subpoena to the criminal defendant. A subpoena is a command from the court that directs individuals to appear at a deposition, hearing, or court proceeding. A subpoena *duces tecum* (under penalty to bring with you) is a command by the court for the individual to produce specific documents or evidence. Criminal defense attorneys and prosecutors use subpoenas, which are actually issued on behalf of the court, as an information-gathering tool. According to Federal Rule of Criminal Procedure (FRCP) 17:

> A subpoena may order the witness to produce any books, papers, documents, data, or other objects the subpoena designates. The court may direct the witness to produce the designated items in court before trial or before they are to be offered in evidence. When the items arrive, the court may permit the parties and their attorneys to inspect all or part of them.[40]

The government may issue a subpoena to the criminal defendant for his social media–related documents or passwords. As will be discussed in Chapter 7, the government can generally obtain social media documents from the social media provider itself. Thus, courts have not really had the opportunity to address the issue of criminal defendants receiving subpoenas for social media–related information. However, the question has arisen in other contexts.

As a general rule, a request for documents by the prosecution via subpoena does not raise Fifth Amendment concerns so long as those documents were voluntarily created by the user. The exception to this rule is when the very production of those documents proves ownership by the user, authenticity of the documents, or requires the user to engage in some mental processes to actually assemble or put together the information requested by the government. In *United States v. Hubbell*, the Supreme Court noted that

> "[t]he act of production" itself may implicitly communicate "statements of fact." By "producing documents in compliance with a subpoena, the witness would admit that the papers existed, were in his possession or control, and were authentic."[41]

Pursuant to a principle known as the foregone conclusion, the likelihood of physical evidence serving as a communication is greatly reduced if the government has prior knowledge of the requested evidence. Professor Susan Brenner sums up this principle as follows:

> If you're telling the government something it doesn't already know, you're testifying; if you're just giving the government something it already knows you have and knows about, you're not testifying. You're just handing over physical evidence.[42]

No court has yet to squarely address the issue of social media passwords and the Fifth Amendment. However, the topic has been raised in other analogous situations with mixed results. To date, the lower courts have gone back and forth on whether requiring someone to turn over a computer password violates the Fifth Amendment. In *United States v. Kirschner,* a 2010 federal court case, the defendant was indicted on three counts of child pornography.[43] Subsequent to the indictment, the defendant received a grand jury subpoena that directed him to produce the password to encrypted files on his personal computer.

The defendant moved to quash the subpoena, arguing that it violated the Fifth Amendment. The court agreed with the defendant, finding that requiring him to disclose the password would be compelling incriminating testimony. This is because the court found the password to be testimonial in nature. According to the court,

> [i]n the instant case, forcing the Defendant to reveal the password for the computer communicates that factual assertion to the government, and thus, is testimonial—it requires Defendant to communicate "knowledge," unlike the production of a handwriting sample or a voice exemplar.[44]

Faced with a similar question in *United States v. Boucher*, the court ultimately came to an opposite conclusion. In *Boucher,* which was decided a year before *Kirschner*, the defendant was crossing the U.S./Canada border when he was designated for secondary inspection by a customs inspector. During the secondary search, a federal agent booted up Boucher's laptop and found 40,000 image files, some of which appeared to be pornographic. When asked by the federal agent whether there was child pornography on the laptop, Boucher said he was unsure because sometimes his downloads included child pornography, which he would then immediately delete.

The federal agent requested assistance from a second agent. This agent asked Boucher how he downloaded files. Boucher, in turn, navigated to the Z drive of the laptop. At this point, the agent began to search the Z drive himself and saw what he believed to be child pornography. The agent then shut down the laptop and arrested Boucher.

The government subsequently obtained a search warrant to search Boucher's laptop but was unable to access the encrypted Z drive. It soon became clear that the only way to open the Z drive was with a password, which Boucher refused to provide. As a result, prosecutors convened a grand jury and had it issue Boucher a subpoena for the password.

Boucher filed a motion to quash the subpoena pursuant to the Fifth Amendment. He argued that providing the password would be compelled testimony that would incriminate him. In response, the government asserted that a password was physical, not testimonial evidence and thus exempt from the Fifth Amendment. The federal magistrate, who makes initial rulings on subpoenas, agreed with Boucher and determined that the subpoena was testimonial. The magistrate judge determined that

Compelling Boucher to enter the password forces him to produce evidence that could . . . incriminate him. . . .

Entering a password into the computer implicitly communicates facts. By entering the password Boucher would be disclosing . . . that he knows the password and his control over . . . drive Z. The procedure is equivalent to asking Boucher, "Do you know the password to the laptop?"[45]

The government appealed the magistrate judge's ruling to the district judge. In the appeal, the government shifted its argument somewhat by stating that

it does not . . . seek the password for the encrypted hard drive, but requires Boucher to produce the contents of his encrypted hard drive in an unencrypted format by opening the drive before the grand jury. In oral argument and postargument submissions, the Government stated that it intends only to require Boucher to provide an unencrypted version of the drive to the grand jury.[46]

This new argument, which was raised before a different judge, proved more successful for the government. Based on the foregone conclusion principle, the district judge overruled the magistrate judge, finding that

Boucher accessed the Z drive of his laptop at the ICE agent's request. The ICE agent viewed the contents of some of the Z drive's files, and ascertained that they may consist of images or videos of child pornography. The Government thus knows of the existence and location of the Z drive and its files. Again providing access to the unencrypted Z drive "adds little or nothing to the sum total of the Government's information" about the existence and location of files that may contain incriminating information.[47]

As demonstrated by this brief discussion, it would take a very unique set of circumstances for the Fifth Amendment to arise with respect to social media. Unfortunately, if an issue were to arise, the case law is not entirely settled in this area. However, it appears that a social media user may, in certain instances, raise a colorable Fifth Amendment argument against turning over social media-related information including passwords to law enforcement.

Part III

Attorneys

In Parts I and II, this book explored the various ways social media has affected both private citizens and law enforcement. In Part III, the book will take a look at the influence of social media on attorneys. Here, the book will cover three specific topics. The first topic to be examined is the methods relied upon by attorneys to obtain information from social media. Next, the book looks at the various ways attorneys employ social media in the everyday practice of law. Finally, Part III concludes with an exploration of the ethical issues that arise from attorneys using social media.

7

Obtaining Social Media Information

In preparing to either prosecute or defend a criminal case, attorneys attempt to obtain information about their opponent's case. Some attorneys, especially defense counsel, rely on pretrial procedures like motions to suppress and bail hearings in order to learn information. Other methods of obtaining information include (1) independent research, (2) subpoenas and warrants, and (3) discovery. These traditional methods, when employed in the context of social media, pose unique challenges, which is the focus of this chapter. However, prior to beginning that discussion, this section will briefly examine the threshold question of why some attorneys have yet to seek out or use social media.

A few attorneys ignore the benefits of social media as a professional tool because they are unaware of the various ways it can assist them. Unlike those in law enforcement, attorneys don't appear to be as attuned to all of the advantages that social media affords the legal profession. This unawareness may be due to the fact that attorneys, as a whole, are older than law enforcement personnel and thus more likely to be Digital Immigrants rather than Digital Natives. Generally speaking, Digital Immigrants are less familiar with Internet-based technology like social media.

Other attorneys are aware of the benefits of social media but don't necessarily know how to mine it for information. Many attorneys falling into this category are stymied by the outdated Stored Communications Act (SCA), which was passed before anyone had even considered developing a social media platform. Enacted in the mid-1980s, this overly complex statute regulates how social media providers may release information to third parties including criminal defense attorneys and prosecutors. At least one court has noted that

> the [SCA] was written prior to the advent of the Internet and the World Wide Web. As a result, the existing statutory framework is ill-suited to address modern forms of communication like [Facebook and Myspace]. Courts have struggled to analyze problems involving modern technology within the confines of this statutory framework, often with unsatisfying results.[1]

The SCA will be discussed in greater detail later in this chapter.

There is a final group of attorneys who are well versed in social media and the many benefits it offers to practitioners, but don't believe that they have the time to use it effectively on a regular basis. Many attorneys falling into this category work for public agencies like the office of the public defender (including appointed outside counsel) or city prosecutor and handle a large number of cases. These attorneys feel that they barely have enough time to read police reports and witness statements before trial, much less investigate social media.

Fortunately for the legal profession and the people they serve, the above-mentioned knowledge gap between Digital Immigrants and Digital Natives appears to be closing as more and more attorneys regardless of age are exhibiting a greater awareness of social media. This is reflected in the increased use of social media by practitioners of all age groups. It is also demonstrated in the courtroom, where the number of cases referencing Facebook, LinkedIn, Twitter, and so on continues to grow at an exponential rate. In addition, attorneys are becoming more comfortable with the SCA and discovering ways around some of its more restrictive components.

Unfortunately, the issue of attorneys with too many cases and too little time is a reoccurring problem—one that manifests itself in other areas of the law, not just with respect to using social media. The problem here is one of resources. While no easy answer exists to this question, there are steps the court and the legal system can take to allow attorneys to make better use of their time (e.g., create work-friendly courtrooms). Some courts have taken this first step by installing computers and Wi-Fi in the courtroom so that attorneys can continue to work on cases while out of the office. Ultimately, the resource question comes down to how the attorney wants to allocate her time. Attorneys will most likely find the necessary time to squeeze in social media so long as cases continue to be won or lost based on how well practitioners use it.

INDEPENDENT RESEARCH

After clearing the knowledge and resource hurdles, the next issue confronting attorneys is determining the best method for acquiring social media–related information. To date, the most common way to obtain information from social media is through independent research conducted by either the attorney or her agent.

As a threshold matter, most practitioners, when conducting independent research, do not concern themselves, at least initially, with the rules of evidence and whether the information discovered on social media will be admissible in a court of law. As will be discussed in Part IV, the rules on getting social media admitted into evidence are somewhat complex. However, regardless of admissibility, the information from social media may still be beneficial. This point was illustrated by a Texas prosecutor from Harris County who stated,

> [e]ven if the use of the person's profile or picture is technically not admissible under the rules of evidence, many times I am able to gather good information that I can use in the cross examination of the witness.[2]

Attorneys generally adhere to three key principles when performing independent social media research: (1) immediacy, (2) completeness, and (3) preservation.[3] The first principle is important because information on social media is user-created, which means that it can change without notice. In addition, the user, at any time, can delete his account or alter his privacy settings by the mere click of a button. Therefore, prudent attorneys begin their investigation of social media as soon as practicable. According to one Los Angeles County district attorney,

> the first thing I do when I get a case is to Google the victim, the suspect, and all the material witnesses. I run them all through Facebook, Myspace, Twitter, YouTube and see what I might get.[4]

The second principle reflects the view that attorneys should not focus solely on finding the proverbial "smoking gun." Granted, some witnesses and criminal defendants make social media investigations fairly easy and straightforward by posting pictures of stolen property on Myspace or admitting through a tweet to fabricating evidence. However, this is not always the case. Furthermore, as more and more individuals realize that social media is regularly relied on in court, this type of information will become increasingly difficult to find.[5]

Attorneys must treat social media research like any other investigation and conduct it thoroughly. This means that attorneys have to look past the obvious, such as photos, and examine things like status updates and mood indicators. Attorneys should also examine the sites of the social media account holder's friends. While social media investigations may not always result in finding the perfect piece of evidence to impeach a witness or increase a defendant's sentence, they can lead the attorney to other important areas. According to an Alcohol, Tobacco, and Firearms spokesperson, investigating social media might not

solve anything, but at least it gives a direction in which to go.[6]

The third key principle is preservation of social media evidence. Preservation occurs in two stages. In the first stage, the attorney, in a written letter, informs social media providers and users that information in their possession should be safeguarded because it will likely be used as evidence in an upcoming criminal trial. If the attorney believes that the social media information is incriminating or exculpatory, that fact should also be included in the letter.

These letters, often referred to as "preservation letters," are important because they decrease the likelihood that individuals who receive them will later claim that the requested information is no longer available because it was either deleted or removed. When sending preservation letters, attorneys should be as specific as possible about the information to be preserved. The letter should also warn recipients that the attorney will assume any destruction of material is done in bad faith since the recipient has been put on notice about its importance. A sample defense preservation letter is available in Appendix B. A sample prosecution preservation letter is available in Appendix A.

The second stage of preservation involves the attorney taking independent steps to safeguard any information she comes across. For example, some attorneys take screen shots of the social media information they discover. Other attorneys print the information. The key here is for the attorney to preserve the information in as close to the same format as how it was discovered. This decreases the likelihood that others will later make claims that the information was doctored or altered in some form or fashion.[7]

Generally speaking, independent research works well for publicly available information on social media. However, not all social media information falls into this category. Many social media users, as illustrated throughout this book, employ a variety of privacy settings to prevent others from viewing their information. In those situations, attorneys must turn to other methods. The next section examines how attorneys use subpoenas, court orders, and warrants to obtain social media information directly from social media users and providers.

Social Media Users and Providers

If a user employs privacy settings limiting public access to her social media site, the attorney may, in certain situations, contact the user directly and attempt to gain access to her site. When making such contact, attorneys, unlike law enforcement, are generally prohibited from using deception. This question about what an attorney must reveal when interacting with others through social media will be discussed in greater detail in Chapter 9, which examines the ethical implications of using social media.

If the attorney's request is rebuffed, the attorney can attempt to subpoena the social media information directly from the user. Here, attorneys generally rely on a subpoena *duces tecum* because they are usually requesting documents from the user. When sending subpoenas to criminal defendants, prosecutors must be attuned to any potential Fifth Amendment issues that may arise. This issue was discussed in greater detail in Chapter 6. In addition to a subpoena, prosecutors also have the option of obtaining a warrant to gather information directly from the social media user.

Generally speaking, subpoenas are liberally granted. When challenged in court, the person sending the subpoena must be able to demonstrate that the information requested is (1) relevant, (2) admissible, and (3) described with specificity.[8] Practically speaking, subpoenas are not routinely litigated in criminal law, except in the area of white-collar crime. As a result, few criminal cases have addressed the question of what constitutes relevancy in the context of social media discovery. However, relevancy is a hotly contested area in the civil arena. The issue of whether social media information is relevant for civil discovery has been addressed both here and in Canada (see, e.g., *Mackelprang v. Fidelity National Title Agency* and *Leduc v. Roman*).[9]

Relevancy also relates to the earlier point of conducting a thorough investigation. The more information the attorney uncovers during her initial independent investigation, the less likely the court will view her subsequent subpoena request as a "fishing expedition." By conducting a thorough and complete investigation, the attorney is more likely to come up with information to support her request for a subpoena.

In the context of criminal law, many practitioners question the usefulness of issuing subpoenas directly to individuals. This is because attorneys doubt whether the recipients will properly comply; many individuals would rather run the risk of contempt of court for failure to properly comply with a subpoena than turn over incriminating evidence. Understanding this reality, attorneys routinely attempt to obtain information from a neutral source. Thus, instead of subpoenaing an individual user, most attorneys prefer sending a subpoena directly to the social media provider. Appendix C contains subpoena point of contacts for various social media providers.[10]

Unfortunately for attorneys, obtaining subpoenaed documents from social media providers is not as easy or straightforward as it might seem. In addition to meeting the requirements of relevancy, admissibility, and specificity, a subpoena to a social media provider must also comply with the SCA. It is this latter requirement that generally serves as the biggest impediment to obtaining information from social media providers via subpoena.[11]

Passed in 1986, the SCA imposes both criminal and civil penalties on social media providers who improperly reveal third-party information under their control to others.[12] Congress's intent behind the SCA was to protect the confidentiality of new forms of communication and data storage that had started to emerge in the 1980s.[13] If properly protected, Congress believed, these new methods of communication would flourish. While some use the SCA and Electronic Communications Privacy Act (ECPA) interchangeably, the SCA is actually a subsection of the ECPA.[14]

As illustrated in Chapter 6, Fourth Amendment protections can be somewhat lacking when applied to electronic communications. The SCA was created to fill this gap in coverage by providing Fourth Amendment–like protections to new forms of communication and data storage. According to one court:

> The SCA was enacted because the advent of the Internet presented a host of potential privacy breaches that the Fourth Amendment does not address.[15]

As written, the SCA offers levels of protection depending on the information requested. For example, under the SCA, certain information may be obtained from a social media provider with a mere subpoena (with or without prior notice to the user); other information requires a special court order (with or without prior notice to the user); and the last category of information requires a search warrant.

This chapter will focus on how the SCA regulates what information social media providers may offer to third parties, including prosecutors, law enforcement, and defense counsel.[16] One major consequence of the statute, which was probably not foreseen when it was originally passed, is that criminal defense attorneys are extremely limited in the amount of third-party or user information that they can receive from social media providers. Although prosecutors and law enforcement aren't as limited as defense attorneys, they nonetheless must meet certain requirements to obtain third-party information from social media providers.

Content Information

As written, the SCA prevents social media providers from giving defense counsel or civil practitioners content information from a user's social media account absent permission from that user.[17] This is true regardless of whether that information is subpoenaed directly from the social media provider. In light of this restriction, defense attorneys have basically three options when it comes to obtaining content information from a social media provider.

First, attorneys can work with the social media account holder. Defense attorneys can try to get the individual social media account holder to consent to access. If the social media account holder will not consent, the defense attorney can turn to the court and request that the account holder be directed to consent or face contempt. This scenario, which, as of late, has been met with mixed success, will be discussed in greater detail later in this chapter.

Second, attorneys can challenge the constitutionality of the SCA.[18] An attorney might argue that the SCA as currently drafted deprives criminal defendants of due process and their right to a fair trial. Courts may look favorably at a constitutional challenge, especially if an attorney can show that the information sought from the social media provider is exculpatory or essential to proving the innocence of the criminal defendant.

Third, defense attorneys can work with prosecutors. As discussed below, the SCA has specific exemptions for the government. Thus, defense counsel can ask the government to request certain content information from the social media provider. Once the government receives the information from the social media provider, they should, theoretically speaking, provide defense counsel with any portion that contains discovery material.

In certain limited situations, a social media provider may provide prosecutors and law enforcement content information from an individual's social media account. To understand when this might occur, it is first necessary to classify the provider as either a provider of remote computing service (RCS) or a provider of electronic communication service (ECS).

An RCS is (e.g., computer storage or processing services)

the provision to the public of computer storage or processing services by means of an electronic communications system.[19]

The statute covering RCS further defines "electronic communications
system" as

any wire, radio, electromagnetic, photo-optical or photo-electronic
facilities for the transmission of wire or electronic communications,
and any computer facilities or related electronic equipment for the
electronic storage of such communications.[20]

An ECS is (e.g., email, phone, IM, or text messages)

any service which provides . . . users . . . the ability to send or receive
wire or electronic communications.[21]

"Electronic storage" is

any temporary, intermediate storage of a wire or electronic transmission thereof; and any storage of such communication by an [ECS] for
purposes of backup protection of such communication.[22]

While the ECS/RCS distinction made sense in 1986, technology has
advanced so much that the terms have become anachronistic. As a result,
applying the ECS/RCS distinction can be somewhat challenging with
respect to social media providers because they might fall into both categories depending on how they are used.[23] When that situation arises, many
courts look at the specific service of the social media provider and classify
it as either ECS or RCS. According to one federal court in Oregon,

[t]oday, most ISPs provide both ECS and RCS; thus, the distinction
serves to define the service that is being provided at a particular time
(or as to a particular piece of electronic communication at a particular time), rather than to define the service provider itself.[24]

If the provider or specific service is an ECS and the information
requested has been stored for less than 180 days, the government needs a
warrant to obtain the information. If the provider or specific service is an
RCS or an ECS and the information requested has been stored for more

than 180 days, the government has the option of using a (1) warrant, (2) court order (18 USC § 2703(d)), or (3) subpoena.[25]

Although a warrant requires more evidentiary support than 2703(d) court orders or subpoenas, it does not require proof beyond a reasonable doubt or clear and convincing evidence, both of which are high standards to meet.[26] Instead, the legal threshold for a warrant is probable cause.

To obtain a 2703(d) court order, the government must provide specific and articulable facts demonstrating reasonable grounds to believe that the information requested is

relevant and material to an ongoing criminal investigation.[27]

The 2703(d) court order is

something like a mix between a subpoena and a search warrant. . . . If the judge finds that the factual showing has been made, the judge signs the order. The order is then served like an ordinary subpoena.[28]

The requirements for a subpoena, which are not difficult to meet, have been previously discussed.

If the government relies on the 2703(d) court order or the subpoena to obtain content information, the social media provider must provide the account holder prior notice. This notice may be delayed under certain circumstances. The SCA allows for a delayed notice of 90 days if the government has

reasons to believe that notification of the existence of the court order may have an adverse result.[29]

An "adverse result" includes (1) endangering the life or physical safety of an individual; (2) flight from prosecution; (3) destruction of or tampering with evidence; (4) intimidation of potential witnesses; and (5) otherwise seriously jeopardizing an investigation or unduly delaying a trial.[30]

Noncontent Information

The ECS or RCS classification and 180-day threshold are irrelevant for noncontent information. Instead, the focus is on the two subcategories of noncontent information. If the government wants a noncontent transactional record, like a log, from a social media provider, it must obtain either a warrant or a 2703(d) court order.[31] For other noncontent information, like the name and address of the account holder, the government need only obtain a subpoena.

The SCA does not require anything from a nongovernmental entity requesting noncontent information. However, most social media providers as part of their voluntary privacy practices require nongovernmental entities to obtain a subpoena to receive noncontent information.

Motion to Quash

As previously mentioned, when attorneys or law enforcement use subpoenas to acquire social media information, they generally do so by sending the subpoena to the social media provider instead of the individual user. This has led to an interesting question about what steps, if any, users can take to prevent the disclosure of their own social media information by social media providers. At present, several barriers exist to prevent social media users from blocking the disclosure of their social media information via subpoena.

First, social media users are not always provided with advanced notice of subpoena requests. As previously discussed, under certain conditions, the SCA allows the government and social media providers to delay notifying users that their information has been subpoenaed. Without prior notice, it is very difficult for social media users to file a timely motion to quash—the traditional legal tool employed to contest or challenge a subpoena.

Assuming the user receives notice beforehand, other issues arise with respect to ownership of the social media information. Does it belong to the user or to the social media provider? If the information belongs to the social media provider, does the user then have standing to challenge its release? "Standing" is a legal term of art and has been defined as follows:

> a legally protectable stake or interest that an individual has in a dispute that entitles him to bring the controversy before the court to obtain judicial relief.[32]

This question of whether defendants have standing in the social media information they create, at least with respect to Twitter, was addressed in *People v. Harris.*[33]

In *Harris,* the government alleged that the defendant, Malcolm Harris, along with several hundred other Occupy Wall Street protesters, illegally marched on the roadway of the Brooklyn Bridge. As a result, many of these individuals including the defendant were charged with disorderly conduct.

On January 26, 2012, the prosecution sent a subpoena *duces tecum* to Twitter. The subpoena sought information including email address and tweets posted from September 15, 2011, to December 31, 2011, for the twitter account @destructuremal which allegedly belonged to Malcolm Harris. The prosecution claimed that they needed this information from Twitter to refute Harris's potential defense that law enforcement either led or escorted him onto the nonpedestrian part of the Brooklyn Bridge. Prosecutors wanted to discredit this defense by introducing the defendant's tweets.

On January 30, 2012, Twitter informed the defendant of the government's subpoena request. The next day the defendant informed Twitter that he would move to quash the subpoena. The defendant's motion to quash was denied on April 20, 2012. Twitter then filed its own motion to quash the subpoena, which was also later denied.

In rejecting the motions to quash by both Malcolm Harris and Twitter, the court determined, at least with respect to the defendant's motion, that he did not have standing in the case. The court based this on the idea that the defendant had no proprietary interest in his tweets—they belonged to Twitter. The *Harris* court reached this conclusion by comparing tweets to bank records. Previous courts have held that individuals do not have "proprietary or possessory interests" in their bank records because they belong to the bank.[34] Here, the *Harris* court determined that tweets were like bank records because Twitter owned them. The court also made note of Twitter's TOS, in place at that time, which reads as follows:

> [users] authorize us [Twitter] to make your Tweets available to the rest of the world and to let others do the same.[35]

The court also found that the defendant's tweets were not protected by the Fourth Amendment. According to the *Harris* court, there was no physical intrusion upon the defendant's tweets. They were obtained from Twitter. In addition, the defendant did not have a reasonable expectation of privacy in his tweets that were broadcast to the world via the Internet.[36] In the eyes of the *Harris* court, Malcolm Harris's situation was much different from that of Katz, who went into an enclosed pay phone booth to discuss his illegal bets with another person. Harris wanted others to read his tweets; Katz only wanted the person on the other end of the telephone line to hear his phone conversation, and he took steps to ensure that his phone call was private.

Not surprisingly, the *Harris* opinion has come under criticism by First Amendment and privacy advocates like the American Civil Liberties

Union (ACLU) and Electronic Frontier Foundation (EFF). They claim that just because a user sends a tweet does not mean that he loses standing to prevent that tweet from being subpoenaed. These organizations contend that the *Harris* decision restricts the ability of individuals to go to court and protect their social media information.

As a result of *Harris*, some have wondered whether other social media providers will follow in the footsteps of Twitter and change their policies to ensure that users maintain greater control and ownership of their information. Subsequent to the *Harris* court's initial decision denying the defendant's motion to quash, Twitter changed its TOS to read as follows:

> [y]ou Retain Your Right To Any Content You Submit, Post Or Display On Or Through The Service.[37]

Additional questions have arisen about standing and what *Harris* means for other social media platforms. Put differently, was *Harris* limited to Twitter or does it apply to other social media platforms like Pinterest, Facebook, Craigslist, Reddit, and the like? It should be noted that in opinions prior to the *Harris* decision, courts have found that social media users do have standing to challenge subpoenas sent to social media providers. For example, in *Crispin v. Christian Audigier*, a civil case involving copyright infringement, the court found that the plaintiff did have standing to object to subpoenas sent by defendants directly to Myspace and Facebook.[38] Thus, it remains to be seen whether the *Harris* opinion will be relegated to Twitter and the specific facts of that case or if it will be expanded to other areas.

DISCOVERY

Besides conducting independent research and contacting social media providers, attorneys may also obtain social media information through discovery.[39] Discovery is a pretrial process governed by the court in which opposing counsel exchange essential information with each other in order to properly prepare for trial. The purpose of discovery is to avoid trial by ambush or trial by surprise. According to the Supreme Court,

> [t]he adversary system of trial hardly is an end to itself; it is not yet a poker game in which players enjoy an absolute right always to conceal their cards until played.[40]

Although discovery occurs in both civil and criminal litigation, it functions differently in each. In criminal law, discovery is much more limited.

In addition, unlike in the civil arena, discovery in the criminal context is not always a two-way street. Due to constitutional considerations, the defendant is not required to turn over as much information as the prosecution. However, one similarity between the two forms of discovery is that failure to turn over discoverable material can lead to a variety of court-imposed sanctions on the parties involved.

Two primary methods exist by which defense attorneys receive information pursuant to discovery. The first is through the rules of criminal procedure. Unlike other areas of law, states throughout the country take different approaches to handling criminal discovery. Yet, despite these variations among jurisdictions, they can be loosely categorized by reference to three basic models: (1) ABA's *Standards Relating to Discovery and Procedure Before Trial* (First Edition); (2) ABA's *Standards for Discovery* (Third Edition); and (3) the Federal Rules of Criminal Procedure (FRCP).[41] This last model will be relied on for this book.

Pursuant to FRCP 16, the prosecution, upon a defendant's request, must disclose the following to the defense: (1) evidence that it intends to use in its case-in-chief; (2) items obtained from the defendant; and (3) relevant written and recorded statements of the defendant.[42] If a defense attorney requests information pursuant to FRCP 16, she is subject to reciprocal discovery requests from the prosecution. Social media–related information held by either prosecution or defense is not exempted from the requirements of FRCP 16.

The second method of obtaining discovery arises from United States Supreme Court cases such as *Brady v. Maryland* and *United States v. Giglio*.[43] *Brady* and its progeny require the prosecution to turn over material information that would exculpate the defendant or reduce his sentence.[44] *Giglio* requires the prosecution to turn over information that may be used to impeach a key government witness on a material point.[45] The disclosure of *Brady* or *Giglio* material is a self-executing duty of the prosecution. Thus, the defense need not first request this information. Furthermore, so-called *Brady* material must be disclosed at both the trial and sentencing stages. Similar to FRCP 16, social media information is not exempted from the requirements of *Brady* and *Giglio*.

An interesting issue has arisen with respect to discovery and social media providers. Generally speaking, the prosecution is only responsible for turning over information in their possession or control. Although a social media provider is not under the general control of the prosecution, they, unlike defense counsel, can obtain content information from the social media provider. Thus, an argument can be made that if the prosecution is put on notice about potentially exculpatory information held by a social media provider, the prosecution has a due process obligation to make an effort to obtain that information. This is one of the reasons why this book suggested earlier that defense attorneys work with the prosecutor's office when attempting to obtain content information from social media providers.

Once an attorney has conducted independent research, issued subpoenas and warrants where applicable, and participated in the discovery process, the next step is to effectively use the information obtained. Chapter 8 will examine the multitude of ways that criminal law attorneys have employed social media in their everyday practice.

8

Using Social Media

Chapter 8 highlights the variety of ways in which attorneys employ social media. At present, attorneys use social media both inside and outside the courtroom. Inside the courtroom, attorneys primarily rely on social media to either bolster or discredit a witness. Other uses of social media include supporting an alibi, demonstrating the defendant's guilt, or investigating jurors. Outside the courtroom, attorneys use social media primarily to communicate with the public. Many attorneys believe that they can have an impact on events inside the courtroom through public opinion.

INSIDE THE COURTROOM

Attorneys rely on social media in all phases of litigation; some even use it prior to actually stepping foot into the courtroom. In one New York case, a defense attorney was able to avoid trial entirely and convince the government to dismiss the charges by sharing his client's Facebook account with the prosecution.[1] The case involved 19-year-old Rodney Bradford, who was charged with a mugging that occurred in Brooklyn at 11:50 a.m. on October 17, 2009.

Bradford denied any participation in the crime. He claimed that he was at home in Harlem when the mugging occurred. His assertion was supported by his father and stepmother, who were allegedly at home with him. However, Bradford was identified in a police lineup. Furthermore, Bradford was already facing additional charges for another alleged robbery.

This appeared to be a fairly typical mugging case that would turn on the credibility of witnesses, except for one additional factor. Bradford had an unbiased, impartial, and unshakable alibi—Facebook. On October 17,

2009 at 11:49 a.m., Bradford posted the following update on his Facebook page:

> on the phone with this fat chick . . . where my i hop [referencing a telephone conversation with his pregnant girlfriend and a recent visit to a pancake restaurant].[2]

When presented with this information, the government verified it with Facebook. The government also confirmed that the status update was posted from an Internet protocol address that matched the one registered to Bradford's father. This led the government to ultimately drop the charges against Bradford. This case is considered one of the earliest examples of social media serving as an alibi for a criminal defendant.

Of course, someone at Bradford's home could have logged into his Facebook account and pretended to be him. That exact scenario may come to fruition in the future as people become increasingly more familiar and comfortable with social media. However, the prosecutor here was satisfied that Bradford had indeed logged into his own account, and it was not some elaborate scheme concocted by a teenager to provide himself an alibi so he could conduct a mugging.

Other examples of social media providing solid evidence of a defendant's innocence include an assault case from Arizona. Here, the defense attorney researched the Myspace page of one of the state's witnesses and discovered a video that actually showed that witness, not his client, starting the fight.[3] This video was admitted into evidence and the defendant was acquitted.

Obviously, defense attorneys are pleased when they turn to social media and discover ironclad alibis or evidence that someone else, other than their client, instigated an altercation. However, those discoveries are increasingly rare. Instead, social media is primarily relied on to support the credibility of the attorney's own witness or call into question the integrity of opposing counsel's witness. Defense attorneys across the country have employed social media to impeach or discredit the government's witnesses.

In one New York case, the defense attorney used social media to impeach the credibility of a police officer.[4] Although the defendant did not obtain an outright acquittal, he avoided a conviction on the more serious charge. In that case, the state of New York charged the defendant with felony possession of a weapon and resisting arrest. The government's key witness was the arresting officer, Vaughan Ettienne.

On cross-examination, defense counsel impeached Ettienne's testimony by presenting information from the officer's Facebook page. For example, defense counsel introduced the fact that on the day of the defendant's arrest Ettienne listed his mood on Facebook as "devious." Ettienne also made comments about the movie *Training Day* in which Denzel Washington plays a rogue police officer. In reference to the movie, Ettienne posted the following:

> Vaughan is watching "Training Day" to brush up on proper police procedure.[5]

Besides investigating the social media pages of witnesses and clients, defense counsel have also obtained valuable information from the social media pages of victims. In Florida, a defendant was accused of stabbing Joseph Hall to death. The defendant claimed that he was acting in self-defense. To help demonstrate that the victim was a violent person and the instigator of the altercation, defense counsel introduced Hall's Myspace page, which was titled "joehallwillkillyourfamily" and featured a violent music video by the band Waking the Cadaver.

Unfortunately for defense counsel, the prosecutor also conducted his own social media investigation. The prosecutor discovered that the criminal defendant's girlfriend had actually invited the victim to the house where the altercation occurred. The prosecution's discovery helped seal the criminal defendant's conviction.

In another case, Oregon attorney Laura Fine represented a teenager charged with forcible rape.[6] The alleged victim told police that she would never willingly have had sex. However, her Myspace page told a different story. On her Myspace page, the alleged victim, who used a very lascivious screen name, talked about parties and sex. Her Myspace page also included some very racy photos. Thinking that the alleged victim would not present well before the grand jury, Fine suggested that the prosecutor call her as a witness, which the prosecutor did. Upon hearing from the alleged victim, the grand jury declined to indict Fine's client.

The aforementioned cases demonstrate how social media investigations permit attorneys to obtain a different view of witnesses. Better than interviewing a neighbor or friend, social media allows the attorney to learn how the witness views himself. Granted, people at times do take on a false online persona or can at times be less than honest. This fact was illustrated earlier in this book in the chapter examining online impersonations. However, that is true in many facets of life. People act differently at work than at home or in front of their family or friends. It is the job of the attorney to wade through this information and separate fact from fiction because arguably nothing is as compelling on cross-examination as using the witness's own words against him.

Like defense attorneys, prosecutors have also learned how to mine social media for important information.[7] When investigating social media, prosecutors focus primarily on the defendant. This is due primarily to two factors. First, some defendants neither call witnesses nor present evidence at trial; thus prosecutors are limited as to what information they can present in court. Second, the best information for prosecutors, to date, has been found primarily on social media accounts belonging to the defendant.

As discussed previously in Chapter 6, criminal defendants place a large amount of incriminating and harmful evidence on social media both intentionally and unintentionally. For example, Matthew Cordle, a 22-year-old Ohio man, created his own YouTube video in which he admitted killing Vincent Canzani in a drunk driving accident. In the video, which received widespread attention in the traditional media, Cordle stated the following:

[m]y name is Matthew Cordle, and on June 22nd, 2013, I hit and killed Vincent Canzani. This video will act as my confession.[8]

Later on in the video Cordle says:

I won't dishonor Victor's memory by lying about what happened. By releasing this video, I know exactly what it means. I'm handing the prosecution everything they need to put me away for a very long time.[9]

Cordle ends the video by exhorting viewers not to drink and drive. After being indicted, Cordle ultimately pled guilty to aggravated vehicular homicide and driving under the influence. He was sentenced to six and a half years in prison.

Not surprisingly, videos like the one produced by Cordle are an uncommon occurrence. This is because most criminal defendants do not place information on social media with the intent that it be used to prosecute them. Instead, it is generally done through negligence. Many criminal defendants fail to realize that their actions on social media, including making harassing posts, tagging incriminating photographs, or sending ill-advised friend requests, can be used to successfully prosecute them.

In one example from Tennessee, the government was able to prove a restraining order violation by showing that the criminal defendant had reached out to the victim and "poked" her on Facebook.[10] Apparently, the defendant did not understand that a Facebook poke constituted contact. According to the judge, a criminal defendant can violate a restraining order both online and offline and contact can be both physical and virtual.

To date, prosecutors have used information from the defendant's social media account at every stage of the trial from bail[11] all the way through to appeal.[12] In a case from Buffalo, New York, a defendant was facing charges of second-degree assault and fourth-degree criminal possession of a weapon.[13] Upon arrest, the defendant's bail was initially set at $5,000. The prosecutor, however, wanted the defendant's bail revoked because he believed the defendant was affiliated with a gang. Therefore, at a bail hearing the government introduced, among other things, the defendant's Myspace page, which showed him

> wearing gang clothing, giving Crips hand signs and even posing with his children and relatives in gang colors.[14]

The defendant's bail was not revoked, but it was raised to $50,000. According to the judge, the increase in the defendant's bail was due in part to

> a Myspace page that gives clear evidence of gang membership.[15]

During trial, prosecutors employ social media in a variety of different ways ranging from impeaching a witness to demonstrating a criminal defendant's motive for committing a crime. In one case, the criminal defendant Laura Ashley Hall was charged with tampering and hindering apprehension.[16] Hall's charges stemmed from her efforts to help Colton Pitonyak dismember a corpse and flee to Mexico. Pitonyak, who had killed Jennifer Cave, wanted to dispose of Cave's body and leave the country.

To demonstrate why Hall would take such drastic steps to help Pitonyak, the state argued that Hall enjoyed playing the role of the gangster's girlfriend. To support this theory, the government introduced Hall's Myspace entry for August 15, 2005, the day Cave died. Under "Summer Plans" Hall wrote,

> I should really be more of a horrific person. Its [sic] in the works.[17]

To date, prosecutors have found their greatest success with social media during sentencing, when the rules of evidence are more relaxed.[18] As will be discussed later, lawyers face some challenges in getting information derived from social media admitted into evidence. At sentencing, the prosecution has successfully used social media to (1) argue for enhancements,

(2) demonstrate the criminal defendant's lack of remorse, and (3) humanize the victim.

In Rhode Island, 20-year-old Joshua was involved in a traffic accident in which another person was seriously injured.[19] According to the prosecution, Joshua had been drinking and speeding. At sentencing, Joshua's attorney argued that his client was truly remorseful and had written apologetic letters to the victim and her family. In response, the prosecution introduced a picture from Joshua's Facebook page showing him at a Halloween party two weeks after the accident dressed in an orange jumpsuit with the nametag "Jail Bird." In remarking about the Facebook photo, the judge stated,

> I did feel that gave me some indication of how that young man was feeling a short time after a near-fatal accident, that he thought it was appropriate to joke and mock about the possibility of going to prison.[20]

The trial judge sentenced Joshua to two years in prison, which was higher than what the typical defendant receives.

In *United States v. Villanueva*, a convicted felon saw his sentence enhanced because the prosecutor presented to the court Myspace photographs and a YouTube video of the defendant brandishing several different firearms.[21] Villanueva appealed his sentence enhancements, arguing that not all the guns were real and that the trial court had no way of knowing when the video had been made. The appellate court, in upholding the trial court, determined that the weapons in the photograph were indeed real and the video had been made after Villanueva's conviction but prior to sentencing.

Information derived from social media has also served as a victim impact statement during sentencing. A victim impact statement has been defined as follows:

> [I]nformation about the financial, emotional, psychological, and physical effects of a violent crime on each victim and members of their immediate family, or person designated by the victim or by family members of the victim and includes information about the victim, circumstances surrounding the crime, the manner in which the crime was perpetrated, and the opinion of the victim of a recommended sentence.[22]

In one case, a victim died as a result of a vehicular homicide.[23] The defendant pled guilty and the only issue was sentencing. The deceased victim's family did not appear in court nor had they submitted any letters to the judge.

Thus, the prosecutor was searching for a way to personalize the impact of the victim's death. The prosecutor turned to the victim's Facebook page. Here is a sampling of what the prosecutor read to the court at sentencing:

I like milkshakes, chocolate milkshakes are my favorite.

I took piano lessons in fourth grade, but I never got very good.

I want to paint my bedroom red.

If I ever get a tattoo, it will be a butterfly on my ankle.[24]

Unfortunately for the prosecutor, she continued to read from the victim's Facebook page and this victim impact statement lost some of its effect.[25] Nonetheless, this case demonstrates how social media can not only speak for a deceased victim, but also provide the court some insight into the victim as a person.

While defense attorneys have not been as successful as prosecutors with social media at the sentencing stage of the trial, they have had some positive outcomes. For example, the criminal defendant's social media page can humanize the defendant and show him in a different light.[26] This is especially valuable after the court hears all the negative evidence presented by the prosecution.

OUTSIDE THE COURTROOM

When employed outside the courtroom, attorneys primarily use social media to shape public opinion about themselves, their clients, or some specific legal issue or problem. Where in the past an attorney might hold a press conference or issue a press release in order to communicate with the public, today's attorney turns to social media. Like most things, this practice has both advantages and disadvantages.

Generally speaking, additional information disseminated by attorneys normally results in a more informed citizenry—one that better understands the criminal justice system and those who operate in it. On the other hand, when using social media attorneys can come across as more informal and less professional, which in turn may lead some to question or lose faith in the criminal justice system as a whole. This concern is especially true for prosecutors who are not only government officials but also responsible for ensuring that justice is fairly administered.

Consider Ray Larson, the district attorney for Lexington, Kentucky, who uses both Twitter and Facebook to offer his views on crime and the criminal justice system. Mr. Larson's Twitter account (handle) is "Ray-theDA." The term is even emblazoned on a superman-like avatar that he prominently features on both his Facebook and Twitter sites. Here is a sample of some of the tweets sent by Mr. Larson:

> [19 Aug 13] MONDAY: after a good weekend now is a great time to get up and get after the bad guys. LET'S GO CRIME FIGHTERS
>
> [16 Aug 13] ERIC HOLDER'S LATEST SCAM: Telling Fed. Prosecutors not to prosecute "low-level" drug cases.
>
> [7 Aug 13] LEX/CRIME BEAT: Hey another Burglary. Isn't that what our Legislature calls a "NON-VIOLENT" Property Crime?[27]

Mr. Larson is not alone in his quest to engage the public via social media. Other prosecutors like Jennifer M. Joyce, a St. Louis circuit attorney, also rely on it to disseminate their views on life and the law. Here is a sample of Ms. Joyce's tweets:

> [13 Aug 13] These scam artists never cease to amaze
>
> [13 Aug 13] What's your opinion? Is 6 months enough time for this repeat offender?[28]

When discussing whether her actions on social media were ethical and legal, Ms. Joyce offered the following explanation:

> An acquittal results in a closed record. It would be inappropriate for me to generate public discussion about a closed record. I regularly tweet about guilty verdicts, even if it's not for the crime originally charged. I highlight staff members on a regular basis, as there are many people in the office and the courts who are excellent public servants. We are very careful about every social media post, and review all content from a legal and ethical standpoint.[29]

Like prosecutors, defense attorneys also employ social media outside of the courtroom. Generally speaking, defense counsel use social media outside of the courtroom in order to bring greater public attention to either themselves or their clients. A few prosecutors have attempted to stop defense attorneys from discussing their case or client on social media. This usually occurs in the form of a motion to the court requesting that the judge issue a gag order on all parties. Many judges, however, are reluctant to grant such orders in light of the First Amendment.

Examples of defense attorneys effectively using social media outside of the courtroom include Mark O'Mara, who successfully represented George Zimmerman in his second-degree murder trial for the death of Trayvon Martin. In this high-profile trial in which race, gun rights, and self-defense played critical roles, O'Mara relied on a variety of different social media platforms to communicate with the general public about the case.

O'Mara offered the following reasoning for why he felt the need to use social media:

> [W]e contend that social media in this day and age cannot be ignored. It is now a critical part of presidential politics, it has been part of revolutions in the Middle East, and it is going to be an unavoidable part of high-profile legal cases, just as traditional media has been and continues to be. We feel it would be irresponsible to ignore the robust online conversation, and we feel equally as strong about establishing a professional, responsible, and ethical approach to new media.[30]

While not all of O'Mara's forays into social media were successful, many were. For example, he ultimately had to shut down his "George Zimmerman Legal Case" Facebook page because of infighting among commenters. However, he used other sites like Twitter to effectively advocate for his client and keep the public informed about the progress of the case.

Prosecutors tried to prevent O'Mara from using social media both before and during the trial. In fact, on three separate occasions, the government filed motions with the court to impose a gag order on all parties involved in the case. In making their request, prosecutors alleged that the information released by the defense team tainted potential jurors. In denying the government's repeated request for a gag order, the judge determined that

> [t]here has not been an overriding pattern of prejudicial commentary that will overcome reasonable efforts to select a fair and impartial jury.[31]

As with Savannah D. in Chapter 1, social media gave the Zimmerman defense team its own voice. With social media, Zimmerman's defense team could circumvent traditional media outlets and reach the public directly. This direct connection to the public allowed them to (1) dispute misinformation about the case; (2) discredit and eliminate fraudulent social media profiles of people claiming to be George Zimmerman; (3) reduce speculation about the case and George Zimmerman; (4) raise funds for George Zimmerman's defense; (5) react to developments in the case in real time; and (6) post relevant legal documents.[32]

Besides using social media to communicate with the general public, the Zimmerman defense team also relied on it in other ways before and during the trial. One particularly unique aspect of how the Zimmerman defense team used social media inside the courtroom involved jury selection. With social media, the defense team was able to not only research jurors but also verify many of their answers during voir dire. In one instance, the defense team was able to get a prospective juror challenged for cause because she failed to disclose a social media relationship with a potential witness. The next section will provide a brief discussion about this burgeoning practice of attorneys using social media to investigate jurors.

INVESTIGATING JURORS

Although it may appear to be a modern-day concept, the practice of attorneys investigating jurors is not new. In fact, it has been around for quite some time. For example, during the 20th century, Clarence Darrow made effective use of juror investigations in the trial of Bill Haywood.[33] However, over time, the practice fell out of fashion with most attorneys. This is because juror investigations were expensive and time consuming. Furthermore, starting in the 1970s, courts gradually made it increasingly difficult to investigate jurors by waiting until the eve or day of trial to make the names of prospective jurors available to attorneys.

Social media, however, has resurrected the practice. With so much personal information now available on social media, attorneys no longer need to expend significant resources to research jurors. Furthermore, attorneys do not need the names of jurors days in advance. In certain instances, attorneys start their investigation right in the courtroom when the judge calls out the juror's name for the first time in voir dire.

In the Digital Age, courts and state bar associations have both approved and encouraged the investigation of jurors. Furthermore, the practice, as illustrated by the Zimmerman defense team, has gained increased acceptance among practitioners.

There are a few trial judges, however, who don't permit attorneys to investigate jurors. Judges in these courts believe that attorneys do not have a right to monitor or investigate a juror. Furthermore, they think that juror investigations not only intrude on the "safety, privacy, and protection against harassment" to which jurors are entitled but also potentially stifle juror willingness to participate in jury service.[34] These judges, however, are in the minority.

Today's attorneys investigate jurors for five primary reasons: (1) to confirm juror answers during voir dire; (2) to discover which jurors are favorable or unfavorable to their clients; (3) to bond with jurors; (4) to monitor juror behavior; and (5) to discover grounds for appeal.[35]

Traditionally, attorneys had few resources at their disposal to verify the answers provided by jurors in questionnaires or during voir dire. For example, if a juror said she didn't know any of the witnesses or parties in the case, the attorneys, for the most part, had to take that answer at face value. Today, an attorney can go online and discover whether a juror is Facebook friends with any of the trial participants, which is exactly what occurred in the Zimmerman trial.

Social media also affords attorneys the ability to better determine which jurors are more likely to be favorable or unfavorable to their respective side. For example, in the Casey Anthony murder trial one prospective juror tweeted the following:

Cops in Florida are idiots and completely useless.[36]

Not surprisingly, the prosecution used one of their peremptory challenges to strike this juror.

Examining a juror's social media site also helps attorneys learn about a juror's personal interests. This in turn facilitates attorney–juror bonding. For example, if an attorney goes on a juror's Facebook page and discovers that he is really into sports, the attorney may make athletic references during the trial. This helps the attorney connect with that particular juror. As explained by one seasoned litigator, it can be quite effective to use

a well-placed metaphor in [a] closing argument tailored to a juror's interest or social views as described on Facebook or Twitter.[37]

Investigating a juror's social media site also allows the attorney to track the juror's online activities during trial. This monitoring has garnered increased value in the Digital Age as jurors routinely violate the courts' rules about conducting improper communications and research during trial. By following a juror's social media site, attorneys may uncover juror misconduct.

In California, a defense attorney discovered that a juror deciding his client's fate had blogged about the case during trial.[38] On his blog, entitled

"The Misanthrope," the juror posted photographs of the murder weapon and criticized court staff. The juror's blog even encouraged questions about the case from the general public.

Finally, some attorneys investigate jurors after a verdict has been reached in an effort to find information on which to base an appeal. Here, attorneys review the juror's social media site in the hopes of discovering some inappropriate remark made by or to the juror during the trial. Some courts, however, do not look favorably on attorneys who wait until after trial to investigate jurors. This is especially true if the attorneys had any prior notice about potential juror improprieties before the verdict was reached.[39]

Subpoenaing a Juror's Social Media Information

When using social media to investigate jurors, one question that arises is how far can attorneys go to look for information? As will be discussed in the next chapter, attorneys can't friend or contact jurors. However, in certain limited situations attorneys can subpoena information from a juror's social media site. *Juror #1 (AR) v. Superior Court of California,* discussed next, illustrates how criminal defense attorneys were able to successfully subpoena information from a juror's Facebook page.

Juror #1 (AR) v. Superior Court of California arose from a 2010 criminal trial in which AR served as jury foreman.[40] At the conclusion of the trial, in which the jury convicted several members of a criminal gang of serious assault, AR friended Juror #5 on Facebook. Upon becoming AR's friend, Juror #5 noticed that AR, despite admonitions from the judge not to do so, had made and received comments about the trial on Facebook. Juror #5 reported this information to the defense attorneys in the case.

Upon learning the information from Juror #5, the defense attorneys sent subpoenas to Facebook and AR. The attorneys wanted to look at AR's Facebook page, which was not publicly available. Facebook, citing the SCA, refused to turn over the postings despite receiving the subpoena. However, Facebook did give AR all of his old postings and then informed him that he could turn those over to the defense attorneys if he so desired. Despite receiving his postings from Facebook, AR refused to turn them over to the defense attorneys. AR claimed that the request by the defense attorneys

violates the SCA, the Fourth and Fifth Amendments to the United States Constitution, and his state and federal privacy rights.[41]

After several court decisions, including two stays by the California Supreme Court, the appellate court sided with defense counsel. Specifically, AR was directed to

> execute a consent form pursuant to the Stored Communications Act (SCA) (18 U.S.C. 2701 et seq.) authorizing Facebook to release to the court for in camera review all items he posted during the trial.[42]

The appellate court determined among other things that the SCA is inapplicable because it applies to

> attempts by the court or real parties in interest to compel Facebook to disclose the requested information.[43]

Here, the compulsion is on AR, not Facebook. The court then made short work of AR's Fourth and Fifth Amendment arguments because they contained no citation to legal authority.

Lastly, the court addressed AR's right to privacy claim. Here, the court pointed out that AR's privacy interest, assuming that it exists, is not an absolute right. This right must be balanced with the criminal defendant's right to a fair trial. The appellate court also added that

> [t]he trial court has the power and the duty to inquire into whether the confirmed misconduct was prejudicial.[44]

At least one legal commentator has questioned whether the court's action here violated the SCA or at least the spirit of the law. According to Professor Orin Kerr, who has written extensively on the SCA,

> compelled consent is not valid consent.[45]

Thus, according to Professor Kerr, Facebook should not turn over AR's posts because the consent it received from AR was coerced or compelled by the judge.

Two problems arise with Professor Kerr's argument. First, Facebook gave AR all of his posts before the court directed him to execute the consent agreement. Second, Professor Kerr elevates the SCA above the criminal defendant's constitutional rights to a fair trial and impartial jurors. If the trial court has credible evidence that a juror has been contacted by outside parties or violated the court's rules on using social media, the court cannot stand idly by; it must investigate or remedy the problem. To do otherwise allows a statute like the SCA to trump the constitutional rights of the criminal defendant.

As this and the previous chapter illustrate, both prosecution and defense attorneys employ social media in a wide variety of different ways. Unfortunately, sometimes attorneys cross the ethical line when they attempt to obtain or use social media. The next chapter will address some of the ethical issues that arise when attorneys attempt to obtain or use social media in either personal or professional settings.

9

Ethical Implications of Using and Obtaining Social Media

All licensed attorneys are subject to the rules of professional and ethical conduct established by the states in which they practice. Failure to abide by these rules can lead to sanctions, including the loss of an attorney's license to practice law. Unfortunately, some attorneys have run afoul of these rules while seeking, obtaining, or using social media. This chapter will examine those missteps while also identifying other ethical problem spots that arise when attorneys interact with others via social media.

To facilitate this examination, this chapter places in two broad categories: on-the-job and off-the-job ethical issues. However, prior to starting the discussion on either category, a threshold question must be examined with respect to whether attorneys even need to familiarize themselves with social media or use it in the practice of law.

Despite its omnipresence in society and growing role in the law, a few attorneys (primarily those classified as Digital Immigrants) believe that they can prevent any problems with social media, ethical or otherwise, by just avoiding it altogether. While this head in the sand approach may, at first blush, sound appealing to those attorneys who fear all things digital or high-tech, it reflects flawed reasoning and if strictly followed could lead to disastrous results not only for the attorney, but also his client.

Among other things, ignoring social media runs contrary to the American Bar Association (ABA) Model Rules of Professional Conduct. Although the ABA Model Rules are nonbinding on attorneys, most states, when drafting their own rules, mimic or closely follow the ABA Model

Rules. Thus, the Model Rules will serve as the guideposts for this chapter. According to ABA Model Rule 1.1, Comment 6, which covers attorney competency,

> [t]o maintain the requisite knowledge and skill, a lawyer should keep abreast of changes in the law and its practice, including the benefits and risks associated with relevant technology.[1]

As this comment indicates, attorneys have a duty to remain current on changes in the practice of law. Obviously, this can be challenging with respect to technology because it constantly progresses, and attorneys can't stay up-to-date on every advancement, new gadget, or technological breakthrough. However, attorneys have to be alert to major trends, especially when these trends significantly alter the actual practice of law.

As illustrated throughout this book, social media is the proverbial "game changer" that has influenced every stage of the criminal justice process. In addition, and arguably most importantly, social media has shaped the outcomes of numerous cases. Defendants have been both acquitted and convicted based on how well the prosecution or defense employed social media. Thus, in order to stay relevant and be in compliance with the ethical rules, attorneys need to be able to both understand and use social media.

In addition to the ABA Model Rules, several courts have addressed the importance of attorneys using and implementing technology like social media. Some courts go so far as to associate the use of social media with attorney competency. The highest state court in Maryland recently noted that

> [i]t should now be a matter of professional competence for attorneys to take the time to investigate social networking sites.[2]

This court aligns with the growing number of courts that view the use of social media as part of an attorney's duty to conduct due diligence and maintain proficiency in the practice of law.

Attorneys who fall below basic proficiency may be subject to claims of malpractice and ineffective assistance of counsel.[3] While malpractice has traditionally been based on a theory of negligence, claims of ineffective assistance of counsel adhere to the test created by *Strickland v. Washington*.[4] According to *Strickland*, for a defendant to succeed on an ineffective assistance of counsel claim, he must demonstrate that his attorney's representation did not meet the standards of a reasonable attorney and that, but for the substandard performance by the attorney, the outcome of his case would have been different.

An example of a defendant successfully raising an ineffective assistance of counsel claim related to social media can be found in *Cannedy v. Adams*.[5] In this case, the defendant challenged his conviction for molesting his stepdaughter (A.G.) on the grounds that his trial attorney provided ineffective representation. At trial, the defendant's theory of defense was that A.G. fabricated her allegations in order to live in another part of the state with her biological father.

On appeal, the defendant claimed that his trial attorney was ineffective because he

failed to present witnesses who could have corroborated [A.G.]'s motives for accusing [the defendant] of molestation.[6]

Apparently, J.C., a friend of A.G., and J.C.'s mother had seen a message on America Online Instant Messenger (service that allows users to sign up with a screen name and communicate online with others using that screen name), which supported the defense's theory that A.G. fabricated the claims of molestation. The message, which had allegedly been posted by A.G. after the molestations occurred, reads as follows:

To everyone whos reading this, the rumors that you've heard are wrong. I just wanted to move to my dad's because everyone hates me, and I don't want to put up with it anymore. Everything that you have heard isnt true. I just made it up so I could get away from it all. I'm living at my dad's where I have friends, and I am very happy. I'm at (redacted) right now but I'm only going to be here for a day so you can reach me at (redacted) if you want to talk.[7]

The defendant found little success with his initial appeal in state court. Thus, he turned to federal court and filed a writ of habeas corpus. The federal judge hearing the habeas motion agreed with the defendant and found that his legal representation was constitutionally deficient because

[e]vidence that A.G. recanted her molestation allegations to her friends was so significant and potentially exculpatory that any reasonable attorney would have sought to admit the evidence.[8]

The judge further determined that the defendant was prejudiced by his attorney because evidence about the message including the witnesses who allegedly saw it might have permitted jurors reasonably to conclude, or at least reasonably to suspect, that: (1) [A.G.] fabricated the allegation; and (2) [A.G.] had a motive to fabricate those allegations because she wanted to move away.[9]

Since both prongs of *Strickland* were met, the federal court granted the defendant's claim of ineffective assistance of counsel. After making this finding, the federal judge then speculated as to why the trial attorney never called the additional witnesses to testify about A.G.'s AOL message. One reason proffered by the judge was that the defense attorney might have been unsure about how AOL Instant Messenger functioned. The judge wrote that the defense attorney might have

misunderstood the workings of AOL Instant Messenger in ways that caused him to depreciate the value of the information.[10]

Cannedy illustrates why attorneys can't ignore social media.[11] In this case, investigation of the victim's social media site was crucial for an adequate defense of the defendant. This investigation included learning how the social media site in question functioned.[12] Due diligence for attorneys in the Digital Age includes not only going to crime scenes, testing evidence, and interviewing witnesses, but also using new techniques like examining and employing social media.[13]

Although the defense attorney in *Cannedy* did not run afoul of the ethical rules, one can easily see how it might occur. The next section will address the potential ethical issues that arise in the context of attorneys seeking, obtaining, or using social media. The first part of this section will address on-the-job ethical issues. The second part will look at ethical issues that occur off the job. Unlike other types of professionals, attorneys can run afoul of ethical rules even for conduct that does not involve the actual practice of law.

ON THE JOB

On-the-job ethical issues for attorneys can be subdivided into three categories. The first subcategory addresses issues that arise when attorneys interact with witnesses and jurors via social media. The second subcategory concerns social media ethical issues involving the attorney–client relationship. The third subcategory deals with issues that occur when attorneys engage their friends or the general public via social media.

Witnesses and Jurors

One of the initial questions that arise with attorneys using social media is whether the ethical rules permit them to examine social media sites that belong to witnesses or jurors. Generally speaking, attorneys may view any social media site (public or private) belonging to a witness or a juror. However, in doing so, the attorney may not contact a juror or a witness who is a represented party.[14] Thus, an attorney may not friend a juror or a witness who is a represented party in order to view her social media site. ABA Model Rule 4.2 states:

> [i]n representing a client, a lawyer shall not communicate about the subject of the representation with a person the lawyer knows to be represented by another lawyer in the matter, unless the lawyer has the consent of the other lawyer or is authorized to do so by law or a court order.[15]

As for contacting a juror, ABA Model Rule 3.5 states

[a] lawyer shall not:

(a) seek to influence a judge, juror, prospective juror or other official by means prohibited by law;

(b) communicate ex parte with such a person during the proceeding unless authorized to do so by law or court order.[16]

This prohibition against contacting jurors and represented witnesses also applies to those acting on behalf of the attorney.

This no-contact rule also covers inadvertent contact or contact automatically generated by the social media provider itself. For example, many users of Twitter read tweets by subscribing to or following a sender's Twitter account. When an individual follows someone's tweets or subscribes to someone's tweets, Twitter generates an automated message alerting the sender that she is now being followed by a specific person.

In examining this type of indirect contact with a juror, the New York City Bar held that the automated response, if the attorney was aware of it, is a violation of the ethical rules.[17] Thus, if an attorney decides to follow the tweets of a juror and the juror receives the automated response from Twitter that she is now being followed by a certain attorney, this would be an ethical violation according to the New York City Bar. Interestingly, the New York City Bar took no position with respect to situations where the attorney was ignorant or unaware of the automated response procedures of the social media site.[18]

There are, however, ways to avoid alerting users that they are being followed on social media. Again using Twitter as an example, some companies that focus on cyber or electronic discovery offer a specialized public follow feature that enables access to all the past tweets of a specific user (up to 3,200 past tweets) and any new tweets in real time. This feature does not generate a formal follow request and therefore the sender of the tweet is unaware that she is being followed.[19]

The aforementioned no-contact rule is inapplicable to witnesses who are *un*represented parties. Here, attorneys may contact or friend these witnesses. However, in making this contact, the rules of ethics require that attorneys be truthful and nondeceptive. As illustrated next, a few attorneys believe that these rules regarding honesty and deception are less applicable in the online world or have greater flexibility when applied to social media.

In Cleveland, Ohio, a prosecutor thought it was ethically permissible to impersonate another individual online in order to interact with potential trial witnesses.[20] In this case, the assistant prosecutor from Cuyahoga County created a fake Facebook profile in which he pretended to be the ex-girlfriend of the criminal defendant whom he was prosecuting for aggravated murder. Using this bogus Facebook profile, the prosecutor friended and then initiated a series of chats with the defendant's two female alibi witnesses who were going to testify that the defendant was on the other side of town when the victim was killed.

During these social media interactions, the bogus ex-girlfriend, who was actually the prosecutor, informed the two women that she was the ex-girlfriend of the defendant and had recently given birth to his child. The bogus ex-girlfriend also attempted to get the witnesses to change or recant their testimony that was favorable to the criminal defendant.

According to the assistant prosecutor, he did nothing wrong. He claimed that

[l]aw enforcement, including prosecutors, have long engaged in the practice of using a ruse to obtain the truth.[21]

The county prosecutor saw it differently and terminated the assistant prosecutor. He found the assistant prosecutor's behavior unethical and added that

[b]y creating false evidence, lying to witnesses as well as another prosecutor, . . . [the assistant prosecutor] has damaged the prosecution's

chances in a murder case where a totally innocent man was killed at his work.[22]

In discussing this incident, one noted legal ethicist stated that the prosecutor might have violated "six" Ohio Rules of Ethics:

tampering with evidence, suborning perjury, becoming a necessary witness, prosecutorial misconduct, misrepresentation of facts, contact with a person represented by counsel and dishonesty.[23]

While it is fairly clear that an attorney cannot lie to an unrepresented witness, it is not entirely clear how much information an attorney must disclose upon initially contacting an unrepresented witness via social media.[24] At present, there is a split in authority with jurisdictions following either the New York City or Philadelphia rule.[25] Under the New York City rule, which is based on an opinion issued by the New York City Bar, an attorney need not disclose the reasons why she is contacting the unrepresented party.[26] According to the opinion,

an attorney or her agent may use her real name and profile to send a "friend request" to obtain information from an unrepresented person's social networking website without also disclosing the reasons for making the request.[27]

This ethics opinion places a high value on conducting and encouraging informal discovery by attorneys. At present, few jurisdictions follow the New York City rule.

In contrast, the Philadelphia rule, which is based on an ethics opinion by the Philadelphia Bar Association Professional Guidance Committee, states that an attorney or her agent may not contact an unrepresented person whom the other side intends to call as a witness without first revealing the purpose for the contact.[28] The opinion, which places a high value on how attorneys are perceived by the public, noted that it is irrelevant if the witness would allow access to her social media site to almost anyone.

This opinion, which predates the New York City ethics opinion, noted that making such contact without informing the witness about the purpose of the contact violates Pennsylvania Rule of Professional Conduct 8.4 (deceit, misrepresentation, dishonesty, and fraud) because it omits a highly material fact—namely, that the attorney who asks to be allowed access to the witness's social media site is doing so only for a pending or future legal proceeding. Currently, most jurisdictions follow the Philadelphia rule.

Once an attorney ethically gains access to the social media site of a witness or juror, the next question becomes, what action, if any, must the attorney take with respect to the information discovered? More specifically, must this information be disclosed to opposing counsel or turned over to the court? As discussed in Part III, information from social media, similar to information uncovered offline, is subject to the Rules of Discovery. Thus, many of the same ethical considerations that arise when deciding whether to disclose such things as police reports, examinations, or witness statements apply to information unearthed from social media.

One caveat concerns jurors. This is because juror information for the most part is nondiscoverable.[29] Only a small number of jurisdictions make information about jurors subject to discovery.[30] Those few states requiring disclosure of juror information generally place the burden solely on the prosecution.[31] The defense, however, must first initiate a discovery request, which is generally limited to information outside of the public domain or somehow inaccessible to defense counsel.[32] A few judges, however, take it upon themselves to direct the parties to exchange information discovered about jurors with each other. This is what occurred in the trial of reputed mobster Whitey Bulger when the prosecution requested permission from the court to investigate prospective jurors.[33]

Despite being nondiscoverable, juror information may still need to be turned over to the court if holding on to such information would violate the rules of ethics. Depending on the jurisdiction and whether the information uncovered involved misconduct, the attorney may have to turn it over to the court. For example, some jurisdictions like New York require attorneys to report all forms of juror misconduct regardless of how it was discovered. New York Rule of Professional Conduct 3.5(d) states

> a lawyer shall reveal promptly to the court improper conduct by a member of the venire or a juror, or by another toward a member of the venire or a juror or a member of her family of which the lawyer has knowledge.[34]

In addition, both the New York Bar Association and the New York County Lawyer's Association have issued ethics opinions informing attorneys that if they discover juror misconduct while investigating a juror's social media site, they must report that information to the court.[35] Other jurisdictions are silent on juror misconduct and only require attorneys to report juror information that is criminal or fraudulent.[36] However, as more and more attorneys use social media to investigate jurors, issues will surely arise with respect to attorneys failing to turn over information related to juror misconduct. Thus, it is highly likely that those jurisdictions that are silent on juror misconduct will modify their rules to require attorneys to report such information in the future.

Finally, besides the ethical considerations, practitioners must weigh the legal ramifications of failing to disclose juror misconduct discovered during an investigation of social media. Most courts look unfavorably on attorneys who unearth juror misconduct but don't bring it forward until after a verdict has been reached.[37] Failure to alert the court to potential issues of juror misconduct may prevent an attorney from raising the claim later.

Clients

As with witnesses and jurors, social media–related ethical issues can also arise when attorneys interact with clients. These issues come up in a variety of different settings ranging from providing advice to discussing case outcomes to settling disagreements.

Generally speaking, attorneys should and do take it upon themselves to review the social media sites of their clients or witnesses, especially if the attorney plans on calling them to testify during trial. If the attorney discovers unhelpful or inappropriate information during her investigation, she should work to defuse it. One prosecutor has noted that when he discovers unfavorable social media information about his witnesses that is either irrelevant or inadmissible, he

address[es] the topic pre-trial with a motion in limine before the judge.[38]

Other attorneys are even more proactive. They regularly offer clients advice on using social media and safeguarding their social media sites. Here, attorneys must be careful about the advice they provide.[39] While the attorney can tell the client to stop using social media or posting information, she may be foreclosed from telling the client to change his privacy settings, shut down his site, or delete information from it. This is because the information on the social media site may be evidence.

As discussed in Part II, social media provides attorneys with a virtual treasure trove of information. If there happens to be evidence on a social media site and an attorney advises her client to delete that evidence or in some way hinder law enforcement or opposing counsel from accessing that evidence, the attorney may have violated the rules of ethics.[40] Pursuant to ABA Model Rule 3.4 (Fairness to Opposing Party and Counsel), a lawyer may not

> [u]nlawfully . . . destroy or conceal a document or other material having potential evidentiary value.[41]

In addition to a potential ethical violation, the attorney runs the risk of being charged criminally with obstruction of justice or tampering with evidence.[42] Interestingly, the New York County Lawyer's Association recently issued an ethics opinion in which it stated that in civil matters an attorney could under certain circumstances advise her client to maximize privacy settings or remove information from social media provided that

> there is no violation of the rules of substantive law pertaining to the preservation of and/or spoliation of evidence[43]

Lester v. Allied Concrete Company, a 2011 civil case, serves as a shining example for attorneys of what advice not to give clients about social media.[44] In *Lester,* the plaintiff (Isaiah Lester) sued the defendant, Allied Concrete Company, for negligence and wrongful death. A truck operated by the defendant had killed the plaintiff's wife.

Prior to trial, the defendant sought production of plaintiff's Facebook account. In making this discovery request, the defendant attached a photo of plaintiff holding a beer can while wearing a T-shirt with the following inscription:

> I ♥ hot moms.[45]

Upon receiving defendant's discovery request, plaintiff's counsel instructed his paralegal to tell Lester to "clean up" his Facebook account because

> we don't want blowups of this stuff at trial.[46]

Lester's lawyer then formulated a plan by which Lester would deactivate his Facebook account. This in turn allowed Lester to state on April 15, 2009, in response to an interrogatory from the defendant, that he did not own a Facebook page.[47] The defendant then filed a motion to compel discovery, and plaintiff's counsel had his paralegal direct Lester to reactive his Facebook account. Upon reactivation, the Facebook account did not have 16 prior photos that had been previously deleted by Lester. On December 16, 2009, during a deposition, Lester testified that he never deactivated his Facebook page.

On August 18, 2010, the defendant filed a motion for sanctions for spoliation of evidence. Spoliation is the "intentional alteration or destruction of a document" that might have been used in litigation.[48] After the hearing, the court found spoliation and ordered that an adverse inference be given at trial and that Lester and his counsel would remain subject to sanctions.

After a three-day trial in December 2010, a jury awarded Lester $8.6 million, which was later reduced by the judge to $4.1 million. On September 1, 2011, the court granted defendant's motion for monetary sanctions against Lester and his counsel. Lester was sanctioned $180,000 and his counsel $542,000—a record amount at the time. In describing the actions of Lester and his attorney, the court found that

> there was an extensive pattern of deceptive and obstructionist conduct.[49]

In July 2013, the Virginia state bar suspended Lester's attorney from the practice of law for five years.

This case demonstrates, among other things, that just because information is deleted from a social media site does not necessarily mean that it is gone forever. Furthermore, this case puts attorneys on notice that they can and will be held accountable for improper ethical conduct regardless of whether it occurs online or offline.

Not all attorney–client problems related to social media concern advice; sometimes the issue is an actual disagreement between the attorney and client that either occurs on social media or spills over to social media. One example from Illinois involved a dispute between an attorney and her client that centered on the attorney's representation of the client. Unfortunately for the attorney, this dispute occurred on Avvo—a social media site that allows individuals to rate an attorney's performance.

This case stemmed from an employment lawyer's representation of a flight attendant who was terminated for assaulting a fellow employee during an actual flight. The flight attendant wanted the lawyer's assistance in obtaining unemployment benefits from the state. After meeting with the client several times and reviewing his work personnel file, the attorney represented him in a telephonic hearing before the Illinois Department of Employment Security (IDES), which is the state agency responsible for determining whether to award unemployment benefits.

Shortly after the hearing and a determination by IDES that the flight attendant was not eligible for unemployment benefits, the flight attendant terminated his relationship with the attorney. Also, at around this time, the flight attendant decided to publicly comment about his attorney's performance on Avvo. The flight attendant made the following posting about his attorney:

> She only wants your money, claims "always on your side" is a huge lie. Paid her to help me secure unemployment, she took my money knowing full well a certain law in Illinois would not let me collect unemployment. [N]ow is billing for an additional $1500 for her time.[50]

This comment was subsequently removed by Avvo. However, the client then posted a second review, which reads as follows:

> I paid Ms. [redacted] $1500 to help me secure unemployment while she knew full well that a law in Illinois would prevent me from obtaining unemployment benefits.

Shortly thereafter, the attorney responded to the client's post on Avvo with her own post, which reads as follows:

> This is simply false. The person did not reveal all the facts of his situation up front in our first and second meeting. [sic] When I received his personnel file, I discussed the contents of it with him and informed him that he would likely lose unless the employer chose not to contest the unemployment (employers sometimes do is [sic]). Despite knowing that he would likely lose, he chose to go forward with a hearing to try to obtain benefits. I dislike it very much when my clients lose but I cannot invent positive facts for clients when they are not there. I feel badly for him but his own actions in *beating up a female coworker* are what caused the consequences he is now so upset about [emphasis added].[51]

The attorney's post eventually came to the attention of the state bar of Illinois, which decided to investigate. Ultimately, the bar issued the attorney a public reprimand for failing to maintain client confidences.[52]

Many in the legal profession feel that the attorney had a right to defend herself from an adverse review in the online court of public opinion, just as an attorney who has been sued for malpractice can defend herself in an actual courtroom. Others think that the attorney went too far when she publicly acknowledged that her client beat up a female co-worker. They believe that the attorney could have successfully defended herself without revealing this additional information.

Friends and the General Public

Besides attorney–client interactions, ethical problems also occur when attorneys seek to engage either their friends or the general public via social media. Issues here generally arise in one of two areas: (1) advertising or (2) legal commentary. Due to the very nature of social media, it can be difficult to distinguish between typical online interactions and advertising.[53] According to one practitioner,

> [a] lot of stuff in social media seems more like a conversation among friends than an ad, but if a lawyer is involved, it may be considered . . . an advertisement under the ethics rule.[54]

If the social media activity is deemed advertising, then it must adhere to specific ethical rules; for example, some states require attorney advertisements to include disclaimers (discussed in greater detail later) or be preapproved. This can be challenging for certain social media platforms like Twitter, which is fluid and involves tweets of 140 characters or less. As a result, some have advocated for modernizing or updating the ethical rules on attorney advertising to reflect the changes brought by social media.

As for legal commentary, this takes a variety of forms ranging from attempts at satire and humor to editorials about current events. The challenge here is determining when an attorney has gone too far. The state bars across the country, which ensure the integrity of the legal profession by enforcing the ethical rules, have to balance their enforcement duties with the attorney's right to free expression. As will be illustrated, some examples of improper attorney commentary on social media are clear-cut ethical violations, while others fall more into a gray area.

Advertising

A recent example from Virginia demonstrates the challenges that the state bar faces when attempting to determine whether an attorney's conduct on social media constitutes advertising. In *Hunter v. Virginia State Bar*, an attorney maintained a blog entitled *This Week in Richmond Criminal Defense*.[55] His blog posts covered a wide range of legal issues;

however, the majority of the posts were dedicated to covering cases in which the attorney obtained favorable results for his clients. The blog was maintained on the website of the attorney's law firm and did not include disclaimers nor did it allow readers to post comments.

After an investigation, the Virginia state bar determined that the attorney's blog constituted advertising and thus, pursuant to the ethical rules governing attorney advertising, required a disclaimer. The attorney disagreed and refused to post the disclaimer, claiming that requiring him to do so would violate his First Amendment rights. According to the attorney, he did not want to use a disclaimer because

> it's not what I want to say. It cheapens the speech when I have to put in front of it, "Oh, by the way, this is for advertising."[56]

The attorney also claimed that his blog consisted of news and commentary, which reflected accurate public information and did not violate any client confidences.

Ultimately, the Virginia state bar determined that because the blog did not have a disclaimer, the attorney had violated Virginia Rules of Professional Conduct 7.1 and 7.2. The Virginia state bar also determined that the attorney violated Virginia Rule of Professional Conduct 1.6 for disclosing confidential client information in his posts. The bar then issued the attorney a public admonition and directed him to remove case-specific content from his blog for which he had not received prior client consent. In addition, the attorney was required to have a disclaimer that complied with Virginia Rule of Professional Conduct 7.2(a)(3) on all case-related posts.

The attorney appealed the Virginia Bar's decision to the Virginia Supreme Court, which ultimately determined that Rules 7.1 and 7.2 as applied to the blog were constitutional but 1.6 was not. The court found that Rule 1.6 violated the attorney's First Amendment rights. The court pointed out that the attorney was blogging about completed cases and the information discussed was in the public record. Arguably, there might have been a different outcome had the attorney blogged about pending cases rather than completed ones.

As for Rules 7.1 and 7.2, the Virginia Supreme Court found them constitutional as applied to the attorney's blog. The attorney had argued that his blog posts were political, not commercial speech and thus worthy of a higher level of First Amendment protection. However, the court saw it differently. While the court did acknowledge that some of the attorney's posts were political in nature (e.g., the attorney critiqued the legal system), the court determined that the majority of the posts were commercial speech. The court made this determination based on the following factors.

1. Attorney's motivation for the blog was partially economic.
2. Most of the posts pertained to positive case results and thus advertised the attorney's lawyering skills.
3. The blog was maintained on the firm's website rather than an independent website.
4. The blog was noninteractive and did not allow for public discourse.

By labeling the posts as commercial speech, it was easier for the Virginia Supreme Court to find that the requirements imposed on the blog posts by the state bar, that is, use of a disclaimer, were indeed constitutional. While the Virginia Supreme Court did not go as far as the Virginia state bar and call the blog misleading advertising, it did determine that the blog had the potential to be misleading.

Commentary

Other instances of ethical misconduct arise when attorneys use social media to provide commentary about clients and pending cases. In Florida, a Miami County public defender lost her job because of comments she made on social media about her client. Apparently, this attorney, whose client had an upcoming trial, was bothered by the trial clothes brought in by the client's family. Using her cellphone, the attorney photographed a pair of leopard print underwear and then posted the photo along with a message on her Facebook page questioning whether this was indeed "proper attire for trial."[57]

Although the attorney's Facebook page was set to private, the judge hearing the defendant's case was told of the page, causing him to declare a mistrial. In addition to the comments made about the underwear, this same attorney had made earlier posts in which she questioned her client's actual innocence. In discussing why this attorney was ultimately terminated, the Miami-Dade Public Defender's Office offered the following statement:

[w]hen a lawyer broadcasts disparaging and humiliating words and pictures, it undermines the basic client relationship and it gives the appearance that he [the defendant] is not receiving a fair trial.[58]

Another assistant public defender lost her job and received a 60-day suspension of her law license for commentary posted on her blog entitled

The Bardd [sic] *Before the Bar—Irreverant* [sic] *Adventures in Life, Law, and Indigent Defense*. Despite the name of the blog, only one-third of the posts related to the attorney's actual work as a public defender. Unfortunately for the attorney, that one-third included posts about her clients and the judges before whom she appeared.

In certain posts, the attorney would refer to clients by their first names, nicknames, or jail identification numbers. She also described, in sometimes graphic detail, the clients' cases, drug use, and other embarrassing and potentially harmful information that was not known to the general public. In discussing one client, identified as "Dennis the diabetic," the attorney posted that

> [h]e was standing there in court stoned, right in front of the judge, probation officer, prosecutor[,] and defense attorney, swearing he was clean and claiming ignorance as to why his blood sugar wasn't being managed well.[59]

The attorney also commented on and critiqued the local judges. She even went so far as to refer to one judge as "Judge Clueless."

In finding that the attorney violated client confidences, the Illinois state bar noted that the attorney's

> blog was open to the public and was not password-protected . . . [the attorney] knew or should have known that the contents of her blog were continuously available to anyone with access to the Internet, and she maintained a site meter on the blog that counted the number of visits to the blog. At some point, . . . [the attorney] posted the following language on her blog:

> Commentary is Both Invited and Appreciated. Let's Get Some Dialogue Going![60]

Criminal defense attorneys are far from alone with respect to making inappropriate social media posts about pending cases. Prosecutors have also made similar missteps. In Florida, a prosecutor, borrowing from the *Gilligan's Island* theme song, posted the following lyrics about his pending trial on Facebook:

> Just sit right back and you'll hear a tale, a tale of a fateful trial that started from this court in St. Lucie County. The lead prosecutor was a good woman, the 2nd chair was totally awesome. . . . Six jurors were ready for trial that day for a four hour trial, a four hour trial The

trial started Tuesday, continued til Wednesday and then Thursday With Robyn and Brandon too, the weasle [sic] face, the gang banger defendant, the Judge, clerk, and Ritzline here in St. Lucie.[61]

Although this case ended in a mistrial, unrelated to the Facebook lyrics, the chief assistant state attorney for St. Lucie County was none too pleased about the actions of this prosecutor. He referred to the incident as a "training moment." He further stated that he would discuss with prosecutors in his office what they should and shouldn't say on social media sites.

The ethical waters become a little less clear when the attorney uses social media to comment about court personnel or a perceived problem in the legal system. Take, for example, a defense attorney in Florida who grew frustrated with the practices of a local judge and went to a blog (*Jaablog*) created by a criminal defense lawyers' group in Broward County to vent his frustrations. The attorney posted the following about the judge:

(1) "I along with several other attorneys, had to endure her ugly, condescending attitude as one-by-one we all went up to the podium and noted that our respective clients had just been arraigned on Oct. 18th as she forced us to decide between saying ready for trial—or need a continuance"; (2) "Every atty tried their best to bring reason to that ctroom, but, as anyone who has been in there knows, she is clearly unfit for her position and knows not what it means to be a neutral arbitec"; (3) "Evil, unfair witch (hereinafter "witch")"; (4) "As my case was on recall for 2 hours, I watched this seemingly mentally ill judge condescend each previous attorney"; and (5) "Judge (not your honor b/c there's nothing honorable about that malcontent) there seems to be a mistake in this case."[62]

Once the Florida Bar became aware of the post it opened an inquiry to determine whether the post violated the state's ethical rules. The state bar eventually determined that the post impugned the judge's qualifications and integrity. The state bar also found that the attorney's post

not only undermined public confidence in the administration of justice, but these statements were prejudicial to the proper administration of justice.[63]

Upon determining that the post had indeed violated the state's ethical rules, the state bar and the attorney in question agreed to settle the matter with a public reprimand and a fine of \$1,250. However, the Florida Supreme Court, which has final approval of any disciplinary action taken against an attorney licensed to practice in Florida, wanted both parties (the attorney and the state bar) to submit legal briefs to the court examining whether the First Amendment protected the attorney's post. In addition to the briefs submitted by both parties, the ACLU filed an amicus brief supporting the attorney's right to make the blog post. The Florida Supreme Court ultimately upheld the actions of the state bar. However, not everyone was in agreement with the outcome.

Some, like Professor Jonathan Turley, did not believe that the attorney's conduct violated the ethical rules. Instead, they distinguished the actions of this attorney from those of other attorneys who post confidential client information. According to Professor Turley,

> [t]he . . . case is materially different from lawyers violating court rules as jurors or revealing confidential information. Here he was criticizing a judge and is being punished for what the court called "arrogant, discourteous and impatient" speech.[64]

OFF THE JOB

The previously discussed examples illustrate how attorneys, while using social media on the job, can violate the rules of ethics. However, this is not the only time that attorneys run into ethical problems with social media. Ethical missteps can also arise when attorneys use social media off the job. This is because, unlike those in many other professions, attorneys, regardless of whether they are actually practicing law, must adhere to the rules of ethics. The following examples illustrate how attorneys can find themselves in ethical hot water for social media conduct unrelated to or completely removed from the actual practice of law.

As discussed in Chapter 4, some jurors ignore the court's prohibitions against using social media. Surprisingly, this problem is not restricted to laypersons: sometimes even attorneys and judges who are called to serve jury duty violate the rules about discussing the case. In one California criminal trial, an attorney, who was called as a juror, never informed the court or the parties during voir dire that he was a licensed member of the California bar nor did he follow the court's rules about discussing the case orally or in writing.[65] In fact, the attorney posted the following about the court's rules regarding discussing the case before all the evidence is submitted or with outside parties before a final verdict:

Nowhere do I recall the jury instructions mandating I can't post comments in my blog about the trial. (Ha. Sorry, will do).[66]

The attorney was ultimately chosen to be on the jury and was made foreman. Throughout the trial the juror made blog posts about the case and jury deliberations. For example, the attorney wrote the following on his blog:

I had sat bulkhead, in the first row on the aisle of the back courtroom benches, during all the voire dire [sic], not saying a word except for when the microphone was handed over, when I quickly iterated my occupation (project manager for technology company, which is more neutral than lawyer, don't ya think?) and connections thru myself or acquaintances to criminal experiences. . . .

The tide thus turned, and for the next hour-and-a-half, the jury in the People v. Donald the Duck slowly congealed into a rational, investigative body of folks who ultimately realized that stealing was wrong, and that we ought to act responsibly. All, that is, except for Brad, the confident, muscular skinhead character with a carefully shaven goatee sitting directly at the head of the table, to my right. This cocky young fellow I had unease about since seeing him lope down the hallway on day one. He had stared at me for just a second or two too long when he first saw me, expecting some sort of acknowledgment to his presence from another white guy. I averted my eyes then and every other chance since during the trial. Now he was sitting next to me.[67]

Once the attorney's actions were discovered, he was investigated by the state bar of California. The attorney, who cooperated with the investigation, admitted to not maintaining the respect due to the courts by failing to disclose that he was an attorney during voir dire. He also acknowledged that he had improperly posted comments about the trial on his blog. The attorney, who had had no prior problems with the state bar, was placed on probation for two years, suspended from the actual practice of law for 45 days, and ordered to retake the Multistate Professional Responsibility Exam (MPRE) (ethics exam for attorneys).

As for the underlying case on which the attorney served, the defendant is currently appealing his conviction. His appeal is based in large part on the actions of the attorney-juror.

Other examples of attorneys running into ethical problems for non-job-related social media use include online impersonation. For example, one attorney in New York impersonated a former classmate on social media.[68] Unlike the example of the Cleveland prosecutor discussed earlier in this chapter, this attorney's impersonation had nothing to do with the actual practice of law. Here, the attorney went on a social media dating site for lesbians and created a bogus profile pretending to be one of his former female classmates. It was never made clear why the attorney impersonated the woman. However, it does not appear that the woman he impersonated had any connection to the attorney's employment.

The attorney's improper use of social media had several negative consequences for him. First, the attorney was criminally charged for his actions. This resulted in him pleading guilty to attempted aggravated harassment, which is a violation of New York Penal Law §§ 110.00 and 240.30, a class B misdemeanor. Second, as a result of his conviction, the state bar charged the attorney with professional misconduct in violation of rule 8.4(b) and (h) of the New York Rules of Professional Conduct (22 NYCRR 1200.0).

Fortunately for the attorney, he accepted responsibility for his actions. In mitigation, the attorney pointed to his years of service in the U.S. Army Reserves, including his deployment to Iraq. The attorney also submitted testimony of a psychotherapist who opined that there was little likelihood of recurrence as the attorney had sought therapy and had since gained insight into his behavior. Ultimately, the bar suspended the attorney from the practice of law for one year.

Other examples of attorneys allegedly acting improperly while using social media in non-work-related activities are not so clear cut. Consider the following Facebook postings made by an assistant United States Attorney (AUSA):

> How are you fixed for Skittles and Arizona watermelon fruitcocktail (and maybe a bottle of Robitussin, too) in your neighborhood? I am fresh out of "purple drank." So, I may come by for a visit. In a rainstorm. In the middle of the night. In a hoodie. Don't get upset or anything if you see me looking in your window . . . kay?

> . . .

> low information voters carried the day for the Dalibama in the last election.

> . . .

> Obama: Why Stupid People Shouldn't Vote.[69]

When asked about his posts, the AUSA said they were unrelated to the United States Attorney's Office.

The U.S. Attorney for the Eastern District of Texas, the AUSA's boss, indicated that he did not agree with the AUSA's comments and that the AUSA did not speak for his office. He also stated that he would "look into" the AUSA's posts. To date, the U.S. Attorney for the Eastern District of Texas has not stated publicly what action, if any, he is going to take against the AUSA.

Some believe that the AUSA, a federal public official, should resign or be removed from his position. Others believe that the AUSA has a First Amendment right to express himself regardless of whether individuals find his comments offensive.

While it does not appear as though the AUSA violated any ethical rules, there is a concern that he has placed his employer, which is responsible for enforcing federal law in the Eastern District of Texas, in a bad light. His comments will also lead some to question whether prosecutions in this district are driven by the defendant's race. To date, at least one criminal defense attorney has filed a motion to collect the prosecution records of this specific AUSA to compare the sentencing of minority and white defendants.

Part IV

Judges

Of all the individuals in the criminal justice process, judges are arguably the least likely to use social media. This is due to their age (most are Digital Immigrants) and the unique role they play in the courtroom. As neutral arbitrators, judges are rarely, if ever, called upon to employ technology to persuade others. However, this is not to say that social media has not influenced their behavior—it has. Part IV will explore the different ways social media has affected judges.

This exploration begins in Chapter 10, which examines how judges themselves use social media. Among other things, this chapter will cover the ethical issues that arise when judges interact with attorneys via social media. Next, Chapter 11 will analyze how judges regulate the social media use of others. Judges must determine to what extent individuals—whether they are attorneys, jurors, witnesses, the media, or spectators—may access and use social media while in the courtroom. Finally, Chapter 12 focuses on how judges assess evidence derived from social media, looking at the steps a judge takes when deciding whether to admit social media–related information into evidence.

10

Personal Use and Ethics

Although judges, at present, may have less of a need for social media than attorneys or law enforcement, many judges nonetheless routinely use it. This chapter discusses how judges employ social media to communicate with both the general public and private individuals. In addition, this chapter examines the problems that arise when judges use social media to conduct independent research.

GENERAL PUBLIC

Like the other groups of individuals examined in the criminal justice system, social media affords judges the opportunity to communicate directly with the general public. At present, the most common social media platforms relied on by judges to reach the general public are Facebook and LinkedIn. These sites are especially popular in jurisdictions where judges are elected and must run for office. According to Judge Susan Criss, one of the first judges to embrace social media from the bench,

> [f]ew judicial campaigns can realistically afford to refrain from using social media to deliver their message to the voting public. Social media can be a very effective and inexpensive method to deliver campaign messages.[1]

In addition to Facebook and LinkedIn, several judges have their own law-related blogs. A trial judge in Minnesota has a blog entitled *Jurors*

Behaving Badly. As the name suggests, this blog examines issues related to juror misconduct.

Other examples of blogging jurists include Justice Judith Ann Lanzinger of the Ohio Supreme Court whose blog is entitled *Justice Judy*. Justice Lanzinger uses her blog to explain to the public legal concepts and processes as well as developments in the law. According to the Chief Justice, the blog

> fulfill[s] the mandate in the Ohio Code of Judicial Conduct, which requires that "A judge should initiate and participate in activities for the purpose of promoting public understanding of and confidence in the administration of justice. In conducting such activities, the judge must act in a manner consistent with this code" . . .

> This blog is a carefully balanced medium for me to fulfill this obligation using the latest information technology. Studies show that today's young people are the most plugged in generation ever. Blogging offers an opportunity to connect with these young people where they now spend most of their time: Online.[2]

Most, if not all, jurisdictions permit judges to blog or join social media platforms like Facebook and LinkedIn.[3] At least one state, Washington, has issued an ethics opinion encouraging judges to blog.[4] The opinion states that

> [t]o the extent that their time permits, they [judges] are encouraged to do so [blog] within the parameters permitted by the Code of Judicial Conduct. Similarly, judges should be encouraged to improve public understanding of the law.[5]

As with other forms of communication, judges must adhere to judicial canons and the rules of professional responsibility when blogging. For example, judges are not allowed to blog about matters pending in their court. In addition, judges should not express opinions about subjects that could lead to their recusal in future or current cases.

PRIVATE INDIVIDUALS

The biggest area of concern in Chapter 10 is the use of social media by judges to interact with private individuals, especially when those private individuals are involved in a case before that particular judge. Most, if not all, jurisdictions permit judges to interact with attorneys via social media.

However, there is a sharp split in opinion as to whether this interaction should continue if the attorney has a case or will appear before the judge. At present, jurisdictions take one of three approaches in addressing this issue.

The first approach, followed by states like Ohio and Kentucky, permits judges to interact via social media with the attorneys appearing before them. South Carolina has gone so far as to say that social media use by judges promotes public confidence in the judiciary because it allows the community to gain a better understanding of the judge. The state of Ohio, however, does warn judges that

> [a]s with any other action a judge takes, a judge's participation on a social networking site must be done carefully in order to comply with the ethical rules in the Code of Judicial Conduct.[6]

The second approach, adopted by states like California, Florida, Massachusetts, and Oklahoma, is the complete opposite of the first. Here, jurisdictions impose an outright ban on judges interacting via social media with attorneys who appear before them. Jurisdictions relying on this approach fear that judges may favor one attorney over another or that people may perceive a potential for favoritism. According to the Massachusetts Committee on Judicial Ethics,

> [a] judge's "friending" *attorneys* on social networking sites creates the impression that those attorneys are in a special position to influence the judge. Therefore, the Code does not permit you to "friend" any attorney who may appear before you.[7]

The third or middle-ground approach, followed by states like New York, takes no official position on the issue. In a 2009 ethics opinion, the New York Committee on Judicial Ethics neither encouraged nor dissuaded judges from friending attorneys who appear before them. The opinion left the issue completely up to the discretion of the judge. The opinion instructs the judge to

> be mindful of the appearance created when he/she establishes a connection with an attorney or anyone else appearing in the judge's court through a social network. In some ways, this is no different from adding the person's contact information into the judge's Rolodex or address book or speaking to them in a public setting. But, the public nature of such a link (i.e., other users can normally see the judge's

friends or connections) and the increased access that the person would have to any personal information the judge chooses to post on his/her own profile page establish, at least, the appearance of a stronger bond. A judge must, therefore, consider whether any such online connections, alone or in combination with other facts, rise to the level of a "close social relationship" requiring disclosure and/or recusal.[8]

The issue has even grabbed the attention of the ABA, which recently issued an advisory opinion on the matter. According to the ABA's Standing Committee on Ethics and Professional Responsibility, it is ethical for judges not only to use social media, but also to friend attorneys so long as they adhere to the judicial conduct rules. This formal opinion also stated that a judge who employs social media is not necessarily required to disclose to the litigants or counsel that the judge has an online connection to a person involved with the case. According to the opinion,

> [w]hen used with proper care, judges' use of ESM (electronic social media) does not necessarily compromise their duties under the Model Code any more than use of traditional and less public forms of social connections such as U.S. mail, telephone, email or texting.[9]

The opinion went on to discuss six specific rules of the Model Code for a judge to consider when using social media:

1. Judges must act in a manner promoting public confidence in the judiciary (Rule 1.2).
2. Judges must avoid ex parte communications (Rule 2.9(A)).
3. Judges must not comment on pending or impending matters (Rule 2.10).
4. Judges should not form relationships with persons or groups that may convey an impression that these people and entities are in a position to influence the judge (Rule 2.4(C)).
5. Judges should not offer legal advice (Rule 3.10).
6. Judges should not use social media to conduct their own independent investigation into pending matters (Rule 2.9(C)).

Finally, this ABA Ethics opinion cautioned judges about the permanency of information in the Digital Age and that online communication lacks in-person visual or vocal cues, which may result in statements being taken out of context or misinterpreted.

In addition to concerns about ethical violations, certain social media relationships maintained by judges have been grounds for recusal and retrial in both civil and criminal cases. To date, at least one criminal defendant has had the trial judge on his case recused because of the judge's social media relationship with the prosecutor.

In *Domville v. State*, the defendant filed a recusal motion for the judge trying his case. The defendant wanted the judge removed because of the judge's social media relationship with the prosecutor who was prosecuting the case.[10] The judge denied the defendant's request, finding that despite his social media connection with the prosecutor he could remain impartial.

On appeal, the Florida Court of Appeals agreed with the defendant and quashed the trial judge's holding with instructions on remand. The appellate court determined that

Domville has alleged facts that would create in a reasonably prudent person a well-founded fear of not receiving a fair and impartial trial.[11]

In siding with the defendant, the appellate court relied on the Florida Judicial Ethics Advisory Committee opinion, which prohibits judges from friending lawyers who appear before them. The court also reasoned that

when a judge lists a lawyer who appears before him as a "friend" on his social networking page, this "reasonably conveys to others the impression that these lawyer 'friends' are in a special position to influence the judge."[12]

Other successful legal challenges can be found in the civil arena. In *Whitley v. Whitley,* a child custody suit, the judge not only exchanged *ex parte* Facebook communications with the attorney representing the father, but also searched for information about the mother online. At the conclusion of the trial, the judge revealed his actions to the respective attorneys representing both the mother and the father. The attorney representing the mother then moved for a new trial and to vacate the judge's decision in the case. Both of these requests were granted. In a subsequent action by the state bar of North Carolina, the judge in this case received a public reprimand for his online activity.[13]

Other attempts at overturning judicial decisions because of the judge's social media relationship with a witness or one of the parties in a case have been less successful. In *Youkers v. State of Texas*, the criminal defendant challenged his conviction in part on the fact that the trial judge was

Facebook friends with the victim's father. The defendant argued that the judge's social media relationship standing by itself demonstrated the trial judge's lack of impartiality.[14]

The appellate court, however, viewed the situation differently. According to the appellate court, designating someone as a Facebook friend, without more, is insufficient grounds to show a lack of impartiality. The court went on to say that

the designation [Facebook friend], standing alone, provides no insight into the nature of the relationship.[15]

Finally, in *Onnen v. Sioux Falls Independent School District*, another civil case, the plaintiff sought a new trial based on the fact that the trial judge received a "Happy Birthday" post on his Facebook Wall from a key witness during trial. The judge did not personally know the witness nor did he invite the Facebook post. The judge then concluded that the "Happy Birthday" post did not cause him to lose his impartiality nor was it sufficient grounds for a new trial.

The South Dakota Supreme Court upheld the trial judge's ruling. In making its determination, the state supreme court found that the post had no relation to the case nor did it improperly influence the judge. The court basically deferred to the judge's discretion on his ability to be impartial. The South Dakota Supreme Court also noted that

where an ex-parte communication is not invited or initiated by the judge, reversible error occurs only if the adverse party is prejudiced by an inability to rebut the facts communicated and if improper influence appears with reasonable certainty.[16]

INDEPENDENT RESEARCH

As discussed earlier, judges, like others in society, sometimes misuse social media. One area of growing concern about improper use of social media by the judiciary is independent research. *Purvis v. Commissioner of Social Security* illustrates how this problem arises. In *Purvis*, the plaintiff was attempting to obtain Social Security benefits for her asthmatic medical condition.[17] The claimant had been previously denied by an administrative law judge (ALJ) and had appealed that decision to federal district court.

The federal judge deciding the case ultimately determined that the plaintiff's request for benefits had to go back to the Social Security office for further proceedings. This fact, however, did not stop the federal judge from expressing her skepticism of the claimant's credibility. The judge noted in her opinion that

> [a]lthough the Court remands the ALJ's decision for a more detailed finding, it notes that in the course of its own research, it discovered one profile on what is believed to be Plaintiff's Facebook page where she appears to be smoking. . . . If accurately depicted, Plaintiff's credibility is justifiably suspect.[18]

While judges can take judicial notice of certain undisputed facts, they should not conduct their own independent investigations into the cases that they preside over. This is because judges, like jurors, must base their decision of liability, guilt, or innocence solely on the evidence submitted by the parties. At times, judges may have to research the applicable law in certain cases; however, they should not extend this research to the specific facts of the case.

This is not to say that judges cannot use social media to verify the honesty of the lawyers appearing before them, which is what some judges have done. In one example from Texas, an attorney, seeking a continuance of a hearing, informed the trial judge that her father had passed away.[19] Later, a partner from this same firm appeared before the judge and told her that the attorney actually needed a month-long continuance. At that point, the judge informed the partner that she had reviewed the attorney's social media site and discovered that the attorney, rather than being in deep mourning over her father's death, was actually bragging about partying. Needless to say, the judge denied the request for an additional continuance of one month.

11

Inside the Courtroom

REGULATING OTHERS

As previously stated, of all the individuals in the criminal justice system, judges might be the least likely to employ social media. This does not mean, however, that they can afford to be oblivious to social media or the rules governing its use. Judges must be cognizant of the various social media platforms and the legal and ethical rules that apply to them. This is because they are responsible for not only regulating their own behavior, but also that of those appearing in court. Judges must decide whether certain activities like blogging or tweeting should take place in their courtrooms.

Unfortunately for judges, the law in this area, like most things related to social media, is still fairly fluid. Courts are grappling with what approach to take when addressing social media in the courtroom. This chapter examines those various approaches to see how well judges are adapting to the new norm—one in which everyone in the courthouse has ready access to social media.

One of the first questions that arise in this area is whether judges can prohibit individuals in the courtroom from using social media. As illustrated earlier, judges have broad discretion to regulate their courtrooms. Chapter 1 discussed Savannah D., who was threatened with contempt of court for posting facts about her case on Twitter and Facebook. Chapter 4 looked at efforts by judges to restrict social media use by jurors. Chapter 11 will examine whether judges may regulate the social media use of attorneys, the media, and the general public.

At present, it appears that most courts allow attorneys to access social media while in the courtroom. The follow-on question then becomes: in what ways can attorneys use social media while in the courtroom? As discussed in Chapter 8, many attorneys employ social media in the court-room to research and investigate jurors. Most courts, but not all, permit the practice. The Supreme Court has yet to affirmatively approve or disapprove of juror investigations. However, at least one state (New Jersey) appellate court (*Carino v. Muenzen*) has determined that attorneys should be allowed to investigate jurors during voir dire.[1]

In *Carino,* a medical malpractice case, plaintiff's counsel was researching jurors on his laptop in the courtroom during voir dire. Defense counsel, who did not have a laptop, objected. The trial judge sustained the defense attorney's objection, finding that plaintiff's attorney failed to provide advance notice to either opposing counsel or the court regarding his intent to conduct such research. In reviewing this trial judge's actions on appeal, the New Jersey appellate court found them to be unreasonable. Interestingly, however, the appellate court did not overturn the jury's verdict favoring the defendant because the attorney for the plaintiff had failed to identify

> a single juror who was unqualified or as to whom he claims he would have exercised a peremptory challenge, even though he has subsequently had the opportunity to perform an Internet search concerning each juror.[2]

One of the biggest questions confronting judges in Chapter 11 is whether to allow individuals to blog or tweet from the courtroom during trial. Some see blogging and tweeting as a negative, arguing that these practices disrupt the sanctity of the courtroom and hinder the administration of justice.[3] Others see blogging and tweeting as a positive and a true benefit to society because they lead to greater transparency of the criminal justice process and allow the public to stay better informed about trials.[4] It appears, at present, that this latter viewpoint is gaining in acceptance as courts are increasingly allowing both the media and the general public to blog and tweet from the courtroom.

Most discussions about whether individuals may use technology in the courtroom begin with an examination of the public's right to attend criminal trials. The Supreme Court has long held that both the media and the public have a right to be present and watch criminal trials. In *Richmond Newspapers Inc. v. Virginia*, the Court wrote:

> [w]e hold that the right to attend criminal trials is implicit in the guarantees of the First Amendment; without the freedom to attend such trials, which people have exercised for centuries, important aspects of freedom of speech and "of the press could be eviscerated."[5]

The Supreme Court, however, has not gone so far as to say that the media and the public have a right to use certain equipment or technology while in the courtroom. This is generally a decision made by the local jurisdiction. Thus, in 1981, when the Supreme Court held in *Chandler v. Florida* that television cameras in the courtroom are not per se violations of the defendant's Sixth Amendment right to a fair and impartial jury, many jurisdictions began establishing rules to allow cameras in the courtroom.[6] Today, every state, whether at the trial or appellate level, has a rule allowing cameras in the courtroom.[7] Most states leave the decision whether to allow cameras up to the discretion of individual judges.

Federal courts have not been so television-friendly and have taken measures, save for a few pilot programs, to curtail their use. The primary method of prohibiting televisions in federal courtrooms has been Federal Rule of Criminal Procedure 53, which is applicable to federal criminal trials and reads, in part, as follows:

[T]he court must not permit the taking of photographs in the courtroom during judicial proceedings or the broadcasting of judicial proceedings from the courtroom.[8]

Those federal judges who want to prohibit blogging or tweeting in their courtroom point to this rule and claim that such activity encompasses "broadcasting."

In *United States v. Shelnutt* the judge denied a reporter's request to send tweets from his courtroom. In making his decision, the judge cited the dictionary definition of "broadcast," which Webster's has defined as "casting or scattering in all directions" and "the act of making widely known."[9] The judge then concluded that "twittering"

would result in casting to the general public and thus making widely known the trial proceedings.[10]

Not all judges, whether federal or state, however, take this view nor do they compare blogging or tweeting to broadcasting. Instead, they compare blogging or tweeting to taking and sharing notes. Other judges simply ignore the current statutory and dictionary definitions of "broadcast," finding them anachronistic and of little help in determining whether they apply to new methods of communication like Twitter.[11]

One early advocate of permitting the media to tweet from the courtroom is Federal District Court Judge Thomas Marten who noted that he didn't see much difference between a journalist sending tweets and taking notes by hand. When asked in 2009 why he allowed a reporter from the *Wichita Eagle* to sit in his courtroom and tweet about the racketeering trial of six accused gang members, he offered the following rationale:

> The more we can do to open the process to the public, the greater the public understanding—the more legitimacy the public system will have in the eyes of the public.[12]

Judge Marten's ruling also served to benefit family members of the criminal defendants who could not travel to attend the trial. These individuals, although not physically present in the courtroom, could still follow the trial by reading the tweets from the *Wichita Eagle*.[13]

Judge Marten is not alone in his belief that allowing media to blog or tweet from the courtroom improves the criminal justice system. When United States District Court Judge Mark Bennett was asked why he allowed a reporter to tweet from his courtroom, he offered the following reasoning:

> I thought the public's right to know what goes on in federal court and the transparency that would be given the proceedings by live-blogging outweighed any potential prejudice to the defendant.[14]

A few state courts like those of Arkansas, Kansas, and Maryland have updated their rules on broadcasting in the courtroom to address other electronic devices and forms of communication. In changing its rules, the state of Kansas discussed some of the policy reasons why updates were needed.

> These electronic devices are redefining the news media, the informational product disseminated, and the timeliness of the content. They also result in new expectations for the court and participants for immediate access to information.
>
> Policies developed to address the court's concerns should include enough flexibility to take into consideration that electronic devices have become a necessary tool for court observers, journalists, and participants and continue to rapidly change and evolve. The courts should champion the enhanced access and the transparency made possible by use of these devices while protecting the integrity of proceedings within the courtroom.[15]

Concerns about blogging or tweeting from the courtroom appear for the most part overblown. More importantly, they don't overshadow the benefits of such activities to the media and the public in general. For example, some are worried that the electronic devices used to blog or send tweets will somehow disrupt the sanctity of the courtroom or distract jurors. This belief ignores the current reality in which smartphones, laptops, and tablets are becoming commonplace in the courtroom as they increasingly replace the pen and paper that people traditionally used to take notes. Furthermore, the trial judge, if she so desires, can instruct those relying on electronic devices to sit in the back of the courtroom so that they draw less attention to themselves.

Another point to consider is the alternative arrangement. If a judge prohibits blogging or tweeting, then individuals have to find different ways to communicate courtroom activities to those who are not present. The most common alternative involves an individual getting up and physically leaving the courtroom every 5–10 minutes, which is a much bigger distraction than someone sitting in the back of the courtroom sending tweets or posting on a blog. This is especially true if the courtroom has a large number of individuals from the media.

A second concern surrounds the idea of sequestration of witnesses. When a trial witness is sequestered she is prohibited from sitting in the courtroom and listening to the testimony of others. As explained by the Supreme Court, the purpose of sequestration is to

exercise a restraint on witnesses tailoring their testimony to that of earlier witnesses, and it aids in detecting testimony that is less than candid.[16]

Some believe that with live blogging and tweeting sequestration loses much of its value because witnesses can go to a blog and find out what other witnesses have testified to. This is exactly what occurred in the criminal environmental trial of *United States v. W.R. Grace,* where the court permitted both journalism and law students to cover the trial by Twitter and blogs.[17] Although the witnesses were sequestered, the court discovered that a key government witness had read about the case online.

While live blogging and tweeting increases the likelihood that witnesses will learn about prior testimony, the potential for harm is not dramatically increased. This is because other entities such as television stations and newspapers are also reporting on the case and providing the public daily information about the trial. Thus, just as the court instructs witnesses not to watch television reports or read newspaper articles about the trial, the court should inform witnesses that they are also prohibited from reading blog posts or tweets pertaining to the trial. If a witness violates this rule, the court, as in *United States v. W.R. Grace,* has the option of either striking the witness's testimony or issuing instructions to the jury about this particular witness's credibility.

The final concern relates to security and the increased potential for revealing the identities of jurors and testifying witnesses. This release of identifying information can be both intentional and unintentional. For example, in Kansas, a reporter caused a mistrial when he inadvertently tweeted a photo of a juror to the general public. The photo violated a state rule that prohibited photographing individual jurors. This prohibition is not unique to Kansas as many states disallow pictures of sitting jurors.[18] While tweeting a photo of a juror is definitely a problem, it is less likely to occur in the future as individuals gain greater familiarity with their electronic devices. Similar to the reintroduction of television into the courtroom after the Supreme Court's ruling in *Chandler v. Florida*, mishaps do occasionally happen, but they are rare.

As for the intentional release of information, it is a real concern that requires increased vigilance by court personnel. In one criminal trial in Cleveland, Ohio, two individuals were observed in the courtroom directing their smartphones at the jury. After jurors complained to the judge, the two were arrested for contempt of court and intimidation of a juror. To reduce the likelihood of this occurring in the future, courts need to be more attentive to those sitting in the gallery. In addition, courts should require all users of electronic devices in the courtroom to gain prior permission from the court before using those devices.

Once a judge decides to allow social media in the courtroom, she has to determine whether to restrict such use to credentialed media. Some courts allow credentialed media to blog and tweet from the courtroom, but not the general public. Creating this type of distinction then requires the court to determine who is a journalist, which can be challenging in the Digital Age. For example, how can the court tell a blogger who has a following larger than the circulation of most mid-sized town newspapers that he is not a journalist? The better course of action is not to limit social media use to credentialed media only.

Despite the potential problems that may arise from allowing blogging and tweeting in the courtroom, the practice is gaining in popularity. In the recent trial involving the prosecution of Dr. Conrad Murray for the involuntary manslaughter death of Michael Jackson, one news agency sent out nearly 1,900 tweets to over 3,000 followers.[19] This increased acceptance of social media in the courtroom may be due to the evolving methods by which news is received and consumed in society. For example, in 2013, it was reported that approximately 30 percent of Americans used Facebook to obtain news.[20] If receiving news by social media becomes the new norm, then blogging and tweeting from the courtroom will help the public stay informed and engaged in criminal trial proceedings.

12

Admitting Social Media into Evidence

As the previous chapters illustrate, those involved in the criminal justice system increasingly rely on social media in their day-to-day lives. Social media is used by criminal defendants to conduct crimes, by law enforcement to run undercover sting operations, and by attorneys as an instrument of discovery. All of these activities generate social media–related information, which may ultimately become evidence in a court of law.

Court systems around the world, including those in the United States, have rules governing what information may be admitted during trial. The purpose of these rules is to ensure that the finders of fact, whether judges or jurors, only rely on certain information when deciding the criminal defendant's guilt or innocence. In the federal court system, the admission of evidence is regulated by the federal rules of evidence. States have similar rules that closely follow the federal rules. Judges must apply these rules to the information submitted by attorneys and offered by testifying witnesses to see whether or not such information should be allowed as evidence.

This chapter examines the application of the evidentiary rules to information derived from social media. This examination will occur by looking at the five traditional evidentiary hurdles that proponents of information must overcome when seeking to admit evidence into a court of law: (1) relevance, (2) authentication, (3) hearsay, (4) best evidence rule, and (5) character evidence.[1] It should be noted that although the aforementioned rules are the most common to arise with respect to information related to social media, they are not the only rules of evidence. Thus, even if the information sought to be admitted into evidence clears these five hurdles, it still might be inadmissible due to another rule.

The primary focus of this chapter is authentication. This rule of evidence, more than any other, presents the greatest challenge with respect to getting social media–related information admitted into court. This is because social media evidence, unlike traditional evidence, is easier to fictionalize, fabricate, and forge. When authenticating social media–related information courts primarily look at two areas: access and control, and distinctive characteristics.

RELEVANCE

The first requirement for getting information, social media-related or otherwise, into evidence is relevance. To be relevant, evidence must

make the existence of any fact that is of consequence to the determination of the action more probable or less probable.[2]

Generally speaking, establishing the relevancy of evidence is not a difficult burden.[3] To be relevant, the evidence could pertain to an element of the case, an affirmative defense, or be used to impeach or undermine the credibility of a witness. At times, however, practitioners do not always reach this initial evidentiary threshold. As the following two examples will illustrate, judges, on occasion, prevent attorneys from admitting certain information into evidence because they find that it is not relevant to the case at hand.

In *Ohio v. Gaskins*, the defendant was convicted of improper sexual contact with two minors (CM and KR). The crime occurred in June 2005.[4] The prosecution's theory of the case, at least according to the trial judge, was that the defendant acted

reckless[ly], that either he knew the age of the victims, . . . , or he was reckless with regard to their age.[5]

At trial, the defendant attempted to introduce into evidence the Myspace profile of CM. According to the defendant, CM claimed on her Myspace page that she was 18 and had been sexually involved with an adult. However, the defendant put no proof forward that he actually saw CM's Myspace profile prior to the unlawful sexual contact. In addition, it was unclear at trial whether CM's Myspace page was created before or after the date of the sexual assault by the defendant.

While the court did permit the defendant to introduce pictures from CM's Myspace page, the court disallowed any questions related to the page itself because the trial judge did not find them relevant. According to the judge,

> what becomes relevant is how they [victims] looked around June 23rd, not how they looked like in October, not how they looked like in February, not how they looked like in December, but how they looked around June of 2005.[6]

On appeal, the trial court's decision was upheld as the appellate court determined that

> [w]hether CM represented herself as eighteen years old after the incident occurred is not relevant. This case centers around Appellant's belief regarding CM's age at the time of the incident.[7]

State v. Corwin offers another example of the trial judge finding information derived from social media lacking in relevancy and thus inadmissible.[8] Here, the defendant was charged with attempted forcible rape and convicted by a jury. On the night of the incident, the defendant and the victim were out drinking with the victim's friends. After visiting at least two bars, the victim and the defendant returned to the defendant's apartment. While at the apartment, the defendant claimed that the two "made out."

The victim told a different story. She stated that the defendant grabbed her and physically restrained her against her will, which in turn left bruises on her body. She also claimed that the defendant attempted to forcibly have sex with her and allowed her to leave his apartment only after he instructed her not to tell anyone what had occurred that night.

At trial, the defendant argued that the victim had misconstrued or incorrectly remembered the events of the night. To support his argument and call into question the victim's testimony, the defendant attempted to introduce into evidence the victim's Facebook page, which included posts related to sex, drinking, and passing out. For example, nine months after the attempted rape, the victim, in writing about another night on the town, posted the following:

> I didn't pass out I just took a little cat nap to get me through the night! I feel A LOT better now th[a]n I did when I first woke up . . . it was a pretty rough night and I have the bruises to prove it.[9]

Here, the trial judge refused to let into evidence the victim's Facebook posts. The judge did not find these posts regarding partying and passing out dispositive to the defendant's guilt or innocence. Put differently, these posts were not relevant to the issue being disputed, which was whether the defendant, on the night in question, attempted to rape the victim.

On appeal, the trial judge's decision was upheld. In reviewing the decision of the trial court, the appellate court noted at the outset that the victim could be impeached by evidence related to her reputation for truthfulness and veracity but not ordinarily by evidence related to specific acts of misconduct. Thus, if the victim had testified that she didn't drink or go out, these pictures could be admitted to impeach her, but that was not the case here. The appellate court then went on to state that

> the information contained in Exhibit A [the victim's Facebook posts] went beyond any evidence even tangentially related to events of the night in question and detailed prior instances of what could be termed misconduct on the part of Victim. Exhibit A contained quotes, information, photographs, and comments about almost all aspects of Victim's life including references to partying, sex, drinking, schoolwork, and at least one sexually suggestive photograph. None of this information is legally relevant to the fact that Appellant was charged with the attempted forcible rape of Victim. Even the quote at issue relating to an instance some nine months after the event in question where Victim might have received bruises after an evening out on the town is legally irrelevant and is not directed at Victim's reputation for truth and veracity. Evidence that Victim had been bruised on another occasion when intoxicated neither proves nor disproves that her bruises on the day of the attempted rape were from an alcohol-related accident, instead of Appellant's violent actions toward her. It was permissible for Appellant's counsel to ask Victim whether she had received bruises in the past after a night of drinking; however, her Facebook profile page was not admissible to challenge her answer on this collateral matter.[10]

AUTHENTICATION

Historically, the bar to get evidence authenticated had not been set very high. Attorneys were only required to establish a foundation sufficient for a reasonable juror to find that the information or item being offered was genuine or what it purported to be. If the judge determined that the foundation provided by the attorney was sufficient, the information or item being offered was introduced into evidence, at which point the jurors (assuming this was not a bench trial) would decide the credibility and weight to attach to that particular piece of evidence. As explained by the notes in the California Evidence Code,

> the fact that the judge permits [a] writing to be admitted in evidence does not necessarily establish the authenticity of the writing; all that the judge has determined is that there has been a sufficient showing of the authenticity of the writing to permit the trier of fact to find that it is authentic.[11]

The purpose behind the authentication requirement is to prevent fraud and innocent mistake by the judge or jury.[12]

Social media has raised the traditionally low authentication requirement to new heights. This is because evidence derived from social media, unlike traditional evidence, can be more easily altered or forged.[13] In addition, individuals, as discussed earlier in Chapter 3, can create entirely bogus social media sites or pretend to be others on social media. In *Griffin v. Maryland*, which will be discussed in greater detail later, the court noted that

> anyone can create a fictitious account and masquerade under another person's name or can gain access to another's account by obtaining the user's username and password.[14]

There are two primary authentication hurdles a proponent of social media evidence must be prepared to address. The first and more basic requirement is simply demonstrating that the evidence being admitted is from the social media site in question. This can be accomplished by having someone with personal knowledge of the social media site testify that the evidence being offered is from that specific site.[15]

The second and more complex requirement is attributing the social media evidence to a specific person.[16] Put differently, the proponent of the evidence must demonstrate that

> the person to whom any words are attributable is actually that person and not another person.[17]

Absent an admission from the individual who created the social media evidence, the practitioner must rely on circumstantial evidence to fulfill the requirements of authentication.[18]

The circumstantial evidence relied on by the courts generally falls into one of two categories. The first category focuses on "access and control" of the social media information. The second category of circumstantial evidence, the one most relied on by the courts, generally focuses on the social media information itself and whether it contains "distinctive characteristics."

Access and Control

When examining the access and control of the social media information, courts generally consider the following:

- Testimony regarding the account holder's exclusive access to the originating computer and social media account.
- Expert testimony concerning the results of a search of the social media account holder's computer hard drive.
- Testimony directly from the social media provider that connects the establishment of the social media account to the person who allegedly created it and also connects the posting sought to be introduced to the person who initiated it.
- Expert testimony on accessing social media accounts and the methods used to prevent unauthorized access.
- The reply doctrine.[19]

Distinctive Characteristics

When examining the distinctive characteristics of the social media information, courts generally consider the following:

- The message or posting contains facts or details known only to that person who allegedly created it.
- The person who allegedly created the social media information subsequently acts in a manner consistent with the message or posting.
- The message or posting was written in a unique manner consistent with the person's method of communication.

To date, the three most prominent cases on authentication of social media information are *Commonwealth v. Williams,*[20] *Griffin v. Maryland,*[21] and *Tienda v. State.*[22] The first two cases reached the high court in their respective states and involved allegations of using social media to influence witness testimony. The last case involved the criminal defendant's own social media account and reached the highest criminal court in the state of Texas.

In *Griffin*, the defendant, Antoine Griffin, was charged with killing Darvell Guest in the women's restroom of Ferrari's Bar in Perryville, Maryland. During Griffin's first trial, which ended in a mistrial, his cousin (Dennis Gibbs) testified that he did not see Griffin

> pursue the victim into the bathroom with a gun.[23]

During the defendant's retrial, Gibbs altered his testimony. He now testified that he saw the defendant and Guest

> go into the bathroom, and that no one else went in. [He] then heard multiple gunshots.[24]

When defense counsel for Griffin enquired about the reason for this change in testimony, Gibbs responded that prior to the start of the first trial he was threatened by Griffin's girlfriend, Jessica Barber. One of Barber's alleged threats came via her Myspace page, which, inter alia, contained the following statements:

> I HAVE 2 BEAUTIFUL KIDS ... FREE BOOZY!!!! JUST REMEMBER SNITCHES GET STITCHES!! U KNOW WHO YOU ARE!![25]

The prosecution offered printouts of these statements in order to explain Gibbs's evolving testimony. However, the prosecution did not call Barber to authenticate the documents and instead relied on its lead investigator. The investigator testified that he knew these printouts belonged to Barber because the Myspace profile where he obtained the information (1) had a picture of Barber and the defendant; (2) referenced her children; (3) had her birthdate; and (4) referenced the defendant's nickname (Boozy).[26]

Upon conviction, the defendant appealed and the intermediate appellate court upheld the trial court's ruling. The defendant then appealed to Maryland's high court, which overruled the intermediate court and remanded the case for a new trial. According to the high court,

> the trial judge abused his discretion in admitting the Myspace evidence ... because the picture of Ms. Barber coupled with her birth date and location were not sufficient "distinctive characteristics" on a Myspace profile to authenticate its printout, given the prospect that someone other than Ms. Barber could have not only created the site, but also posted the "snitches get stitches" comment.[27]

The court then went on to discuss possible alternative methods for authenticating social media evidence: (1) question the purported creator of the social media information; (2) search the computer of the person who purportedly created the social media information; or (3) have the social media provider link the social media information to the person who purportedly created it.

In *Commonwealth v. Williams*, which was decided while *Griffin* was on appeal, the defendant Dwight Williams was convicted of first-degree murder for the shooting death of Izaah Tucker.[28] At trial, a witness for the government, who appeared a bit reticent on the stand, testified that the defendant had a gun on the night of the murder. The witness further testified that prior to trial she had received four Myspace messages from the defendant's brother, Jesse Williams, urging her not to testify or to claim a lack of memory.

According to the witness, she knew the messages were from Jesse because his picture was on his Myspace account and he used the screen name "doit4It." The witness also testified that she responded back to three of the four Myspace messages sent by Jesse. The prosecution offered the Myspace messages into evidence to explain why the witness appeared reluctant to testify. Defense counsel did not initially object to the witness's testimony about the Myspace messages; however, counsel did eventually move to strike the testimony.

On appeal, the Massachusetts Supreme Judicial Court found the admission of the witness's testimony about the Myspace messages to be in error. The court determined that

> while foundational testimony established that the messages were sent by someone with access to [the defendant's brother's] Myspace Web page, it did not identify the person who actually sent the communication.[29]

However, due to strong evidence of the defendant's guilt, the error was not sufficient to overturn the defendant's conviction.

Two important points deserve highlighting in the *Williams* case. First, the court did not address the issue of the reply doctrine and the fact that the witness testified that she responded to three of the four Myspace messages from Jesse Williams. Had the court applied the reply doctrine, it might have been more inclined to find the Myspace messages admissible.

Second, in making its determination that the admission of the Myspace messages was an error, the court compared social media communication to a telephone call, saying:

a witness's testimony that he or she has received an incoming call from a person claiming to be "A," without more is insufficient evidence to admit the call as a conversation with "A."[30]

This comparison of social media to the telephone, like other analogies discussed in this book, misses the mark. Social media, unlike the telephone, offers a variety of different ways to prove a user's identity. This point will be illustrated in the next case, *State v. Tienda,* where the court, in contrast to *Griffin* and *Williams,* was much more amenable to admitting social media–related information into evidence.

In *Tienda*, the defendant, Ronnie Tienda Jr., was charged with the drive-by murder of David Valadez. As part of its case-in-chief, the prosecution relied on evidence from the defendant's Myspace account at trial. For example, the government introduced the defendant's main profile page, which included the following quotes:

If you ain't BLASTIN, You ain't Lastin

I live to stay fresh!! I kill to stay rich!!

RIP, David Valadez[31]

Along with the quote referencing David Valadez was a music link to the song played at his funeral. The government also introduced a photo of the defendant displaying his electronic ankle monitor with the following quote:

str8 outta jail and n da club[32]

To authenticate this Myspace evidence the government did not rely on the defendant. Instead, it used the victim's sister, Priscilla Palomo. She was the same person who initially found the defendant's Myspace profiles (he had three different ones) and offered them to the police.[33]

At trial, the defense objected to the Myspace information being admitted, arguing that it had not been properly authenticated. After the trial judge denied the defense's objection, counsel for the defendant cross-examined Palomo. During cross examination, Palomo admitted that it was possible to create a bogus Myspace page. She also admitted that the information reportedly written on Tienda's Myspace page was known to others. Yet, despite these answers and the best efforts of defense counsel, Tienda was convicted. He subsequently appealed.

On appeal, the appellate court determined that the trial court did not abuse its discretion in admitting the Myspace evidence. The appellate court pointed out that (1) the Myspace pages were registered to a person with the defendant's nickname and legal name; (2) the photographs were clearly of the defendant; and (3) the defendant's profile referenced the victim and his murder along with the defendant's home monitoring. In comparing this case to *Griffin*, the appellate court noted that

> [t]here are far more circumstantial indicia of authenticity in this case than in Griffin.[34]

Finally, the appellate court stated that

> [i]t is, of course, within the realm of possibility that the appellant was the victim of some elaborate and ongoing conspiracy. Conceivably some unknown malefactors somehow stole the appellant's numerous self-portrait photographs, concocted boastful messages about David Valadez's murder and the circumstances of that shooting, was aware of the music played at Valadez's funeral, knew when the appellant was released on pretrial bond with electronic monitoring and referred to that year-long event along with stealing the photograph of the grinning appellant lounging in his chair while wearing his ankle monitor. But that is an alternate scenario whose likelihood and weight the jury was entitled to assess once the State had produced a prima facie showing that it was the appellant, not some unidentified conspirators or fraud artists, who created and maintained these Myspace pages.[35]

As *Griffin, Williams,* and *Tienda* demonstrate, state courts have not been entirely consistent in their handling of authentication issues related to social media.[36] Some have rigidly adhered to the circumstantial evidence requirement, while others have not. One of the major difficulties for the courts in applying the rules of authentication is that they attempt to do so by comparing social media to other methods of communication. For example, some courts want to compare social media to email. Other courts, as in *Williams,* compare social media to a telephone. However, as illustrated in the Introduction, neither email nor the telephone is directly analogous to social media.

Another challenge with consistency in this area is that individuals have different views on authentication. Some believe that the rules of evidence are somewhat paternalistic and underestimate the abilities of the jury to discern the truth. Individuals following this philosophy believe that the court should err on the side of letting in more information and allowing the jury to separate fact from fiction. Proponents of allowing in more information also believe that if problems exist with the evidence, the other side will point them out, which is what the defense attempted to do in *Tienda*.

Others believe that the court should take an active role in shielding jurors from potentially bogus or fabricated evidence. One problem with this latter viewpoint is that jurors are increasingly taking it upon themselves to use social media to uncover their own evidence, as illustrated in Chapter 4. Thus, some believe that it is better to allow more information, not less, even if the court is somewhat doubtful of its authenticity; that way attorneys have a better idea of what the jury is considering and can challenge that information in court.

HEARSAY

The third requirement for admitting evidence is overcoming any hearsay issues. *Hearsay* as defined by Federal Rule of Evidence (FRE) 801(c) is

a statement, other than one made by the declarant while testifying at the trial or hearing, offered in evidence to prove the truth of the matter asserted.[37]

In the context of social media, hearsay can take the form of updates, messages, and photograph captions. Unlike authentication, the hearsay inquiry for social media evidence is fairly straightforward.

The first step in any hearsay analysis is to determine whether the evidence is a statement made by a person. Information generated automatically by machines is ordinarily not considered a statement. By way of example, certain social media providers use a time stamp whenever an individual posts information on his account. This time stamp would not be a statement so long as it was automatically computer generated.[38] However, the other information in the post would be a statement.[39]

Next, the court has to consider whether the statement is offered for the truth of the matter asserted. For example, in *People v. Valdez*, the government introduced the defendant's Myspace page not for the truth of any express or implied assertions on the Myspace page but to corroborate a victim's statement to investigators and as foundation for testimony by a gang expert.[40]

If the evidence is both a statement and offered for the truth of the matter asserted, then the judge must determine whether the statement is excluded from the definition of hearsay. For example, certain prior witness statements are excluded from the definition of hearsay pursuant to FRE 801 (d)(1).[41] In addition, certain admissions by party opponents are excluded from the definition of hearsay pursuant to FRE 801(d)(2).[42] At least one legal commentator has suggested that a "Like" on Facebook could be deemed an admission and thus be excluded from the definition of hearsay. According to this individual,

Facebook "likes" are most properly viewed as manifestations of belief in an existing statement rather than independent statements, and therefore "likes" constitute adoptive admissions under the Federal Rules of Evidence.[43]

If all the above requirements are met and the statement fits the definition of hearsay, the judge should finally look at whether an exception to the general prohibition against admitting hearsay evidence exists. There are numerous exceptions to the hearsay rule. The more commonly used exceptions for admitting hearsay evidence derived from social media include present sense impression,[44] excited utterance,[45] public records,[46] and business records.[47]

BEST EVIDENCE RULE

The fourth requirement in admitting evidence concerns the best evidence rule, otherwise known as the original writing rule. FRE 1002 states that

[a]n original writing, recording, or photograph is required in order to prove its content unless these rules or a federal statute provides otherwise.[48]

The best evidence rule arises when an attorney attempts to prove the contents of a writing, recording, or photograph.[49] This typically occurs when the writing is itself the item a proponent wants to prove or a proponent wants to prove a matter by using a writing as evidence of that matter. To properly apply the best evidence rule, the judge must

determine when "the contents" of a writing, recording or photograph actually are being proved, as opposed to proving events that just happen to have been recorded or photographed, or those which can be proved by eyewitnesses, as opposed to a writing or recording explaining or depicting them.[50]

In re T.A. illustrates how the best evidence rule works in a social media context.[51] In this case the juvenile (T.A.) was adjudicated delinquent in two counts of felonious assault with firearm specifications. His charges stemmed from shooting a firearm at the house of A.P., who resided at the residence with her son. T.A. shot at the house because earlier that day he had fought with A.P.'s son. Shortly after the shooting, a neighbor provided A.P. printouts of T.A.'s Myspace page, which included T.A.'s photograph and an admission from T.A. about the shooting.

In testifying at trial A.P., over defense counsel's objection, relied on information she received from T.A.'s Myspace page (e.g., pictures of T.A.). The prosecution, however, never admitted into evidence T.A.'s Myspace page. On cross-examination, A.P. acknowledged that one of the ways she was able to identify T.A. as the shooter was through photographs she observed on his Myspace page. Upon appeal the appellate court found that based on the best evidence rule, it was error, albeit harmless error, to allow A.P. to testify about T.A.'s Myspace page because the photographs were never admitted into evidence. In this case, the best evidence would have been T.A.'s Myspace page, because that is where A.P. verified T.A.'s identity.

CHARACTER EVIDENCE

The fifth requirement for the admission of evidence concerns FRE 404. Section (b) of this rule reads as follows:

> Evidence of a crime, wrong, or other act is not admissible to prove a person's character in order to show that on a particular occasion the person acted in accordance with the character.
>
> ... This evidence may be admissible for another purpose, such as proving motive, opportunity, intent, preparation, plan, knowledge, identity, absence of mistake, or lack of accident.[52]

United States v. Phaknikone provides an example of how the issue of improper character evidence arises with respect to social media.[53] In *Phaknikone*, the government charged the defendant, Souksakhone Phaknikone, with robbing seven banks at gunpoint. At trial, the government claimed that the banks were robbed in a similar "gangster style," including the method by which the robber held the gun. To prove its theory that the defendant committed these crimes, the government offered at trial, among other things, the defendant's Myspace page, which included the following:

1. The defendant's profile page that listed the name "Trigga" with "$100 bills . . . float[ing] down the screen."
2. His subscriber report, listing the full name "Trigga FullyLoaded" and email address "gangsta_trigga@yahoo.com."
3. Two photographs, including one of the defendant bearing a tattoo, holding a handgun sideways (apparently gangster style), with a child and another man as passengers.

The government argued that this Myspace evidence was needed to prove the defendant's identity and show the defendant's method (modus operandi) by which he committed the bank robberies. The defendant objected, arguing that it was improper character evidence and unduly prejudicial. The trial court ultimately allowed the evidence in and the defendant was convicted.

On appeal, the Eleventh Circuit Court of Appeals agreed with the defendant with respect to the admissibility of the Myspace evidence. The appellate court found that

[a]lthough the photograph may portray a "gangster-type personality," the photograph does not evidence the modus operandi of a bank robber who commits crimes with a signature trait.[54]

For the Eleventh Circuit Court of Appeals, the Myspace information was a classic example of bad character evidence that Rule 404(b) was created to prevent. The appellate court went on to say that

[t]he Myspace evidence is not evidence of identity. . . . The subscriber report proved nothing more than Phaknikone's nickname. . . . The photograph of a tattooed Phaknikone, his face completely visible, in a car, holding a handgun sideways in his right hand, and with a child as a passenger, proves only that Phaknikone, on an earlier occasion, possessed a handgun in the presence of a child. Although the photograph may portray a "gangster-type personality," the photograph does not evidence the modus operandi of a bank robber who commits his crimes with a signature trait. The Myspace evidence is not evidence of a modus operandi and is inadmissible to prove identity.[55]

Unfortunately for the defendant, the court of appeals did not overturn his conviction. The appellate court determined that although the Myspace evidence was inadmissible, it was harmless error. The appellate court reached this decision based on the overwhelming evidence of the defendant's guilt, including his confession in which he admitted to participating in at least four of the bank robberies.

One takeaway from the *Phaknikone* case is that while there is a virtual treasure trove of information on social media, prosecutors, like defense attorneys, have to be careful in how they use that information, especially at trial. Attorneys can't be in such a rush to get anything social media–related into evidence that they forget about the traditional evidentiary rules. Fortunately for the prosecution, there was overwhelming evidence of Phaknikone's guilt, otherwise the push to have his Myspace page introduced as evidence might have led to a new trial for the defendant.

Conclusion

Social media has and continues to impact every aspect of the criminal justice system from the initial commission of the crime all the way through to the investigation and prosecution. The underlying question surrounding social media's influence is whether it has strengthened or weakened the criminal justice system as a whole. This question may best be answered by briefly exploring social media's role vis-à-vis private individuals, law enforcement, attorneys, and judges.

For some private individuals like crime victims, social media has been a boon. Social media provides them a virtual soapbox in which to voice their views about the criminal defendant, the criminal act itself, and the criminal justice system as a whole. In certain instances, this process of taking to social media to share experiences with a few friends or the entire world can be quite therapeutic for crime victims. In addition, and arguably more importantly, when crime victims take to social media they provide society a firsthand look at the criminal justice system, unfiltered by others like traditional media. This information offered by crime victims facilitates discussion and examination of the criminal justice system, which can result in improvements and necessary reforms. Overall, one must rate the impact of social media on crime victims as a positive.

On the other side of the spectrum of crime victims are criminal defendants. For them, social media has opened up a whole new world, one in which their pool of victims has grown exponentially. In the Digital Age, criminal defendants are no longer constrained by the physical proximity of their victims; they can now reach millions of people, many of whom live thousands of miles away.

Interestingly, the introduction of social media into the criminal justice system has not led to the creation of a vast array of new crimes. In fact, to date, only two additional crimes (flash mobs and online impersonation) have been created. What has changed are the methods by which traditional crimes are now committed. Harassment serves as a typical example. In the past, a crime like harassment might require a criminal defendant to interact physically or telephonically with the victim. In the Digital Age, social media allows the criminal defendant to harass the victim through a variety of methods, including unwitting third parties who may not even know that they are harassing the victim. Third-party harassment works because, unlike past forms of communication, social media allows people to more easily (1) approximate human interaction, (2) conceal their true identity, and (3) take on the persona of another.

At present, criminal defendants appear to have the upper hand over law enforcement with respect to employing social media. This, however, may be short lived as law enforcement continues to incorporate social media into its crime-fighting strategies. Furthermore, legislators and prosecutors are now taking proactive steps to prevent criminal defendants from exploiting social media for criminal purposes. By way of example, several states have passed laws banning certain criminal defendants from social media. Other measures include requiring criminal defendants to disclose past criminal convictions on their personal social media sites (Digital Scarlet Letters).

Social media's biggest threat to the criminal justice system, at least with respect to private individuals, arises from jurors. Although law enforcement is able to combat the negative effects of criminal defendants employing social media, there is no real counterbalance to jurors improperly using social media. In contravention of court rules, jurors use social media to discuss the case with others, including outside parties. In the Digital Age, judges find it increasingly difficult to fulfill their role as gatekeepers and control what information jurors receive and whom they communicate with. According to the past president of the American Society of Trial Consultants, Dr. Douglas L. Keene,

> [i]f a burglar can't resist checking his Facebook status while in the high adrenaline process of burglarizing your home, what's to stop a juror during courtroom tedium.[1]

At present, the best deterrence for preventing jurors from improperly using social media appears to be improved jury instructions. The problem with relying on jury instructions is that they are only instructions—nothing more. In order for instructions to be effective, jurors must follow them.

Thus, jury instructions must be written in such a manner as to create the optimum atmosphere for acceptance. This includes telling jurors why following these instructions is vital to the success of the adversarial system.

Social media's influence on law enforcement has been more evenly split. On one hand, adoption of social media by law enforcement has allowed them to counter the evolving methods relied on by criminal defendants. On the other hand, many are concerned about the privacy implications that arise when law enforcement uses new technology not only to apprehend suspects but also to investigate and monitor others. The big concern here is whether law enforcement's use of social media will lead to the erosion of privacy rights for society as a whole.

At present, the constitutional limitations placed on law enforcement's use of social media are premised on Supreme Court precedents that primarily involve the telephone. For example, the Supreme Court has made a distinction between content and noncontent information as it relates to the telephone. Generally speaking, content information (what a user sends another user), when communicated over equipment owned by a third party, is protected by the Fourth Amendment. Noncontent information (what the entity or user transmits to facilitate the transmission), when communicated over equipment owned by a third party, is not protected by the Fourth Amendment. This content vs. noncontent distinction works with respect to the telephone because its functionality can be neatly segregated (phone conversation vs. numbers dialed). The same, however, cannot be said for social media where users rely on a variety of different methods to communicate (e.g., tweets, email, status updates, instant messages, pictures, videos, wall comments, geographic check-ins, etc.).

Since the Supreme Court has not yet addressed social media in the context of the Fourth Amendment, it is entirely too early to tell whether social media has had a negative or positive impact on law enforcement as it relates to safeguarding the privacy rights of citizens. That answer will have to wait until the court provides better guidance on how far it is willing to go in allowing the police to use social media to combat crime.

Next are attorneys. As with most technological innovations, attorneys struggle, at least initially, with adopting and applying social media to the actual practice of law. As a result, the legal system experienced a few examples of attorneys mishandling cases and making ethical misjudgments due to a lack of familiarity with social media. However, it appears, at present, that most attorneys understand and appreciate the value of social media; it has become one more tool in the arsenal of the skilled practitioner. Furthermore, and arguably most importantly, through social media, attorneys provide more, not less information to the finder of fact, whether that person is a judge or juror. Thus, with respect to attorneys, social media should be viewed as a positive development.

Finally, there are judges. The big concern here is how judges regulate the use of social media in the courtroom. A few judges, who could be deemed Luddites, believe that social media should be completely banned from the courtroom. Most judges, however, understand that they can neither turn back time nor place the genie back in the bottle; therefore, they allow social media in some form or fashion inside the courtroom. While permitting social media in the courtroom comes with some drawbacks (e.g., it makes sequestering witnesses more challenging), those disadvantages appear to be vastly outweighed by the advantages.

Among the chief benefits is greater accessibility to courtroom proceedings. By allowing tweeting or blogging from the courtroom, judges help the public stay informed and engaged in courtroom proceedings. This is especially true for those who can't physically attend courtroom proceedings or who rely on social media as their primary news source. The courts, like society, must adapt to how individuals receive and access information in the Digital Age.

Overall, it appears that social media has done more to strengthen than weaken the criminal justice system. This is primarily due to the fact that social media provides the key players in the criminal justice system an opportunity to communicate directly with the public. This direct unfiltered contact does pose some dangers; for example, criminal defendants can reach more victims, and jurors have greater opportunities to discuss the case with third parties. However, these concerns, while worrisome, are offset by the benefits brought by social media.

These advantages include increased public understanding of the rule of law. When individuals take to social media to discuss a case or the legal system, society as a whole becomes better educated about the legal process. The public is also made aware of potential problem areas that need to be addressed and corrected within the criminal justice system.

Another advantage involves increased transparency. Several judges, who allow both the media and private individuals to blog or tweet from the courtroom, have remarked about how the practice leads to more openness. Both openness and transparency lead to greater confidence in the administration of justice, which in turn increases the likelihood that the public will accept the final outcome of a case regardless of whether a defendant is found guilty or innocent.

Appendix A
Sample Preservation Request Letter (Law Enforcement)

1 January, 2015

Custodian of Records
America Online, Inc.
22000 AOL Way
Dulles, VA 20166
ATTN: Compliance and Investigation Unit
Fax: 703.265.2305
Re: Preservation Request

Dear Sir/Ma'am:

The below listed account is subject to an ongoing criminal investigation at this agency, and it is requested that said account and all e-mail, and any other information contained herein, be preserved pending the issuance of a search warrant. (Specify any information you may want, i.e., unread, read, sent email, account histories, buddy lists, profiles, detailed billing (log on and log off times) payment method, etc. . . .)

Name: John X. Doe
Address: 1234 Any Street, Anytown, U.S. 12345
Phone: 123.456.7890

Screen Names: Johndoe, JohnXYDoe, XYZDoe
Possible AOL Account #:_____
Credit Card #:_____

If you have any questions concerning this request, please contact me at . . .

Sincerely,
Joe Prosecutor

Appendix B
Sample Preservation Request Letter (Defense Counsel)

January 1, 2015

Facebook
Attn: Security Department
1601 South California Avenue
Palo Alto, California 94304
Re: People of the State of California v. Smith
        Case No: 123456

Dear Sir/Ma'am:

Our firm represents Mr. Tim Smith in the above-referenced matter. You are hereby requested to preserve and prevent from destruction or alteration all records and contents of the [email/social networking/cellphone/text message/bbm/i.m./etc.] account of Jane Smith D.O.B. November 9, 1970.

The records and contents referred to in the preceding paragraph are evidence in a pending criminal case, and we are informed and believe that exculpatory evidence is contained in the records and contents and thus in your possession. We might choose to subpoena copies of the records and contents at a later date, but for the present we wish to have all records and contents preserved as evidence.

Please acknowledge your intention to comply with our request by emailing Jim Smith at our firm, at Jim.Smith@hotmail.com, within 48 hours of your receipt of herein correspondence.

Thank you for your prompt attention to this matter.

Most Sincerely,
Jim Smith
Attorney at Law

Appendix C
Subpoena Point of Contact

1. Facebook
Facebook Security
1601 South California Avenue
Palo Alto, CA 94304
Fax: 650.644.3229
Email: subpoena@facebook.com

2. Myspace
2121 Avenue of the Stars
Suite 700
Los Angeles, CA 90067
Phone: 1.888.690.2882

3. Twitter
Twitter, Inc.
c/o Trust & Safety
1355 Market Street
Suite 900
San Francisco, CA 94103
Phone: 415.222.9958

4. Google
Google Legal Investigations Support
1600 Amphitheater Parkway
Mountain View, CA 94043
Phone: 650.253.3425
Fax: 650.249.3429
Email: uslawenforcement@google.com

5. Craigslist
craigslist
1381 9th Avenue
San Francisco, CA 94122
Custodian of Records
Email: legal@craigslist.org
(send request as a PDF file)
Fax: 415-504-6394

6. LinkedIn
Legal Department
2029 Stierlin Court, Suite 200
Mountain View, CA 94043
Phone: 650.687.3600
Fax: 650.810.2897

Appendix D
Model Instructions

Introduction: Serving on a jury is an important and serious responsibility. Part of that responsibility is to decide the facts of this case using only the evidence that the parties will present in this courtroom. As I will explain further in a moment, this means that I must ask you to do something that may seem strange to you: not to discuss this case or do any research on this case. I will also explain to you why this rule is necessary and what to do if you encounter any problems with it.

Communications: During this trial, do not contact anyone associated with this case. If a question arises, direct it to my attention or the attention of my staff. Also, do not discuss this case during the trial with anyone, including any of the attorneys, parties, witnesses, your friends, or members of your family. This includes, but is not limited to, discussing your experience as a juror on this case, the evidence, the lawyers, the parties, the court, your deliberations, your reactions to testimony, exhibits, or any aspect of the case or your courtroom experience. "No discussion" extends to all forms of communication, whether in person, in writing, or through electronic devices or media such as: email, Facebook, Myspace, Twitter, instant messaging, BlackBerry messaging, iPads, iPhones, iTouches, Google, Yahoo!, or any other Internet search engine or form of electronic communication for any purpose whatsoever if it relates to this case.

After you retire to deliberate, you may begin to discuss the case with your fellow jurors and only your fellow jurors. I will give you some form of this instruction every time we take a break. I do that not to insult you or because I don't think that you are paying attention. I do it because, in my experience, this is the hardest instruction for jurors to follow. I know of no other situation in our culture where we ask strangers to sit together watching and listening to something, then go into a little room together and not talk about the one thing they have in common, that which they just watched together.

There are at least three reasons for this rule. The first is to help you keep an open mind. When you talk about things, you start to make decisions about them, and it is extremely important that you not make any decisions about this case until you have heard all the evidence and all the rules for making your decisions, and you will not have heard that until the very end of the trial. The second reason is that, by having conversations in groups of two or three during the trial, you will not remember to repeat all of your thoughts and observations to the rest of your fellow jurors when you deliberate at the end of the trial. The third and most important reason is that by discussing the case before deliberations, you increase the likelihood that you will either be influenced by an outside third party or that you will reveal information about the case to a third party. If any person tries to talk to you about this case, tell that person you cannot discuss the case because you are a juror. If that person persists, simply walk away and report the incident to me or my staff.

Research: Do not perform any research or make any independent personal investigations into any facts, individuals, or locations connected with this case. Do not look up or consult any dictionaries or reference materials. Do not search the Internet, Web sites, or blogs. Do not use any of these or any other electronic tools or other sources to obtain information about any facts, individuals, or locations connected with this case. Do not communicate any private or special knowledge about any facts, individuals, or locations connected with this case to your fellow jurors. Do not read or listen to any news reports about this case. The law prohibits a juror from receiving evidence not properly admitted at trial. If you have a question or need additional information, contact me or my staff. I, along with the attorneys, will review every request. If the information requested is appropriate for you to receive, it will be released in court.

In our daily lives, we may be used to looking for information online and we may "Google" things as a matter of routine. Also, in a trial it can be very tempting for jurors to do their own research to make sure they are making the correct decision. However, the moment you try to gather information about this case or the participants is the moment you contaminate the process and violate your oath as a juror. Looking for outside information is unfair because the parties do not have the opportunity to refute, explain, or correct what you discovered or relayed.

The trial process works through each side knowing exactly what evidence is being considered by you and what law you are applying to the facts you find. You must resist the temptation to seek outside information for our system of justice to work as it should. Once the trial ends and you are dismissed as jurors, you may research and discuss the case as much as you wish. You may also contact anyone associated with this case.

[Questions by the judge to the jury: Are there any of you who cannot or will not abide by these rules concerning communication or research with others in any way during this trial? Are there any of you who do not understand these instructions?]

Ramifications: If you communicate with anyone about the case or do outside research during the trial, it could lead to a mistrial, which is a tremendous expense and inconvenience to the parties, the court, and, ultimately, you as taxpayers. Furthermore, you could be held in contempt of court and be subject to punishment such as paying the costs associated with having a new trial. If you find that one of your fellow jurors has conducted improper communications or research or if you conduct improper communications or research, you have a duty to report it to me or my staff so that we can protect the integrity of this trial.

Notes

PREFACE

1. John G. Browning, *Facing Up to Facebook in the Classroom*, ABA Volume 43 Issue 3 (2012).
2. For an example, see *Course Descriptions*, University of Dayton School of Law.
3. Kim Russell, *Detroit Students Organize Fights Online and Then Post Videos in Practice Called Cyber-Banging*, ABC ACTION NEWS, WXYZ.COM (Jan. 27, 2012).
4. Hayes Hunt and Brian Kint, *Juries and Social Networking Sites*, THE CHAMPION (Dec. 2013).
5. Pew Internet Research, *Teens, Social Media and Privacy*, May 21, 2013, Aaron Smith Duggan.
6. EXPERIAN MARKETING SERVICES, THE 2012 DIGITAL MARKETER: BENCHMARK AND TREND REPORT 79 (2012), available at http://www.experian.com/simmonsresearch/register-2012-digital-marketer.html.
7. Tom Webster, *The Social Habit 2011*, EDISON RESEARCH (May 29, 2011).
8. *John Doe v. Prosecutor, Marion County, Indiana* (Trial Court) Case No. 1:12-cv-00062-TWP-MJD (S.D. Ind. June 22, 2012).
9. *Citizens United v. Federal Election Commission*, 588 U.S. 310 (2010).
10. Jeffrey Bellin, *Applying Crawford's Confrontation Right in a Digital Age*, 45 TEXAS TECH. L. REV. 33 (2012).

11. A. H. Maslow, *A Theory of Human Motivation*, 50 PSYCHOL.REV. 370 (1943) (listing and discussing the basic human needs in order of importance).

INTRODUCTION

1. Leslie Horn, *NYPD Social Media Unit Goes After Criminals Online*, PCMAG.COM (Aug. 10, 2011); see also, John Browning, A LAWYER'S GUIDE TO SOCIAL NETWORKING: UNDER-STANDING SOCIAL MEDIA'S IMPACT ON THE LAW (2010).
2. Tonia Moxley, *Social Media Gives Virginia Tech Police a Host of New Eyes*, ROANOKE.COM (June 16, 2013).
3. Heather L. Griffith, *Understanding and Authenticating Evidence from Social Networking Sites*, 7 WASH. J.L. TECH & ARTS 209 (2012).
4. *Social Media and the Rules on Authentication*, 43 U. TOL. L. REV. 367 (2012).
5. *Avatar*, SECONDLIFE.COM (last visited Jan. 17, 2014).
6. *Doe v. Myspace, Inc.*, 474 F. Supp. 2d 843 (W.D. Tex. 2007).
7. Danah M. Boyd and Nicole B. Ellison, *Social Networking Sites: Definition, History, and Scholarship*, 13 JOURNAL OF COMPUTER-MEDIATED COMMUNICATION 210 (2008).
8. Carolyn Elefant, *The "Power" of Social Media: Legal Issues & Best Practices for Utilities Engaging Social Media*, 32 ENERGY L.J. 1 (2011).
9. NAIC, *The Use of Social Media in Insurance* (2012).
10. Merriam-Webster (last visited Jan. 17, 2014).
11. Carolyn Elefant, *The "Power" of Social Media: Legal Issues & Best Practices for Utilities Engaging Social Media*, 32 ENERGY L.J. 1 (2011).

CHAPTER 1: CRIME VICTIMS

1. *Janet Reno v. American Civil Liberties Union*, 521 U.S. 844 (1997).
2. Abigail Pesta, *Thanks for Ruining My Life*, NEWSWEEK (Dec. 10, 2012).
3. *Id.*
4. Bruce Schneier, *The Court of Public Opinion Is About Mob Justice and Reputation as Revenge*, WIRED (Feb. 26, 2013).
5. *Id.*

CHAPTER 2: VIRTUAL DEPUTIES

1. Hayley Guenther, *Social Media Detectives Help Deputies Catch Criminals*, NWCN.COM (April 11, 2013).
2. Kirsten Crow, *Waco Police Tout Success of Facebook Page*, WACOTRIB.COM (May 20, 2013).
3. Dave Neal, *Reddit Apologizes for Role in Boston Witch Hunt*, THE INQUIRER (Apr. 23, 2013). See also http://blog.reddit.com/2013/04/reflections-on-recent-boston-crisis.html.
4. Ohio Revised Code Annotated § 2921.22.
5. Julia Dahl, *Steubenville Rape Case: How Drunk Is Too Drunk to Consent to Sex*, CBS NEWS (March 13, 2013).
6. See Sandra Guerra Thompson, *The White-Collar Police Force: "Duty to Report" Statutes in Criminal Law Theory*, 11 Wm. & Mary Bill of Rts. J. 3, 37 n.188 (2002) ("MASS. GEN. LAWS ANN. ch. 268, § 40 (West 2002) (establishing a duty to report crimes of rape, murder, manslaughter, or armed robbery if at the scene of the crime and can report without danger to self; any failure to do so is punishable by a fine of $500.00 to $2,500.00) . . . R.I. GEN. LAWS § 11-56-1 (2001) (establishing a duty to assist at the scene of an emergency if one can do so without danger to self, any violators of which may be found guilty of a petty misdemeanor punishable by imprisonment not to exceed six months, a fine no greater than $500.00, or both) . . . WASH. REV. CODE ANN. § 9.69.100 (West 2002) (establishing a duty to report for any witness of a violent or sexual offense against a child or any violent offense, violations of which are punishable as a misdemeanor).
7. See, e.g., FLA. STAT. § 794.027 (2014); MINN. STAT. § 604A.01 (2014); VT. STAT. ANN. tit. 12 § 519 (2014).
8. *Nielsen and Twitter Establish Social TV Rating*, NIELSEN (Dec. 17, 2012).
9. Instagram Press Center, INSTAGRAM, http://instagram.com/press/ (last visited Feb. 1, 2013).
10. Josh James, *How Much Data Is Created Every Minute?*, DOMO (June 8, 2012).

CHAPTER 3: CRIMINAL DEFENDANTS

1. *United States v. Sayer*, Criminal Nos. 2:11-CR-113-DBH, 2:11-CR-47-DBH (May 15, 2012).
2. *People v. Fernino*, 851 N.Y.S. 2d 339 (N.Y. Crim. Ct. 2008).

3. *Griffin v. State*, 995 A. 2d 791 (Md. 2011).

4. *United States v. Elonis*, No. 11-13, 2011 WL 5024284 (E.D. Pa. Oct. 20, 2011).

5. *A.B. v. State*, 863 N.E. 2d 1212 (Ind. Ct. App. 2007), vacated 885 N.E. 2d 1223 (Ind. 2008); *Layshock v. Hermitage Sch. Dist.*, 412 F. Supp. 2d 502 (W.D. Pa. 2006).

6. Tina Susman, *Facebook Identity Theft: Probation Deal for Woman Who Trashed Ex?* LA TIMES (Mar. 20, 2012).

7. *United States v. Drew*, 259 F.R.D. 449 (C.D. Cal. 2009).

8. Computer Fraud and Abuse Act, 18 USC §1030.

9. *Myspace Services Terms of Use Agreement*, Myspace.com (June 10, 2013).

10. MO. REV. STAT § 565.090 (2013).

11. *State v. Vaughn*, 366 S.W. 3d 513 (Mo. 2012). (The Missouri Supreme Court recently determined that Section 6 of MO. REV. STAT § 565.090 (2013) was constitutional but that Section 5 was not.)

12. Susan Brenner, CYBERCRIME: CRIMINAL THREATS FROM CYBERSPACE 87 (2010).

13. Elizabeth Windsor, https://twitter.com/Queen_UK (last visited Dec. 27, 2013).

14. Jeff Bahr, *No Jail Time for Woman Accused in ID Theft*, THE OBSERVER ONLINE (Mar. 28, 2012).

15. *Id.*

16. Judy Lin, *George Bronk Sentenced for Facebook Stalking*, HUFFPOST San Francisco (July 22, 2011).

17. *Id.*

18. Erik Brady and Rachel George, *Manti Te'o's "Catfish" Story Is a Common One*, USA TODAY (January 18, 2013).

19. *Id.*

20. California Penal Code § 528.5 (WEST 2014).

21. Victor Luckerson, *Can You Go to Jail for Impersonating Someone Online*, TIME (Jan. 22, 2013); Texas Penal Code Annotated § 33.07(a) (West 2013).

22. California Penal Code § 528.5(a) (West 2014).

23. Communications Decency Act, 47 U.S.C. §230(c).

24. *Doe II v. Myspace, Inc.*, 96 Cal. Rptr. 3d 148 (2009).

25. *Id.*

26. Jacqueline Lipton, *Combatting Cyber-Victimization*, 26 BERKELEY TECH. L.J. 1103 (2011).

27. *Watts v. United States*, 394 U.S. 705 (1969).

28. *United States v. Elonis*, No. CRIM. A. 11-13 (E.D. Pa. Oct 20, 2011).

29. Sean Coughlan, *Teachers Warn of Online Threats from Pupils*, BBC NEWS (Apr. 6, 2012).

30. Coley Harvey, *Tweets from FSU Player About Killing Cops Upset Fraternal Order of Police Leaders*, ORLANDO SENTINEL (August 1, 2012).

31. *Griffin v. State*, 19 A.3d 415 (Md. 2011).

32. Graeme McMillan, *Student Pleads Guilty to Threatening President Obama on Facebook*, DIGITAL TRENDS (May 23, 2012).

33. *United States v. Jeffries*, 10-CR-100 (E.D. Tenn. Oct. 22, 2010).

34. *United States v. Jeffries*, 692 F. 3d 473 (6th Cir. 2012).

35. Interstate Communications Act 18 USC § 875(c).

36. *United States v. Wheeler*, No. 12-cr-0138-WJM (D. Colo. May 10, 2013) (noting that under 18 USC § 875(c) the government must prove three elements: "(1) a transmission in interstate [or foreign] commerce; (2) a communication containing a threat; and (3) the threat must be a threat to injure the person of another" and defining a "true threat" as "a declaration of intention, purpose, design, goal, or determination to inflict punishment, loss or pain on another, or to injure another or his property by the commission of some unlawful act").

37. *United States v. Elonis*, No. CRIM. A. 11-13 (E.D. Pa. Oct 20, 2011).

38. *Id.*

39. *Id.*

40. Compare Cal. Penal Code § 422 (discussing threat) with Cal. Penal Code § 646.9 (discussing stalking).

41. 47 U.S.C. §223(a)(1)(C) (2006). The Harassment Act does not cover non-anonymous communications. Furthermore, this statute is inapplicable to indirect communications with a victim. Thus, it would not apply to such activity like Twitter or blogs. In addition, it does not apply to situations where the harasser poses as the victim.

42. Josh White, *Girl Who Posed as Boy on Facebook Arrested for Stalking*, WASHINGTON POST (May 12, 2010).

43. Federal Interstate Stalking Punishment and Prevention Act (FISPPA), 18 USC §2261A(1).

44. *Id.*

45. *Id.*

46. *United States v. Cassidy*, 814 F. Supp. 2d 574 (D. Md. 2011).

47. *Id.*

48. *Id.*

49. *Id.*

50. *Id.*

51. *Id.*

52. *Id.*
53. *Id.*
54. *Id.*
55. *Id.*
56. Erica Goode, *Craigslist Used in Deadly Ploy to Lure Victims in Ohio*, NY TIMES (Dec. 2, 2011).
57. Maria Cramer and Shelley Murphy, *Files Tell More About "Craigslist Killer,"* BOSTON GLOBE (April 1, 2011).
58. Corky Siemaszko, *Philadelphia Mom Eley London Allegedly Tried to Hire a Hit Man over Facebook to Kill Baby's Father*, N.Y. DAILY NEWS (June 14, 2011).
59. Interview by Big Think with Bill Wasik, Senior Editor, HARPER'S MAGAZINE, June 3, 2009.
60. Andrew Blankstein and Kimi Yoshino, *The Game's "Telephone Flash Mob" Delayed Responses to Robberies*, L.A. TIMES (Aug. 13, 2011).
61. Pat Galbincea, *Flash Mob Ordinances Become Law in Cleveland Minus Mayor Frank Jackson's Signature*, CLEVELAND.COM (Dec. 12, 2011).

    The specific components of the new law are as follows:
    – Inciting to riot: No person shall knowingly engage in conduct designed to incite another to commit a riot. This supplement ordinance targets the individual(s) who organize a riot and would be a misdemeanor of the first degree.
    – Riot: No person shall participate with four or more others in a course of disorderly conduct in violation of Section 605.03, including but not limited to a community event, place of business, or any City of Cleveland property, facility, or recreation area. This amending ordinance focuses on the individuals participating in a riot and would be a misdemeanor of the first degree.
    – Criminal tool: This ordinance includes "electronic media device" as part of the listing of criminal tools under section 625.08 of the Codified Ordinances of Cleveland. This amending ordinance would be a misdemeanor of the first degree.

62. Margot E. Kaminski, *Incitement to Riot in the Age of Flash Mobs*, 81 U. CIN. L. REV. 1 (2012).
63. *Bill to Crack Down on Flash Mobs in Montgomery County*, NBC WASHINGTON (Dec. 12, 2011).
64. Mark Sweney, *Facebook Users Risk Identity Theft, Says Famous Ex-Conman*, THE GUARDIAN, March 20, 2012.
65. An exception to this general rule was *In re Rolando*, 129 Cal. Rptr. 3d 49 (Cal. Ct. App. 2011), as modified on denial of reh'g (Aug. 10,

2011). (A juvenile court maintained a conviction for identity theft where the juvenile lacked an economic motive for his actions.)

66. 18 USC §1028(a)(7) (2014).

67. 18 USC §1028(d)(7) (2014).

68. *United States v. Kowal*, 527 F. 3d 741 (8th Cir. 2008).

69. *Flores-Figueroa v. United States*, 556 U.S. 646 (2009).

70. Jacqueline Lipton, *Combatting Cyber-Victimization*, 26 BERKELEY TECH. L. J. 1103 (2011).

71. *In re Andre B.*, No. D060024, 2012 WL 5353806 (Cal. Ct. App. Oct. 31, 2012).

72. *Id.*

73. *Id.*

74. *Illinois Lawmakers Crack Down on Social Media "Flash Mobs,"* AP (May 19, 2013); see also, 730 Ill. Comp. Stat. 5/5-5-3.2(28)(c)(8) (2014).

75. *Id.*

76. *John Doe v. Prosecutor, Marion County, Indiana*, No. 1:12-cv-00062-TWP-MJD, 2012 WL 2376141 (S.D. Ind. June 22, 2012).

77. *Id.*

78. Ind. Code § 35-42-4-12(d) (2012).

79. *John Doe v. Prosecutor, Marion County, Indiana*, No. 1:12-cv-00062-TWP-MJD, 2012 WL 2376141 (S.D. Ind. June 22, 2012).

80. *Id.*

81. *John Doe v. Prosecutor, Marion County, Indiana*, 705 F. 3d 694 (7th Cir. 2013).

82. *Id.*

83. *John Doe v. Bobby Jindal et al.*, 853 F. Supp. 2d 596 (M.D. La. 2012).

84. *Id.*

85. H.B. 249, 2012 Leg. Reg. Sess. (La. 2012).

86. James Grimmelmann, *Saving Facebook*, 94 Iowa L. Rev. 1137 (2009).

87. Charles Wilson, *Judge Upholds Ind. Facebook Ban for Sex Offenders*, AP (June 24, 2012).

88. Richard M. Guo, *Stranger Danger and the Online Social Network*, 23 BERKELEY TECH. L. J. 617 (2008).

89. Jim Edwards, *Facebook Targets 76 Million Fake Users in War on Bogus Accounts*, BUSINESS INSIDER, March 5, 2013.

90. *How Can I Report a Convicted Sex Offender?*, FACEBOOK, https://www.facebook.com/help/2100081519032737 (last visited Jan. 23, 2014).

91. Arthur Bright, *The Judge Would Like to Be Your "Friend,"* DIGITAL MEDIA LAW PROJECT (Sept. 4, 2009).

92. *John Doe v. Prosecutor, Marion County, Indiana*, 566 F. Supp. 2d 862 (S.D. Ind. 2008).
93. *Doe v. Nebraska*, 2009 U.S. Dist. LEXIS 121104 (D. Neb. December 30, 2009).
94. Nathaniel Hawthorne, THE SCARLET LETTER (1850).
95. Josh Wolford, *New Louisiana Law Gives Sex Offenders a Scarlet Letter on Facebook*, WEB PRO NEWS (June 25, 2012); see also LA. REV. STAT. ANN § 15:542/1(D)(1).
96. Michael Martinez, *New La. Law: Sex Offenders Must List Status on Facebook, Other Social Media*, CNNTECH (June 21, 2012).
97. William Livingston, *"Have You Been Drinking Tonight, Ms. Prynne?" Ohio's Scarlet Letter for OVI/DUI Offenders: A Violation of First Amendment Protection Against Compelled Speech*, 59 CLEV. ST. L. REV. 745 (2011).

CHAPTER 4: JURORS

1. Thaddeus Hoffmeister, *Google, Gadgets, and Guilt: Juror Misconduct in the Digital Age*, 83 UNIVERSITY OF COLORADO LAW REVIEW 409 (2012).
2. Thaddeus Hoffmeister, *Investigating Jurors in the Digital Age: One Click at a Time*, 60 U. KAN. L. REV. 611 (2012).
3. *People v. Jamison*, 899 N.Y.S. 2d 62 (N.Y. Sup. Ct. Aug. 18, 2009).
4. The Honorable Dennis M. Sweeney, Circuit Court Judge (Retired), Address to the Litigation Section of the Maryland State Bar Association: *The Internet, Social Media and Jury Trials—Lessons Learned from the Dixon Trial* (Apr. 29, 2010).
5. Jonathan Oosting, *From the Facebook FAIL Files: Macomb County Juror Could Face Contempt Charges After Posting About "Guilty" Defendant During Trial*, MLIVE (August 30, 2010).
6. Urmee Khan, *Juror Dismissed from a Trial After Using Facebook to Help Make a Decision*, THE TELEGRAPH, (Nov. 24, 2008).
7. Thaddeus Hoffmeister, *"Are You Single" Juror Uses Facebook to Contact Attorney*, JURIES BLOG (Aug 9. 2012).
8. Nielsen, STATE OF THE MEDIA: SOCIAL MEDIA REPORT (2012).
9. Sonya Colberg, *For Some Oklahomans, Social Media's Addictive: On One Popular Medium, Users Collectively Log 8 Billion Minutes per Day on the Site*, THE OKLAHOMAN (Oct. 25, 2009).
10. Ariel Kaminer, *The Torturous Trials of the Idle Juror*, NY TIMES, Oct. 1, 2010.

11. *United States v. Fumo*, No. 06-319, 2009 WL 1688482 (S.D. W. Va. June 17, 2009).

12. Paula Hannaford-Agor, *Google Mistrials, Twittering Jurors, Juror Blogs, and Other Technological Hazards*, 24 COURT MANAGER 42 (Summer 2009).

13. *State v. Dellinger*, 696 S.E. 2d 38 (W. Va. 2010).

14. Howard Mintz, *Jurors Must Lay Off Twitter, Facebook, iPhones and All Else for Barry Bonds Trial*, SAN JOSE MERCURY NEWS (March 6, 2011).

15. Greg Moran, *Revised Jury Instructions: Do Not Use the Internet*, SIGN ON SAN DIEGO (Sept. 13, 2009).

16. Josh Lowensohn, *Memento for Patent Jurors: 42 Articles They Missed During Trial*, CNET (Aug. 30, 2012).

PART II: LAW ENFORCEMENT

1. *Bradley v. Texas*, 359 S.W. 3dd 912 (Tex. Crim. App. 2012). ("Facebook . . . will undoubtedly play an ever-increasing role in identifying and prosecuting suspects.")

CHAPTER 5: COMMUNITY RELATIONS

1. Kirk Johnson, *Hey @SeattlePD: What's the Latest?*, NYTIMES (Oct. 1, 2012).

2. Kirsten Crow, *Waco Police Tout Success of Facebook Page*, WACO TRIBUNE (May 20, 2013).

3. Michele Coppola, *Tweeting Your Way to Better Community Relations*, TECH BEAT (Summer 2013).

4. Kayla Van Dyne, *Yorkville PD Posting Arrests to Facebook*, TIMES LEADER ONLINE (June 22, 2013).

5. Teri Figueroa, *Police Hope Social Media Will Bring Tips*, UTSANDIEGO (June 9, 2013).

6. Fran Jeffries, *Mom Upset Over Facebook Posts from Clayton Police of Son's Death*, ATLANTA JOURNAL CONSTITUTION (Feb. 19, 2013).

CHAPTER 6: PREVENTION, APPREHENSION, AND INVESTIGATION

1. Huey Freeman, *Police Find Facebook Can Help in a Crisis*, HERALD REVIEW (July 15, 2013).

2. Megan K. Scott, *Justin Bieber's Manager Arrested in Mall Frenzy Case*, BILLBOARD (March 24, 2010).

3. *Teen Pop Star Justin Bieber Discovered on YouTube*, ABC NEWS (Nov. 14, 2009).

4. Edward Marshall, *Burglar Leaves His Facebook Page on Victim's Computer*, JOURNAL NEWS (Sep. 16, 2009).

5. Bill Archer, *Like Button Leads to Obstruction of Justice Charge*, BLUEFIELD DAILY TELEGRAPH (Sep. 14, 2012).

6. Carlin Miller, *Facebook Fugitive Chris Creggo Gives Police Plenty of Help. Current Status: "Arrested,"* CBSNEWS (Feb. 9, 2010).

7. Eyder Peralta, *Betrayed by Metadata: John McAfee Admits He's Really in Guatemala*, NPR.org (Dec. 4, 2012).

8. Hayes Hunt and Brian Kint, *Juries and Social Networking Sites*, THE CHAMPION (Dec 2013). "There are over 20 unique metadata fields associated with individual Facebook posts and messages—unique ID of a user's account, author's display name, when a post was created, message recipients, etc."

9. Clay Carey, *Cops Using YouTube to Find Criminals*, USA TODAY (Feb. 8, 2010).

10. Kiyoshi Martinez, *Student Arrested After Police Facebook Him*, DAILY ILLINI (Aug. 1, 2006).

11. *Surrey Police Turns to Social Media Website in Burglaries First*, THIS LOCAL LONDON (Aug. 6, 2013).

12. KJ Lang, *Facebook Friend Turns into Big Brother*, LACROSSE TRIBUNE (Nov. 19, 2009).

13. Rocco Parascandola, *New York Police Dept. Issues First Rules for Use of Social Media During Investigation*, NEW YORK DAILY NEWS (Sep. 11, 2012).

14. John Lynch and Jenny Ellickson, *Obtaining and Using Evidence from Social Networking Sites*, U.S. DEPARTMENT OF JUSTICE COMPUTER CRIME & INTELLECTUAL PROPERTY SECTION (March 3, 2010).

15. *Statements of Rights and Responsibilities—4. Registration and Account Security*, FACEBOOK (March 26, 2010).

16. *Myspace Services Terms of User Agreement*, MYSPACE (June 10, 2013).

17. U.S. Constitution IV Amendment.

18. *Olmstead v. United States*, 277 U.S. 438 (1928).

19. *Id.*

20. *Katz v. United States*, 389 U.S. 347 (1967).

21. *Id.*

22. *Id.* (Harlan, J., concurring).

23. *Id.*

24. *Id.*

25. *Smith v. Maryland*, 442 U.S. 735 (1979).

26. *Id.*

27. *Id.*

28. *Id.*

29. Monu Bedi, *Facebook and Interpersonal Privacy: Why the Third Party Doctrine Should Not Apply*, 54 B.C. L. Rev. 1 (2013).

30. Laura J. Tyson, Comment, *A Break in the Internet Privacy Chain: How Law Enforcement Connects Content to Non-Content to Discover an Internet User's Identity*, 40 SETON HALL L. REV. 1257 (2010). ("Every Internet modem has a unique serial number called a media-access-control (MAC) address, on which the ISP relies to distinguish one modem from another, such as the modem that connects the house located at 10 Main Street from the modem that connects the house at 12 Main Street. The ISP automatically assigns a unique number—the IP address—to the modem at each of its subscriber's locations. Thus, the ISP uses the IP address to identify different households.")

31. Robert Ditzion, Note, *Electronic Surveillance in the Internet Age: The Strange Case of Pen Registers*, 41 AM. CRIM. L. REV. 1321 (2004).

32. Orin Kerr, COMPUTER CRIME LAW (WEST, 2013).

33. Robert Ditzion, Note, *Electronic Surveillance in the Internet Age: The Strange Case of Pen Registers*, 41 AM. CRIM. L. REV. 1321 (2004).

34. *United States v. Joshua Meregildo et al.*, 883 F. Supp. 2d 523 (U.S. District Court for the Southern District of New York, 2012).

35. *Id.*

36. *Id.*

37. *Id.*

38. *R.S. v. Minnewaska Area Sch. Dist.* No. 2149, F. Supp. 2d 1128 (D. Minn. Sept. 6, 2012) (finding that a sixth grader had reasonable expectation of privacy in private messages exchanged via her password-protected Facebook account); see also *Crispin v. Christian Audigier, Inc.*, 717 F. Supp. 2d 965, 991 (C.D. Cal. 2010) (holding that "webmail and private messaging [are] . . . inherently private").

39. U.S. Constitution V Amendment.

40. Federal Rule of Criminal Procedure (FRCP) 17(c)(1).

41. *United States v. Hubbell*, 530 U.S. 27 (2000).

42. Susan Brenner, *Fifth Amendment Bummer*, CYBERCRIME (March 6, 2009).

43. *United States v. Kirschner*, 823 F. Supp. 2d 665 (2010).

44. *Id.*

45. *In re Grand Jury Subpoena to Sebastien Boucher*, No. 2:06-mj-91, 2007 U.S. Dist. Lexis 87951 (D. Vt. 2009).

46. *In re Grand Jury Subpoena to Sebastien Boucher*, No. 2:06-mj-91, 2009 U.S. Dist. Lexis 13006 (D. Vt. 2009).

47. *Id.*

CHAPTER 7: OBTAINING SOCIAL MEDIA INFORMATION

1. *Konop v. Hawaiian Airlines, Inc.*, 302 F. 3d 868 (9th Cir. 2002).

2. Kendall Kelly Hayden, *The Attorney and Social Media, THE PROOF IS IN THE POSTING How Social Media Is Changing the Law*, 73 TEX. BAR J. 188 (2010).

3. John Browning, A LAWYER'S GUIDE TO SOCIAL NETWORK-ING: UNDERSTANDING SOCIAL MEDIA'S IMPACT ON THE LAW, 53 (2010).

4. Robin Sax, *Watch What You Say . . . Online*, HUFFINGTON POST (last visited June 19, 2009).

5. John Browning, A LAWYER'S GUIDE TO SOCIAL NETWORK-ING: UNDERSTANDING SOCIAL MEDIA'S IMPACT ON THE LAW, 53 (2010).

6. Tresa Baldas, *Social Media Postings Sometimes Leads to Jail Time*, DETROIT FREE PRESS (June 16, 2013).

7. *In re Cory P.*, 2012 Ohio 5453.

8. *United States v. Stevenson*, 727 F. 3d 826 (8th Cir. 2013).

9. *Mackelprang v. Fidelity National Title Agency of Nevada Inc.*, 2007 WL 119149 (D. Nev. 2007) and *Leduc v. Roman* (2009) Can. LII 6838 (Can. Ont. S.C.).

10. The following Web site also maintains the legal addresses and points of contact for various social media providers: http://www.search.org/programs/hightech/isp/.

11. 18 U.S.C. § 2701, et seq.

12. 18 U.S.C §§ 2707 (b), (c).

13. S. Rep. No. 99-451, at 1-4 (1986); *United States v. Councilman*, 418 F. 3d 67 (1st Cir. 2005). Thomas Dukes Jr. and Albert C. Rees Jr., *Military Criminal Investigations and the Stored Communications Act*, 64 A.F. L. Rev. 103 (2009). ("The basic premise of the SCA is that customers of ISPs, cell phone companies, and web-based e-mail providers should receive statutory privacy protections for the account, transactional, and content data that these third party providers maintain on behalf of the customer.")

14. *Crispin v. Christian Audigier, Inc.*, 717 F. Supp. 2d 965 (C.D. Cal. 2010).

15. *Quon v. Arch Wireless Operating Co., Inc.*, 529 F.3d 892, 900 (9th Cir. 2008) (citing Orin S. Kerr, *A User's Guide to the Stored*

Communications Act, and a Legislator's Guide to Amending It, 72 GEO. WASH. L. REV. 1208 (2004)).

16. See *O'Grady v. Superior Court*, 139 Cal. App. 4th 1423 (2006); *Flagg v. City of Detroit*, 252 F.R.D. 346 (E.D. Mich. 2008); *Viacom Int'l v. YouTube*, 253 F.R.D. 256 (S.D.N.Y. 2008); *In re Subpoena Duces Tecum to AOL, LLC*, 550 F. Supp. 2d 606 (E.D. Va. 2008).

17. Orin S. Kerr, *A User's Guide to the Stored Communications Act, and a Legislator's Guide to Amending It*, 72 GEO. WASH. L. REV. 1208 (2004).

18. See, for example, *California Criminal Defense Law Firm Wallin & Klarich Seeks Court Order to Obtain Electronic Communications from Facebook, Myspace*, PRWEB (July 27, 2009).

19. 18 U.S.C § 2711(2).

20. 18 U.S.C § 2510(14).

21. 18 U.S.C § 2510(17)(A).

22. 18 U.S.C § 2510(17).

23. See *Crispin v. Christian Audigier, Inc.*, 717 F. Supp. 2d 965 (C.D. Cal. 2010).

24. *In re U.S.*, 665 F. Supp. 2d 1210, 1214 (D. Or. 2009).

25. 18 U.S.C § 2711(2).

26. Illana Katan, *Cloudy Privacy Protections: Why the Stored Communications Act Fails to Protect the Privacy of the Communications Stored in the Cloud*, 13 VAND. J. ENT. & TECH. L. 617 (2011).

27. 18 U.S.C § 2703(d).

28. Orin S. Kerr, *A User's Guide to the Stored Communications Act, and a Legislator's Guide to Amending It*, 72 GEO. WASH. L. REV. 1208 (2008).

29. 18 U.S.C § 2705(a)(1)(A).

30. 18 U.S.C § 2705(a)(2)(A)-(E).

31. 18 U.S.C § 2703(d).

32. The Free Dictionary (last checked Sep. 9, 2013).

33. *People v. Harris*, 945 N.Y.S. 2d 505 (N.Y. City Crim. Ct. 2012).

34. *Id.*

35. *Id.*

36. *Id.*

37. *Terms of Service*, TWITTER (June 25, 2012).

38. *Crispin v. Christian Audigier, Inc.*, 717 F. Supp. 2d 965 (C.D. Cal. 2010). (In this civil case, a federal court held that the plaintiff had standing to quash subpoenas served on social media platforms because plaintiff had a "personal right in information in his or her profile and inbox on a social networking site.")

39. *United States v. Drummond*, No. 1:09-cr-00159, 2010 U.S. Dist. LEXIS 29981 (M.D. Pa. Mar. 29, 2010) (defendant's Myspace pictures showing that he had large amounts of cash and held a gun were provided through discovery).

40. *Williams v. Florida*, 399 U.S. 78 (1970).

41. Yale Kamisar et al., ADVANCED CRIMINAL PROCEDURE (13 Ed.), WEST, 2012.

42. Thomas C. Frongillo and Daniel K. Gelb, *It's Time to Level the Playing Field—the Defense's Use of Evidence from Social Networking Sites*, 34 CHAMPION 14, 15 (2010). (Many states have criminal procedure rules that mimic or closely follow the federal rules.)

43. *Brady v. Maryland*, 373 U.S. 83 (1963); *Giglio v. United States*, 405 U.S. 150 (1972).

44. *Brady v. Maryland*, 373 U.S. 83 (1963).

45. *Giglio v. United States*, 405 U.S. 150 (1972); see also R. Michael Cassidy, *Plea Bargaining, Discovery, and the Intractable Problem of Impeaching Disclosures*, 64 VAND. L. REV. 1429 (2011).

CHAPTER 8: USING SOCIAL MEDIA

1. Sophia Yan, *The Facebook Defense: Social Networking as Alibi*, NY TIMES (Jan. 21, 2010).

2. *Id.*

3. John G. Browning, *What Lawyers Need to Know about Social Networking Sites*, Dallas Bar Ass'n (Feb. 2009).

4. Jim Dwyer, *The Officer Who Posted Too Much on Myspace*, NY TIMES (March 10, 2009).

5. *Id.*

6. Stephanie Francis Ward, *Myspace Discovery*, A.B.A. J. (Jan. 2007).

7. *State v. Bell*, 145 Ohio. Misc. 2d 55 (Com. Pl. 2008).

8. Kisa Miela Santiago, *Man Who Confessed to Drunken Driving in Viral Video Gets 6 1/2 Years*, CNN (Oct 24, 2013).

9. *Id.*

10. Ki Mae Heussner, *Tennessee Woman Arrested After Facebook "Poke,"* ABC NEWS (Oct. 12, 2009).

11. Thomas J. Prohaska, *Myspace Page Used Against Gang Suspect*, BUFFALO NEWS (Jan. 23, 2009).

12. Phillip K. Anthony and Christine Martin, *Social Media Go to Court: Litigators Find There's More to Web 2.0 Than What Jurors Put on Their Facebook Profiles*, RECORDER (SAN FRANCISCO) (February 20, 2009).

13. Thomas J. Prohaska, *Myspace Page Used Against Gang Suspect*, BUFFALO NEWS (Jan. 23, 2009).

14. *Id.*

15. *Id.*

16. *Hall v. Texas*, 283 S.W. 3d 137 (Tex Ct. App 2009).

17. *Id.* ("Hall listed her screen name as 'DocPhantasm' and her favorite quote as the following statement from horror writer Peter Straub: 'You're part music and part blood, part thinker and part killer. And if you can find all of that within you and control it, then you deserve to be set apart.' Hall also listed, among her favorite films, several that had violent crime themes: *Pulp Fiction, Scarface, Carlito's Way, Heat,* and *Donnie Brasco*. At least two of the films, the State pointed out, had scenes involving the dismemberment of bodies. Elsewhere on the page, under 'About Me,' Hall commented, 'Uh, don't be like me. Not a role model! Also, I'm really quite bored. Entertain me?' Under "Clubs and Jobs," she similarly opined that "I hate my job. Working is for losers." Under 'Looking For,' Hall indicated, 'Whatever I can get.'")

18. *State v. Altajir*, 123 Conn. App. 674 (Conn. App. Ct. 2010). (The prosecutor used photographs from a defendant's Facebook page to demonstrate that the defendant violated the terms of his probation.)

19. Eric Tucker, *Facebook Used as Character Evidence, Lands Some in Jail*, USA TODAY (July 16, 2008).

20. *Id.*

21. *United States v. Villanueva*, 315 Fed. Appx. 845 (11th Cir. 2009).

22. Oklahoma Statute § 142A-1 (Definitions) (2014).

23. Reading Random, *BLONDE JUSTICE BLOG* (March 28, 2010), Blondejustice.blogspot.com.

24. *Id.*

25. *Id.* The prosecutor continued to read the following: "I prefer men with shaved or waxed chests. My favorite class at the gym is stripper aerobics."

26. Ken Strutin, *The Role of Social Media in Sentencing Advocacy*, N.Y. L.J. (Sep. 28, 2010).

27. Twitter account of district attorney Ray Larson, https://twitter.com/RaytheDA.

28. Twitter account of St. Louis circuit attorney Jennifer M. Joyce, https://twitter.com/JenniferJoyceCA.

29. *Social Media: The "New" Courthouse?* ABA: LEGAL TECH RESEARCH CENTER (December 11, 2012).

30. *Why Social Media for George Zimmerman?* GEORGE ZIMMERMAN LEGAL CASE, http://www.gzlegalcase.com/index.php/press-releases?start=48 (last visited 28 Aug. 2013).

31. Lizette Alvarez, *Judge in Trayvon Martin Case Denies Request for Silence*, NY TIMES (Oct. 29, 2012).
32. Lizette Alvarez, *Social Media, Growing in Legal Circles, Finds a Role in Florida Murder Case*, NY TIMES (Nov. 2, 2012).
33. Geoffrey Cowan, THE PEOPLE V. CLARENCE DARROW 179 (1993).
34. *In re Globe Newspaper Co.*, 920 F.2d 88 (1st Cir. 1990).
35. Thaddeus Hoffmeister, *Investigating Jurors in the Digital Age: One Click at a Time*, 60 University of Kansas Law Review 611 (2012).
36. *Tweet Helps Bounce Would-Be Juror in Casey Anthony Trial*, CBSMIAMI (May 14, 2011).
37. Christopher B. Hopkins, *Internet Social Networking Sites for Lawyers*, 28 TRIAL ADVOC. Q. 12 (Spring 2009).
38. Michelle Sherman, *The Anatomy of a Trial with Social Media—The Jury*, SOCIAL MEDIA LAW BLOG (Dec. 14, 2010).
39. Thaddeus Hoffmeister, *U.S. v. Daugerdas: A Cautionary Tale About Investigating Jurors*, CHAMPION (2012).
40. *Juror Number One v. Superior Court*, 142 Cal. Rptr. 3d 151(Cal. Ct. App., 2012).
41. *Id.*
42. *Id.*
43. *Id.*
44. *Id.*
45. Orin Kerr, *Can a Judge Order Individuals to Consent to Facebook Disclosing Their Status Updates?* THE VOLOKH CONSPIRACY (June 1, 2012).

CHAPTER 9: ETHICAL IMPLICATIONS OF USING AND OBTAINING SOCIAL MEDIA

1. MODEL RULES OF PROFESSIONAL CONDUCT R. 1.1 comment 6 (2012).
2. *Griffin v. State*, 995 A. 2d 791 (Md. Ct. Spec. App. 2010).
3. *People v. Hardaway*, No. 284980, 2009 Mich. App. LEXIS 1912 (Mich. Ct. App. Sept. 17, 2009).
4. *Strickland v. Washington*, 466 U.S. 668 (1984).
5. *Cannedy v. Adams*, No. ED CV 08-1230-CJC(E) 2009 WL 3711958 (C.D. Cal. Nov. 4, 2009).
6. *Cannedy v. Adams*, 706 F. 3d 1148 (9th Cir. 2013).
7. *Id.*
8. *Id.*

9. *Id.*

10. *Id.*

11. See, e.g., *Commonwealth v. Williams*, 926 N.E. 2d 1162 (Mass. 2010). MODEL RULES OF PROF'L CONDUCT R 1.1 (1983). ("A lawyer shall provide competent representation to a client. Competent representation requires the legal knowledge, skill, thoroughness and preparation reasonably necessary for the representation.")

12. The Association of the Bar of the City of N.Y. Commission on Professional Ethics, *Formal Opinion 2012-2: JURY RESEARCH AND SOCIAL MEDIA*, New York City Bar. ("Indeed, standards of competence and diligence may require doing everything reasonably possible to learn about the jurors who will sit in judgment on a case.")

13. See generally, Jenny Roberts, *Too Little, Too Late: Ineffective Assistance of Counsel, the Duty to Investigate, and Pretrial Discovery in Criminal Charges*, 31 FORDHAM URB. L.J., 1097 (2004).

14. *Formal Opinion No. 2005-164, Communicating with Represented Persons: Contact Through Web Sites and the Internet*, OREGON STATE BAR (Aug. 2005); N.Y. State Bar Association Commission on Professional Ethics, *Opinion #843*, NEW YORK STATE BAR ASSOCIATION (Sep. 10, 2010).

15. MODEL RULES OF PROFESSIONAL CONDUCT 4.2 (1983).

16. MODEL RULES OF PROFESSIONAL CONDUCT 3.5 (1983).

17. The Association of the Bar of the City of N.Y. Commission on Professional Ethics, Formal Opinion 2012-2: JURY RESEARCH AND SOCIAL MEDIA, New York City Bar. The ABA has taken a slightly different approach on this issue. See, ABA COMMITTEE ON ETHICS AND PROFESSIONAL RESPONSIBILITY, Formal Opinion 466, Lawyer Reviewing Jurors' Internet Presence (April 24, 2014)."

18. *Id.*

19. See, e.g., *XI Social Discovery: Social Media Discovery and Web Collection*, XI UNIFIED SEARCH & EDISCOVERY FOR VIRTUAL CLOUD & HYBRID ENVIRONMENTS.

20. James McCarty, *Cuyahoga County Prosecutor Fired After Posing as an Accused Killer's Girlfriend on Facebook to Try to Get Alibi Witnesses to Change Their Testimony*, CLEVELAND PLAIN DEALER (June 6, 2013).

21. *Id.*

22. *Id.*

23. Jack Marshall, *A Prosecutor Lies, But It's for a Good Cause*, ETHICS ALARMS (July 5, 2013).

24. MODEL RULES OF PROFESSIONAL CONDUCT R. 8.4 (1983).

25. ABA Commission on Ethics and Professional Responsibility, *Formal Opinion 319* (1967).
26. N.Y. State Bar Association Commission on Professional Ethics, *Opinion #843*, NEW YORK STATE BAR ASSOCIATION (Sep. 10, 2010).
27. The Association of the Bar of the City of N.Y. Commission on Professional Ethics, *Formal Opinion 2010-2: OBTAINING EVIDENCE FROM SOCIAL NETWORKING SITES*, NEW YORK CITY BAR.
28. The Philadelphia Bar Association Professional Guidance Committee, *Opinion 2009-02* (March 2009).
29. Thaddeus Hoffmeister, *Investigating Jurors in the Digital Age: One Click at a Time*, 60 U. KAN. L. REV. 611 (2012).
30. See *State v. Bessenecker*, 404 N.W.2d 134 (Iowa 1987) (en banc) (limiting access to juror information by county attorneys and requiring county attorneys to disclose to the defense any juror information obtained); *Commonwealth v. Smith*, 215 N.E. 2d 897, 901 (Mass. 1966) (allowing the defense access to juror information obtained by the government).
31. *State v. Bessenecker*, 404 N.W.2d 134 (Iowa 1987) (requiring prosecutors to disclose to the defendant any rap sheets on jurors acquired by court order).
32. See Jeffrey F. Ghent, *Right of Defense in Criminal Prosecution to Disclosure of Prosecution Information Regarding Prospective Jurors*, 86 A.L.R. 3d 571 (1978) ("Rule 421(a) of the Uniform Rules of Criminal Procedure makes it the duty of the prosecuting attorney, on the defendant's written request . . . , to allow access at any reasonable time to . . . 'reports on prospective jurors'"). Jurisdictions not requiring the release of such information by the prosecutor to defense counsel include Florida, Louisiana, and Texas. See *Monahan v. State*, 294 So. 2d 401, 402 (Fla. Dist. Ct. App. 1974) (holding that the trial court did not err in denying the criminal defendant's request for discovery of juror records); *State v. Jackson*, 450 So. 2d 621, 628–29 (La. 1984) (denying defendant's appeal because the records did not impact his voir dire); *Martin v. State*, 577 S.W.2d 490, 491 (Tex. Crim. App. 1979) ("The State has no obligation to furnish counsel for accused with information he has in regard to prospective jurors" (quoting *Linebarger v. State*, 469 S.W.2d 165, 167 (Tex. Crim. App. 1971))).
33. AP, *Bulger Judge Allows Juror Background Checks* (May 25, 2013).
34. New York Rule of Professional Conduct 3.5(d) (MCKINNEY 2013).
35. The Association of the Bar of the City of N.Y. Commission on Professional Ethics, Formal Opinion 2012-2: JURY RESEARCH AND SOCIAL MEDIA, New York City Bar; N.Y. County Lawyers'

Association, Commission on Professional Ethics, *Formal Opinion No. 743*, NYCLA.ORG.

36. Thaddeus Hoffmeister, *Investigating Jurors in the Digital Age: One Click at a Time*, 60 U. KAN. L. REV. 611 (2012).

37. *United States v. Daugerdas*, 757 F. Supp. 2d 364 (S.D.N.Y. 2010).

38. Kendall Kelly Hayden, *The Attorney and Social Media, THE PROOF IS IN THE POSTING, How Social Media Is Changing the Law*, 73 TEXAS BAR JOURNAL 188 (March, 2010).

39. Molly McDonough, *First Thing Lawyer Tells New Clients: Shut Down Facebook Account*, A.B.A. J., Feb. 9, 2010).

40. MODEL RULES OF PROFESSIONAL CONDUCT R 3.4(a) (1983) (prohibiting lawyers from unlawfully altering or destroying evidence and from assisting others from doing so).

41. ABA Model Rule 3.4 (Fairness to Opposing Party and Counsel).

42. 18 U.S.C §§ 1503, 1512, 1519.

43. N.Y. County Lawyers' Association, Committee on Professional Ethics, *Formal Opinion No. 745: Advising a Client Regarding Posts on Social Media Sites*, NYCLA.ORG.

44. *Lester v. Allied Concrete Co.*, 83 Va. Cir. 308 (Va. Cir. Ct. 2011).

45. *Id.*

46. *Id.*

47. *Id.*

48. Brian D. Wassom et al., *Wassom on Social Media Law Chp. 20*.A.

49. *Lester v. Allied Concrete Co.*, 83 Va. Cir. 308 (Va. Cir. Ct. 2011) (final order).

50. Mike Frisch, *Attorney Charged with Confidentiality Breach in Response to Unfavorable AVVO Review*, LEGAL PROFESSION BLOG (Sep. 5, 2013).

51. Debra Cassens Weiss, *Lawyer's Response to Client's Bad Avvo Review Leads to Disciplinary Complaint*, ABA JOURNAL (Sep. 12, 2013).

52. *Id.*

53. Steven Seidenberg, *Seduced: For Lawyers, the Appeal of the Social Media Is Obvious. It's Also Dangerous*, ABA JOURNAL (Feb. 1, 2011).

54. *Id.*

55. *Hunter v. Virginia State Bar ex rel. Third Dist. Comm.*, 285 Va. 485 (Va. 2013).

56. Frank Green, *Panel: Richmond Lawyer Broke Rule*, RICHMOND TIMES DISPATCH (Oct. 18, 2011).

57. Martha Neil, *Lawyer Puts Photo of Client's Leopard-Print Undies on Facebook; Murder Mistrial, Loss of Job Result*, ABA JOURNAL (Sep. 13, 2012).

58. *Id.*
59. *In the Matter of Kristine Ann Peshek*, No. 09 CH 89, 2009 Ill. Atty. Reg. Disc. LEXIS 206 (The Hearing Board of Ill. Attorney Registration and Disciplinary Committee) (Aug. 25, 2009).
60. *Id.*
61. Melissa Holsman, *Facebook Poem Gets Prosecutor in Hot Water*, SUN SENTINEL (April 22, 2010).
62. Jonathan Turley, *Florida Supreme Court Upholds Sanction Against Lawyer Who Called Judge a "Witch" on a Blog*, RES ISPA LOQUITOR (Sep. 30, 2009).
63. *Id.*
64. *Id.*
65. Unfortunately, this is not the only example of an attorney being less than honest during voir dire. See, for example, Thaddeus Hoffmeister, *U.S. v. Daugerdas: A Cautionary Tale About Investigating Jurors*, CHAMPION (Dec. 2012).
66. Rosalind Greene and Jan Mills Spaeth, *Are Tweeters or Googlers in Your Jury Box*, ARIZONA ATTORNEY (Feb. 2010).
67. *McNeely v. Hernandez*, Report and Recommendation to Deny Amended Petition for Writ of Habeas Corpus (July 12, 2010).
68. Debra Cassens Weiss, *Lawyer Gets Suspension for Impersonating College Acquaintance on Lesbian Dating Website*, ABA JOURNAL (July 23, 2013).
69. Brooke Crum, *U.S. Attorney Under Scrutiny for Facebook Posts*, HOUSTON CHRONICLE (Aug. 13, 2013).

CHAPTER 10: PERSONAL USE AND ETHICS

1. *Youkers v. State*, 400 S.W. 3d 200 (Tex. App. 2013) (quoting Judge Susan Criss, *The Use of Social Media by Judges*), 60 THE ADVOCATE (TEX.) 18 (Fall 2012).
2. Judith Ann Lanzinger, *About the Justice Judy Blog*, JUSTICE JUDY, http://justicejudy.blogspot.com/ (last visited Nov. 24, 2013).
3. Sam Jones, *Judges, Friends, and Facebook: The Ethics of Prohibition*, 24 GEORGETOWN JOURNAL OF ETHICS 281 (2011).
4. State of Washington Ethics Advisory Commission, *Opinion 09-05*, WASHINGTON COURTS (Nov. 17, 2009).
5. *Id.*
6. Board of Committee on Grievances and Discipline, *Opinion 2010-7*, THE SUPREME COURT OF THE OHIO (December 3, 2010).

7. *CJE Opinion No. 2011-6: Facebook: Using Social Networking Web Site*, THE MASSACHUSETTS JUDICIAL BRANCH, SUPREME JUDICIAL COURT (Dec. 28, 2011).
8. N.Y. Advisory Committee on Judicial Ethics, *Opinion 08-176* (Jan. 29, 2009).
9. ABA COMMITTEE ON ETHICS & PROFESSIONAL RESPONS-IBILITY, *Formal Opinion 462, Judge's Use of Electronic Social Networking Media* (Feb. 21, 2013).
10. *Domville v. State*, 103 So. 3d 184 (Fla. Dist Ct. App. 2012).
11. *Id.*
12. *Id.*
13. *Public Reprimand: B. Carlton Terry, Jr., District Court Judge, Dist. 22*, INQUIRY NO. 08-234 (April 1, 2009).
14. *Youkers v. Texas*, 400 S.W. 3d 200 (Tex. App.2013).
15. *Id.*
16. *Onnen v. Sioux Falls Independent School District*, 801 N.W. 2d 752 (S.D. 2011).
17. *Purvis v. Commissioner of Social Sec.*, 2011 WL 741234 (D.N.J., Feb. 23, 2011).
18. *Id.*
19. Molly McDonough, *Facebooking Judge Catches Lawyer in Lie, Sees Ethical Breaches #ABAChicago*, ABAJOURNAL (July 31, 2009).

CHAPTER 11: INSIDE THE COURTROOM

1. *Carino v. Muenzen*, A-5491-08T1, 2010 WL 34448071 (N.J. Super. Ct. App. Div., Aug. 30, 2010) (per curiam), cert. denied, 13 A. 3d 363 (N.J. 2011) (table decision).
2. *Id.*
3. Richard M. Goehler, Monica L. Dias, and David Bralow, *The Legal Case for Twitter in the Courtroom*, 27 COMM. LAWYER 14 (2010).
4. *Id.*
5. *Richmond Newspapers Inc. v. Virginia*, 448 U.S. 555 (1980).
6. *Chandler v. Florida*, 449 U.S. 560 (1981).
7. Nancy Marder, *The Conundrum of Cameras in the Courtroom*, 44 ARIZ. ST. L. J. 1490 (2012).
8. Federal Rule of Criminal Procedure 53.
9. *United States v. Shelnutt*, 2009 WL 3681827 (M.D. Ga. 2009).
10. *Id.*

11. *State v. Komisarjevsky*, 2011 WL 1032111 (Conn. Super.), 39 Media L. Rep. 1727, 51 Conn. L. Rptr. 485.

12. Roxana Hegeman, *Live Coverage Boosts Access to Federal Courts*, USATODAY (Mar. 6, 2009).

13. Richard M. Goehler, Monica L. Dias, and David Bralow, *The Legal Case for Twitter in the Courtroom*, 27 COMM. LAWYER 14 (2010).

14. Debra Cassens Weiss, *Judge Explains Why He Allowed Reporter to Live Blog Federal Criminal Trial*, ABAJOURNAL (Jan 16, 2009).

15. *Media Coverage of Judicial Proceedings*, Rule 1001, SUPREME COURT OF KANSAS (Oct. 18, 2012).

16. *Geders v. United States*, 425 U.S. 80 (1976).

17. Jury Instructions and Order, *United States v. W.R. Grace*, No. 05-07-M-DWM (D. Mont. 2009).

18. Rachel Bunn, *Reporter's Tweeted Photo of Juror Leads Judge to Declare Mistrial in Murder Prosecution*, Reporters Committee for Freedom of the Press (April 16, 2012).

19. Bruce Carton, *Is Tweeting from the Courtroom by Reporters Too Distracting for Jurors?*, LEGAL BLOG WATCH (April 6, 2012).

20. Amy Mitchell et al., *The Role of News on Facebook*, PEW RESEARCH JOURNALISM PROJECT (Oct. 24, 2013).

CHAPTER 12: ADMITTING SOCIAL MEDIA INTO EVIDENCE

1. Steven M. Cerny, *The Intersection Between Social Networking and Litigation: Discovery and Authentication of Social Media Evidence*, 1 REYNOLDS COURTS & MEDIA L. J. 479 (2011).

2. Norman M. Garland, *An Overview of Relevance and Hearsay: A Nine Step Analytical Guide*, 22 S.W. U. L. REV. 1039 (1993).

3. *Lorraine v. Markel*, 241 F.R.D. 534 (D. Md. 2007) ("Once Evidence has been shown to meet the low threshold of relevance . . .").

4. *State v. Gaskins*, No. 06CA0086-M (Ohio App. 9 Dist. Aug. 13, 2007).

5. *Id.*

6. *Id.*

7. *Id.*

8. *State v. Corwin*, 295 SW 3d 573 (Mo. Ct. App. S.D. 2009).

9. *Id.*

10. *Id.*

11. *People v. Valdez*, 135 Cal. Rptr. 3d 628, 633 (Ct. App. 2011) (citing Cal. Evid. Code § 1400 (West 1995) (alteration in original)).

12. Lawrence Morales, *Social Media Evidence: "What You Post or Tweet Can and Will Be Used Against You in a Court of Law,"* 60, THE ADVOCATE (Texas) 32 (2012).

13. *People v. Fielding,* 2010 WL 2473344 (Cal. Ct. App. June 18, 2010); see also, Brian Krebs, *Hackers Latest Target Social Networking Sites,* WASHINGTON POST (Aug. 9, 2008); Riva Richmond, *Stolen Facebook Accounts for Sale,* NY TIMES (May 3, 2010); Heather Kelly, *83 Million Facebook Accounts Are Fakes and Dupes,* CNN (Aug. 02, 2012).

14. *Griffin v. Maryland,* 19 A.3d. 415, 421 (Md. 2011).

15. David I. Schoen, *The Authentication of Social Media Postings,* ABA SEC. OF LITIGATION, TRIAL EVIDENCE (May 17, 2011).

16. FED R. EVID. 901(a).

17. Byron L. Warnken, *Social Networking Sites and Criminal Litigation,* PROFESSOR BYRON L. WARNKEN'S BLOG (Jan. 3, 2011).

18. Steven M. Cerny, *The Intersection Between Social Networking and Litigation: Discovery and Authentication of Social Media Evidence,* 1 REYNOLDS COURTS & MEDIA L. J. 479 (2011).

19. *Jazayeri v. Mao,* 94 Cal. Rptr. 3d 198 (Cal. Ct. App. 2009). ("If a letter or telegram is sent to a person and a reply is received in due course purporting to come from that person, there is sufficient evidence of genuineness.")

20. *Commonwealth v. Williams,* 926 N.E. 2d 1162 (Mass. 2010).

21. *Griffin v. State,* 19 A.3d 415 (2011).

22. *Tienda v. State,* 358 S. W. 3d 633 (Tex. Crim. App. 2012).

23. *Griffin v. State,* 995 A. 2d 791 (Md. Ct. Spec. App. 2010).

24. *Id.*

25. *Id.*

26. *Id.*

27. *Griffin v. State,* 419 Md. 343 (Md. 2011).

28. *Commonwealth v. Williams,* 926 N.E. 2d 1162 (Mass. 2010).

29. *Id.*

30. *Id.*

31. *Tienda v. State,* No. 05-09-00553-CR (Tex. App. Dec. 17, 2010).

32. *Id.*

33. *Tienda v. State,* 358 S. W. 3d 633 (Tex. Crim. App. 2012). In order to authenticate Tienda's Myspace page, the government also relied on multiple photos "tagged" to the defendant's Myspace accounts and subscriber reports from Myspace, which stated that the accounts "were created by a 'Ron Mr. T,' and . . . 'Smiley Face,' which is the appellant's widely known nickname. The account holder purported to

live in 'D TOWN,' or 'dallas,' and registered the accounts with a 'ron-nietiendajr@' or 'smileys_shit@' email address." *Id.*

34. *Id.*
35. *Id.*
36. Ira P. Robbins, *Writings on the Wall: The Need for An Authorship-Centric Approach to the Authentication of Social-Networking Evidence*, 13 Minn. J. L. Sci. & Tech. 1 (2012).
37. FED. R. EVID. 801(c).
38. *United States v. Hamilton*, 413 F.3d 1138 (10th Cir. 2005).
39. Steven Goode, *The Admissibility of Electronic Evidence*, 29 REV. LITIG. 1 (2009).
40. *People v. Valdez*, 135 Cal. Rptr. 3d 628 (Cal. Ct. App. 2011).
41. FED. R. EVID. 801(d)(1).
42. FED. R. EVID. 801(d)(2). See also, *State v. Greer*, 2009 WL 2574160, Ohio Ct. App. 2009.
43. Molly McPartland, *An Analysis of Facebook "Likes" and Other Nonverbal Internet Communication Under the Federal Rules of Evidence*, 99 IOWA L. REV. 445 (2013)
44. FED. R. EVID. 803(1).
45. FED. R. EVID. 803(2).
46. FED. R. EVID. 803(8).
47. FED. R. EVID. 803(6).
48. FED R. EVID. 1002.
49. Steven Goode, *The Admissibility of Electronic Evidence*, 29 REV. LITIG. 1 (2009).
50. *Lorraine v. Markel*, 241 F.R.D. 534 (D. Md. 2007).
51. 2011 WL 6145742 Ohio App. 8 Dist., 2011.
52. FED. R. EVID. 404(b).
53. *United States v. Phaknikone*, 605 F. 3d 1099 (11th Cir. 2010).
54. *Id.*
55. *Id.*

CONCLUSION

1. Hilary Hylton, *Tweeting in the Jury Box: A Danger to Fair Trials?*, TIME (Dec. 29, 2009).

Index

About the Author

Thaddeus A. Hoffmeister is a law professor at the University of Dayton. He primarily teaches and writes on topics related to criminal law, juries, privacy, and technology. His published works include "Google, Gadgets, and Guilt: The Digital Age's Effect on Juries," *University of Colorado Law Review*; "Investigating Jurors in the Digital Age: One Click at a Time," *University of Kansas Law Review*; and "Crimes, Prosecution and Evidence," a book chapter in *Social Media and the Law*. Professor Hoffmeister also edits two blogs that discuss juries and social media.